Alberta H. Klemp

THE SMALL SECTS IN AMERICA

The
SMALL SECTS
IN AMERICA

Revised Edition

By ELMER T. CLARK

NEW YORK   NASHVILLE

ABINGDON-COKESBURY PRESS

THE SMALL SECTS IN AMERICA

SET UP, PRINTED, AND BOUND BY THE
PARTHENON PRESS, AT NASHVILLE,
TENNESSEE, UNITED STATES OF AMERICA

PREFACE TO THE REVISED EDITION

WHEN THE ORIGINAL EDITION OF THIS BOOK WAS PUBLISHED A DOZEN years ago, no other study had attempted to bring together information concerning the numerous little religious bodies that were, for the most part, unknown to even well-informed persons. It was hoped that the volume would stimulate interest in the subject and lead to the production of a more nearly adequate report.

That hope has been partially fulfilled, for, whether stimulated or not by this book, the subject of our divided denominations has occupied the attention of numerous students who have since written about religious life in America. None of these, however, has attempted to describe or even to list the various groups. This book has therefore remained as the only publication of its kind.

The recognition accorded it in both popular and scholarly circles, and the continuing demand for it since war conditions forced it out of print, have indicated the need for a new and enlarged edition, while changes in the subject matter and the experiences derived from criticisms indicated that certain revisions should be made. These, however, have been held to the minimum. Some expressions that proved objectionable to certain groups have been eliminated, statistics have been brought up to date, and an appendix and Index of Religious Bodies have been added to include a list of nearly all the bodies, with brief descriptions of a few that belong to categories not adequately discussed in the text. The general nature and content remain unchanged.

Over the intervening years I have continued gathering data on the smaller church groups in this country, and I have accumulated masses of their literature. The material has been diligently sought for and carefully studied for nearly a quarter of a century. But it must be emphasized that the written descriptions in this book are my own. Experiments were made in securing statements from representatives of the various groups, or in having statements revised by them, but these only proved that I myself must bear the responsibility, for good or ill. The attempts resulted in endless repetitions of doctrines held in common by all the churches, identical words and phrases used with varying meanings, scriptural phrases and language that conveyed no clear-cut meaning to the reader, obscuring of tenets and observances that indicated the main differences between groups, and even outright propaganda. A glance at the United States *Census of Religious Bodies* will show the results of that procedure.

It should not be necessary to insist that I have tried to maintain an objective attitude and to write with sympathy. But there have been many difficulties, and it is probably too much to expect that I have pleased everybody. Some of the groups are very reticent about their own history and practices, and some have objected to the use in this book of materials plainly published in their own literature, which was supplied by them to me as authoritative.

In justice to all the groups it must be pointed out that emphasis has been placed upon distinctive principles and the points wherein they differ from others rather than upon the points of general agreement. It seems pointless to state in each case that the group under discussion believes in the existence of God, the divinity of Christ, the immortality of the soul, and salvation by faith. This may have the unfortunate effect of making some of the groups seem "peculiar" or "erratic," when, as a matter of fact, their peculiarity is confined to but one or a few points. It is important, therefore, to remember that among most of the religious bodies agreements are far more numerous and important than differences. In spite of superficial appearances the churches are nearly all alike, and the strife or contention between them has been greatly exaggerated.

It should also go without saying that no disparagement is meant by the word "sect." No fine distinctions of definition are drawn between churches, denominations, and sects, and the words may be found used interchangeably. As a glance at Webster will show, all religious bodies may be, and often are, referred to as sects; the "sects" in continental Europe are the very bodies which in America are the largest denominations, the Methodists, Baptists, and others.

While disagreeing at many, perhaps at most, points with the attitudes, beliefs, and interpretations of these small sects, I deem them quite important in our religious milieu; I have respect for their adherents' sincerity and recognize spiritual values in their service. I have endeavored to maintain a strictly unbiased, certainly an unprejudiced and sympathetic, attitude, in so far as this is possible to one outside their own circle of believers. In the small sects one sees religion as it springs naturally from the naïve and simple heart that craves touch with the supernatural, and is unaffected by the conventions and the scientific leanings of a sophisticated society.

In the compilation of the Index and in manuscript preparation, I express my gratitude to my associate, Miss Georgina Johnston, and my secretaries, Mrs. Elma S. Brunner and Miss Florence Mitchell, and to the others of my staff.

ELMER T. CLARK

CONTENTS

INTRODUCTION

THE PROBLEM AND THE DATA

THIS BOOK IS CONCERNED WITH AN INTERESTING AND NEGLECTED phase of religious life in the United States. The principles of religious freedom, untrammeled access to and the right of individual interpretation of the Holy Scriptures, and the privilege of worship according to the individual conscience, which were promulgated by the Protestant Reformation and have found their fullest expression in America, have given rise to a multiplicity of religious sects in this country. In 1947 there were approximately 74,000,000 persons in the United States affiliated with some religious body, this being about one half of the estimated total population as of that date. By far the greater number of these were members of a very few large denominations, more than 90 per cent of them belonging to two dozen bodies. There are, however, more than four hundred different religious groups in the country. Most of these are very small groups, about half of them having fewer than seven thousand adherents each. This book undertakes a study of these small sects, concentrating especially on more than one hundred that are unusual and relatively unknown.

The data of the study have been difficult of access. Little mention of most of the sects discussed is found in the general religious literature of the country. Weak and poverty-stricken, not many of them publish literature of their own, save ephemeral tracts and newspapers of limited circulation. The investigation has accordingly been under considerable handicap and has required years of study and research. The sources of the data have been as follows:

1. Statistical data have been drawn from the United States *Census of Religious Bodies* and the statistics gathered annually by the *Christian Herald*. Many figures are uncertain; and all are, of course, subject to constant changes. There is no attempt to secure exact accuracy herein, but figures are given when available only for the purposes of indicating in general the size of various bodies.

2. Such literature as is published by the sects themselves has been laboriously gathered and carefully studied. Since these materials are, for the most part, in the form of leaflets, pamphlets, and newspapers,

inaccessible and unknown save to the members of the small bodies, the securing and study of them has been really original research.

3. Information has been secured by means of correspondence and the circulation of question lists. The first approach was made to the executive educational officer of the group, the secretary, chairman, or editor of the board or committee of education, where such organizations exist and could be contacted. In other cases reliance was placed on the individuals selected by the director of the census to furnish statements of history, doctrine, and work for the decennial census reports. Such persons have been assumed to possess authority to speak for their groups. When contact was once established with these individuals, a rather prolonged correspondence generally ensued, fuller information being thus secured and doubtful points cleared up. A comprehensive question list was filled out and returned by the representatives of about one hundred bodies.

4. Direct access to a large number of sects was secured by personal visitation. Over a period of several years I visited the headquarters or the spokesmen of fifty or more sects in half the states of the country. Much firsthand information not available, or not clearly stated in the literature and questionnaire, has thus been secured.

Since a volume could be written about any one of the sects, requirements of space imposed necessary limitations to the study. Brief historical sketches covering many groups have been included, but no attempt has been made to write detailed or exhaustive histories. Points of doctrine and practice wherein the sects generally agree with the great and well-known denominations have been passed over. Bodies with which the general public are more or less familiar have not been stressed, though many of them are quite small. The racial Catholic bodies, such as the Albanian, Bulgarian, Greek, Russian, Serbian, and Syrian churches, have likewise been omitted because they differ little from the parent bodies with which informed persons are familiar. Sects that are essentially non-Christian, such as the Theosophists, Spiritualists, Vedantists, and Bahais, have been excluded by considerations of space, but they are discussed briefly in the appendix.

CHAPTER I

THE SECTARIAN SPIRIT IN
AMERICAN CHRISTIANITY

READERS OF CURRENT LITERATURE FREQUENTLY ENCOUNTER DESCRIP-
tions of the sorry state of religion and dire predictions of its decline and
approaching elimination as an influential social factor.[1] One such prophet
has written a book to show just how morality, hitherto bolstered by
religion, is to be maintained by science after its erstwhile prop has been
removed.[2] Another solemnly assures us that in a cross-country automobile
journey of sixteen thousand miles he found only one religious person,
wherefore "Christianity is hardly to be considered at all as a force in
American life" [3]—this in a land where church members have given billions
to build and maintain their churches and religious institutions. Such
discouraging pictures are, of course, as old as Christianity itself. They are
not, however, supported by the factual data on the subject, certainly not
by the statistical record of the population's allegiance to and the consequent
growth of religious bodies. These data, on the contrary, show that
organized religion is one of the most tremendous social factors in our
contemporary life, and from the beginning of our national existence to the
present day its growth has kept pace with the increase of our population.[4]

Our Religious Constituency. There are around 250,000 churches in the
United States, and these have a membership of approximately 74,000,000
persons, 60,000,000 of whom are above thirteen years of age.[5] Comparison
with the general population estimates of the same date shows that a
considerable majority of all the adults in the United States are members
of religious organizations. The 200,000 Sunday schools have more than

[1] A good example of such literature is Barnes, *The Twilight of Christianity.*
[2] Parshley, *Science and Good Behavior.*
[3] Markey, *This Country of Yours.*
[4] One wonders as to the sources of information of those who deprecate the influence of religion
in this country. Where, for example, did Markey travel and whom did he interview? There is
scarcely a hamlet in the land wherein on any Sunday he would not find assembled groups of
persons, to many of whom religion means more than any other concern.
[5] All figures cited, which are given in round numbers, are from the United States *Census of
Religious Bodies,* the *Christian Herald,* and the *Yearbook of American Churches* (1947).

25,000,000 officers, teachers, and scholars. The value of church buildings reaches $4,000,000,000, plus $500,000,000 for ministerial residences. If parochial school buildings, homes for children and the aged, and similar institutions, are added, the grand total value of church property is found to approximate $7,000,000,000. The expenses of the churches in normal prewar times ran to nearly a billion dollars annually.

Such are the facts derived from the available statistics. It would be a mistake, however, to draw the conclusion, as many do, that "half the American people have no religion," for these figures by no means present a true picture of our religious life. It is certain that a far larger proportion of our people have some kind of religious faith and affiliation.

In the first place, the statisticians do not even claim to present all the data. The *Christian Herald* list includes only denominations having at least 50,000 members, and derives its huge total of nearly 74,000,000 from reports of 54 groups, leaving 300 or more entirely out of its enumeration. While it is true that these 54 account for a very large majority of all church members, it is also true that the 300 omitted have several million adherents. The United States census reaches more groups than any other agency, but its 1936 report listed more than fifty bodies from which no figures were obtained.

Any careful investigator will soon discover that there are thousands of religious and quasi-religious groups which have not been, and probably cannot be, reached by the ordinary statistical processes. In every city they will be found meeting in hotel parlors, rented rooms, "store front" churches, auditoriums or tabernacles, and residences; on any Saturday many of their advertisements will be found on the religious-news pages of the newspapers. The rural areas contain many of these unknown and unenumerated congregations, and they are numerous among the Negroes everywhere. Leaders of the pentecostal movement do not hesitate to declare that there are more churches of that type in most of our cities and states than all others combined, Protestant, Catholic, and Jewish; these are nearly all independent groups, most of them being "store front" congregations, and many of which regard denominational affiliation or even a membership record as unscriptural.

There are numerous New Thought, healing, "psychology," mystic, and esoteric cults of various kinds that are not counted in the various enumerations. Among these are Unity, The Great I Am, Aquarian, Mental Metaphysics, Biosophical, Chapel of Truth, Church of the Truth, Divine Science, Divine Truth, Universal Peace, New History, High Watch, and many other groups. Some of these, such as Unity, are widespread and attract thousands of people. In some cases they would be regarded by most people as only quasi-religious, but they hold the spiritual attachment of their adherents and claim to bring them into right relations with God. Their members would certainly not care to be classed as irreligious.

In the second place, the number of religious persons would be greatly increased by a uniform system of counting. Among Protestants the usual practice is to include only those who voluntarily join the church after reaching "years of discretion," and who continue some form of maintenance of membership. Roman Catholics, on the other hand, count by families, and claim all those who were baptized in infancy, without much regard to their later attitudes and actions. The statistics of Jewish "congregations" are almost identical with the total Jewish population. This difference in method of computation greatly exaggerates the strength of Roman Catholicism as compared with that of Protestantism, and omits millions who give assent to religious doctrines and are as closely related to the church as are multitudes of those who are claimed and counted among the Catholics and Jews.

The actual number of believing Protestants in this country is probably nearer 75,000,000 than the 44,000,000 indicated by the enumeration of the denominations.

The Sectarian Milieu. There are around four hundred religious denominations of all kinds in the United States; the exact number at any given time is uncertain, because changes are constantly occurring and obscure sects are not easy to locate. The United States census of 1936, the last official enumeration, listed 310 bodies, including 54 on which no statistics were available.

This amazing medley is largely due to our principle of religious liberty and the Protestant doctrine of free access to, and individual interpretation of, the Bible. However, no church anywhere has been able to avoid splits and schisms, and this is true of non-Christian religions as well as of Christian churches. It will probably remain true as long as theological convictions are regarded as important. The Roman Catholic Church, which is often supposed to possess a unity that is lacking in Protestantism, has actually experienced more divisions than any other; in fact it may be said that every other Christian group in the world represents a break from Catholicism. In the United States today there are eleven Orthodox churches and six Old Catholic bodies which, in the main, accept Catholic theology but reject the Roman system and the authority of the pope. Furthermore, among the various orders of the Catholic Church there are differences and animosities as marked as those which exist between the various Protestant denominations, but actual separation is prevented by the overhead authority of the hierarchy.

Contrary to popular belief, the same situation exists among the Jews. Although they are all embraced in one ethnic category, they are divided in America into four different denominations, three of which have different creeds, separate churches, and their own theological seminaries. These Jewish sects are called the Orthodox, Conservative, Reformed, and Restitutionist. The differences between Orthodox and Reformed Jews are at least as marked as the differences between Methodists, Baptists, and Presbyterians.

It is worthy of note that comparatively few of these denominations are really indigenous to American soil in the matter of origin; it has in fact been asserted that Mormonism and Christian Science alone constitute our distinct contribution to the multitude of religious sects in the world.[6] There are seventy bodies which are distinctively foreign or racial, such as the Dunkers or German Baptists, Eastern Orthodox Churches, Lutherans, Mennonites, Moravians, Scandinavian Evangelical bodies, Schwenkfelders, and Old Catholic Churches; several others, such as the Quakers, Plymouth Brethren, Jews, Roman Catholics, and the Reformed bodies, have foreign traditions and antecedents, though they have become more or less thoroughly Americanized. Even those bodies which have attracted the allegiance of the largest groups of our people, the Methodists, Presbyterians, Baptists, and Episcopalians, are all foreign importations. The fact that most of our sects came to us from Europe, at least in the parent stems, is frequently overlooked by those who regard sectarian diversity as a peculiarly American phenomenon.

Most of our denominations are quite small; some, indeed, are almost microscopic. Eight groups that are listed as denominations have only one congregation each, and one of these has only thirteen members. There are more than fifty denominations with fewer than ten local churches and as many more that have fewer than one thousand members. More than half the sects have less than 7,000 adult members, and only 33 have as many as 200,000 members each; the latter, however, include considerably more than 90 per cent of all the church members in the country.

Nearly all American sects are geographically localized. Only nine are represented in each state by at least one church, and several are concentrated in one state only. No state has churches of all the denominations; the largest number of sects are found in Pennsylvania, followed in order by Ohio, New York, and Illinois.

Many of these small American sects are unknown to most people. The Apostolic Overcoming Holy Church of God, Two-Seed-in-the-Spirit Predestinarian Baptists, United Zion's Children, Yorker Brethren, Church of God and Saints of Christ, Church of Daniel's Band, Pillar of Fire, Free Christian Zion Church of Christ, Hutterian Brethren, Old Order Amish,

---

[6] Bass, *Protestantism in the United States*, p. 26.

House of Prayer, Church Triumphant—that these and many others are in existence would doubtless be surprising information to many persons. But their size and obscurity do not argue their unimportance. Though any one of these tiny sects may in itself be uninfluential and insignificant, the total body of such holds the loyalty of hundreds of thousands of people. That such a multitude do not fit into the religious niches in which most of us feel comfortable, but find their spiritual needs satisfied in sects which to others seem vagrant and absurd, is a fact of profound psychological moment. Many of these little sects have some sort of survival value; indeed they have survived in the American environment quite as long as the great denominations, since they were planted here in early colonial days. From every angle, therefore, it would seem that the small sects are worthy of closest study.

The Confusion of Tongues. One who regards the present as an "age of doubt" has evidently failed to study the convictions of the small sects; for one familiar with the doctrines steadfastly held by multiplied thousands, and even millions, of their adherents will rather be impressed with the amazing credulity of a large section of our population. Many strange beliefs are cystallized in the dogmas of these churches. Some of them are undergirded by erratic interpretations of Scripture. Trivial differences of opinion have caused groups to split up into various independent denominations. It is difficult to see how the voices speaking to the American conscience in the name of God could be more completely confused. And yet this very confusion is a psychological phenomenon of much importance.

The Church of the Living God, "Christian Workers for Fellowship," insists that Jesus Christ, David, Job, and many other biblical characters were Negroes; Christ was a son of David and David was most certainly a Negro, for did he not say, "I am become like a bottle in the smoke"? Amish Mennonites, during the whole course of American history, have regarded buttons, suspenders, and top buggies as sinful; men wear hooks and eyes, while women keep their heads covered according to the biblical injunction. Dozens of sects expect the immediate personal second coming of Christ, and their pictures of what will then occur are lurid and bloody in the extreme. Foot-washing sects are numerous; the River Brethren split into "one-mode" and "two-mode" denominations, the former holding that the same brother should both wash and dry, the latter insisting that each act must be performed by a different individual.

Primitive Baptists are opposed to missions and Sunday schools. Several bodies insist that they are not "denominations" and refer to all other than themselves as "sectarian churches." The Plymouth Brethren are split into eight branches, but they remain steadfast in their intention of forming a basis of union for all Christians and refusing to be called a denomination. The Church of Christ in Christian Union has 86 congregations with 3,500 members, yet it seriously proposes to unite all Christians on its own platform, believing it alone is solidly based on Scripture. This sect has no monopoly on that aim, however, for many others have the same ambition. The Churches of Christ "speak where the Scriptures speak and are silent where the Scriptures are silent," and on that basis they forbid the use of organs in the churches and the organization of benevolent boards. Other sects also are convinced that God looks with favor upon tuning forks and congregational singing, but has no ear for other forms of music.

The Church Triumphant holds to "Koreshanity," and teaches that we live on the inside of a hollow world. The Liberal Church has developed an "Uncle Sam's Religion" and made a creed of the constitution of the United States. A full score of denominations declare that they have no creed or "man-made doctrines," but their beliefs and scriptural interpretations are as elaborate as any. Several sects "talk in unknown tongues." A vision granted to a Negro cook on the Santa Fe Railway, revealing the fact that the Negro race is descended from the ten "lost" tribes of Israel, was the origin of the Church of God and Saints of Christ. The twelve "apostles" of the Catholic Apostolic Church obtain office by divine appointment only; all are now dead, the last dying in 1901, and since the Lord has seen fit to appoint no successors the members have for fifty years been "waiting upon the Lord for whatever it may please Him to do."

A multitude of persons accept the odd philosophies and interpretations of the sects and find therein that inner unity and spiritual wholeness they cannot discover elsewhere. This very fact prevents the careful student from dismissing them lightly. It may be a peculiar type of mind which is convinced that God is interested in whether his worshipers sing with or without instrumental accompaniment, but it is a real type, and there are some 400,000 American minds in that category. That so many persons attach moral meaning to what most people regard as trivial details is a psychological problem in itself.

Economic Influence in the Rise of Sects. All denominations began as sects, and the evolution of a sect into a church has followed a routine. In the background of nearly all sects there is a strong economic influence. These groups originate mainly among the religiously neglected poor, who find the conventional religion of their day unsuited to their social and psychological needs. This is true of Christianity itself, which was three hundred years old before it attracted considerable numbers of the socially well-placed. Finding themselves ill at ease in the presence of an effete and prosperous *bourgeoisie,* their emotional natures unsatisfied by a middle-class complacency, their economic problems disregarded by those who have no such problems to meet, and their naïve faith and simple interpretations smiled upon by their more cultured fellows, the poor and ignorant revolt and draw apart into groups which are more congenial. They elevate the necessities of their class—frugality, humility, and industry—into moral virtues and regard as sins the practices they are debarred from embracing. Those pinched by economic circumstances look askance at theatergoing, card playing, and "putting on of gold and costly apparel," but indulge in the same when their earthly fortunes improve. Their standards of conduct are invented from the simple lives they are compelled at all events to lead and which are congenial to their simplicity. They give free rein to their emotions and attribute the pleasant thrills thereof to a divine agency. They look for an escape from their hard lot into a heaven of bliss and comfort which is foreign to their workaday existence, and usually picture a coming time when the judgments of society shall be reversed and they shall change places with the prosperous and comfortable, who shall be cast down while the pious poor shall be exalted. They espouse their tenets with almost fanatical devotion and regard themselves as the true beloved of God. Thus the sect is born, out of a combination of spiritual need and economic forces.

Wrote Troeltsch:

The really creative, church-forming, religious movements are the work of the lower strata. Here only can one find that union of unimpaired imagination, simplicity in emotional life, unreflective character of thought, spontaneity of energy and vehement force of need, out of which an unconditioned faith in a divine revelation, the naïvete of complete surrender, and the intransigence of certitude can rise.[7]

In the second generation the sect begins to lose its character. The need for indoctrination of the young in the peculiar doctrines arises, and those who are trained in the sect seldom espouse its principles with the same devotion of those who were initiated therein by personal experience. The virtues of frugality and industry bear fruit in prosperity, and when prosperity comes the reasons for the sectarian revolt disappear and the manner of life against which the fathers rebelled is embraced by their children. Thus the spiritual need and economic forces which in one generation drew the sect out of the church turn about to transform the sect into a church. The last century witnessed the completion of this process in the case of Methodism. The Church of the Nazarene is now in the period of transformation.

John Wesley, the creator of a typical sect of the poor and ignorant, clearly foresaw this evolutionary process.

[7] Quoted by Niebuhr, *The Social Sources of Denominationalism*, p. 29.

I do not see how it is possible in the nature of things for any revival of religion to continue long. For religion must necessarily produce both industry and frugality, and these cannot but produce riches. But as riches increase so will pride, anger, and love of the world in all its branches.

The process was under way in his time.

The Methodists in every place grow diligent and frugal; consequently they increase in goods. Hence they proportionately increase in pride, in anger, in the desire of the flesh, the desire of the eyes, and pride of life. So, although the form of religion remains, the spirit is swiftly vanishing away.

Wesley had indeed a formula to prevent this development. He could not and ought not to prevent people from gaining all they could. But

what way can we take, that our money may not sink us into the nethermost hell? There is one way and there is no other way under heaven. If those who gain all they can, and save all they can, will likewise give all they can, then the more they gain, the more they will grow in grace, and the more treasures they will lay up in heaven.[8]

In propounding his remedy for the prevention of "pride, anger, and love of the world" Wesley did not take into account the psychology of the rich, who are not disposed to give away all the fruits of their frugality and industry; we have witnessed the completion of the process he feared, for Methodism has graduated from the ranks of the sects and has become a typical church of the *bourgeoisie*.[9]

The sects themselves do not recognize the economic factor in their history, though it frequently stands out plainly in their protest against elements which only wealth can secure—fine churches, organs, costly raiment, jewelry, indulgence in worldly amusements, and the like. In the sectarian mind the causes of divergence are theological. In some cases there is the alleged discovery of new truth, sometimes by special revelation; but more frequently the trouble lies in the neglect or abandonment by the churches of doctrines or practices which the protestants consider fundamental. Wherefore the sects are usually looking backward; in their own minds they are recovering primitive Christianity, maintaining the integrity of the Bible, preserving true religion and the experience thereof, or restoring the church to pristine purity. In all this, of course, economics figures prominently. It is the growth in wealth and culture that brings about

[8] Wesley, "Thoughts Upon Methodism," *Works* VII, 317.

[9] Exceptions to the general rule that sects originate and flourish among the ignorant poor are found in certain egocentric sects like Christian Science, Unity, and the so-called New Psychology, which offer physical comfort by mental processes, and the esoteric groups like the Vedantists, Bahais, and Theosophists, which speculate on mystic themes.

the departures from the early status and standards against which the schismatics protest.

In several ways the economic influence operates to bring about changes in theological emphases and ecclesiastical polity which are objectionable to the conservative mind and to those unblessed by the economic development. In the first place, increase in wealth eliminates the frontier simplicity and creates an atmosphere of affluence uncongenial to simple souls. Fine edifices appear, in which well-dressed and bejeweled congregations worship to the accompaniment of instrumental music and salaried choirs. Class distinctions emerge and social life within the church partakes of the "worldly" spirit. The favorite taboos of the poor, against dancing, theatergoing, and similar exercises, weaken, and the difference between the "saved" and "unsaved" becomes less apparent. In the minds of the conservative element, and those debarred by circumstances from participation in the general affluence, the church has grown apostate and worldly. Revolt ensues and a sect is born.

This process brought about two of the largest schisms of recent times in American Protestantism. The Disciples of Christ originated in the early nineteenth century in a "restoration" or back-to-the-Bible movement, the leading spirits of which were Alexander Campbell and Barton Stone. With the passing of frontier conditions cultural forces began to affect the group and a controversy over instrumental music and the organization of a missionary society with money dues, which began near the middle of the century, led to a movement to "restore the restorationists," which finally resulted in the emergence of the Churches of Christ as a separate sect. Indeed this and similar controversies have split the total body of Disciples into not less than six "mutually hostile and exclusive groups," [10] later to be mentioned.

Then growth in wealth and bigness undermines the democratic spirit and eliminates simplicity in ecclesiastical polity. There emerges a need for overhead boards, general officers, and money with which to support a benevolent program. A distinction comes about between connectional "leaders" and the plain ministry and people. In some quarters jealousies and distrust result. Many become uncomfortable in the presence of "machinery," for which they find little warrant in scripture, and chafe under the demands made upon them. Revolt is the result.

Such is the story of the beginnings of many small sects. As already mentioned, the Disciples split asunder over their missionary organization, made necessary by their growth. Among the Methodists the episcopacy and autocracy in government have always been stumbling blocks to many;

[10] Garrison, *Religion Follows the Frontier*, p. 297.

directly or indirectly the original Methodist body has sloughed off forty or fifty sects; these elements figured in nearly all the schisms and nearly all the resulting sects simplified and democratized their polity.

In the third place, the advance of education modifies doctrinal emphases, modes of religious expression, and methods of propaganda within the churches. In recent years the advance of science and historical criticism has profoundly influenced the theories of biblical inspiration and authority in the leading evangelical denominations; the literal accuracy of the Genesis stories, the nature of God, the reality of the devil, hell, and heaven, the doctrine of sin, and many other ideas have been greatly modified. A study of the beliefs of seven hundred ministers and two hundred theological students on fifty-six points of doctrine, made by Professor George Herbert Betts, indicates that the change of theological opinion has been more drastic than most churchmen have imagined.[11] Betts found that only 80 per cent of these ministers believed in the Trinity, 47 per cent in the Genesis account of creation, 68 per cent in the possibility of miracles, 60 per cent in the existence of the devil, 71 per cent in the Virgin Birth, 57 per cent in heaven as a place, 53 per cent in hell. When the replies of traditionally conservative Lutherans were omitted all these percentages were even more startling. Among students of theology the divergence from traditional orthodoxy is still more marked. This modification in belief has been accompanied by an almost total elimination of emotional expression, radical conversion experiences, and the revival method in the great denominations. Religious education has supplanted these phenomena which were fundamental to frontier religion and dear to thousands of simple souls. All this development has been accompanied by uneasiness and protest and has been responsible for many schisms and the creation of many sects.[12]

What Is A Sect? Sectarianism is a matter of spirit rather than form, organization, or size, hence it is not possible to define closely the term "sect." Even the greatest religious bodies, especially the largest of all, the Roman Catholic Church, has many characteristics of sectarianism, while very small bodies, like the Quakers and various racial groups, have long since graduated from the ranks of the sects and become churches.

In view of the gradual passing of the sect into a church, a process which

---

[11] Betts, *The Beliefs of 700 Ministers.* Being a study of opinions based on questions open to a variety of interpretations, many of them incapable of being answered by a categorical "yes" or "no," its accuracy must be greatly discounted. Only trends may be inferred therefrom.

[12] The economic influence in religion has been most ably discussed by Tawney, *Religion and the Rise of Capitalism;* also Niebuhr, *The Social Sources of Denominationalism,* and Sombart, *Quintessence of Capitalism.* The forerunner of the economic interpretation was Troeltsch, *Soziallehren der Christlichen Kirchen und Gruppen,* and Weber, *Gesammelte Aufsatze Zur Religionssoziologie.* See Tawney's criticism of the extreme positions of Troeltsch and Weber, pp. 319-21.

rarely begins until the second generation and may require several generations for its completion, it is plain that there is no clear-cut line between the two. A definition is accordingly difficult or impossible to formulate in terms that include all the elements of the sect and exclude all those of the church; even the names employed to designate the two bodies are more or less arbitrarily chosen; all claim to be churches and all repudiate the term sect as applied to themselves.

Niebuhr has attempted something like a definition by pointing out the distinctive features of each. The sect, he holds, is a voluntary association, while the church is "a natural social group akin to the family or nation." One joins the sect, but is born into the church; this difference is only partially accurate, however, since some process of joining is required by the churches as well as the sects. Churches, continues Niebuhr, "emphasize the universalism of the gospel, while sects are exclusive in character, appeal to the individualistic element in Christianity, and emphasize its ethical demands." Further, church membership rests largely on social obligation, while the sects usually "demand some definite type of religious experience." The church attaches importance to the means of grace which it administers, to its doctrines, sacraments, official clergy, its system of training the young, and the general social conventions. The sect rather insists on experience, "the priesthood of all believers," an ordinary or lay clergy, and separateness from "the world." [13]

The sect has a strong attachment to certain definite or concrete earmarks of its own, such as peculiarities of worship, literal interpretation of scripture, specific form of emotional reaction, rejection of "innovations" which depart from alleged ancient practices, and the disproportionate elevation of some tenet like premillenarianism or the state of the dead. The breadth and liberal attitude of the conventionalized church is foreign to the sect; the latter usually looks upon the former as apostate and regards itself as the "true church" and its practices alone as conforming to the biblical and divinely-sanctioned pattern. A narrow dogmatism is perhaps the most nearly universal characteristic of the typical sectarian spirit. Beyond these general specifications it is scarcely possible to define the church or the sect.

Different Types of Sects. Various attempts have been made to designate categories into which churches, denominations, or sects naturally fall. They are frequently designated as *ritualistic or sacramentarian,* as the Roman Catholic and Episcopalian; *experiential or emotional,* as the Methodist and allied bodies; *intellectual or doctrinal,* as the Presbyterian, Unitarian, and similar groups; and *racial,* as the Jews. McComas names three great types: the *intellectual, feeling,* and *action* types.[14]

[13] Niebuhr, *op. cit.,* pp. 17, 18.
[14] See McComas, *The Psychology of Religious Sects,* chs. vi-vii.

These categories are supposed to correspond to the mental make-up of the persons who find their spiritual cravings satisfied by the teaching or worship practices of the various bodies. Such classifications, it seems plain, can hold good for the sects only in their early or formative stages, when individuals are free to respond to the type of worship which best suits their natures. In the case of the long-established and conventionalized churches the *teaching* process has entered to eliminate the principle of voluntary selection by imposing denominational attachments on persons without regard to their psychological needs. Originally the Methodists were a pure experimental or emotional type, and few entered the fold save through a definite conversion experience or feeling reaction; today, however, training and social pressure fill The Methodist Church with the sons and daughters of Methodists, few of whom have undergone a definite experience and many of whom are no doubt temperamentally incapable of the radical emotional upheaval.[15] Similarly, many modern Presbyterians doubtless know or care little about the stern logic and hair-splitting intellectualism of the early Calvinistic theology. Social considerations have brought into all the churches persons of various psychological make-up and temperament, and the worship has been so modified that all are comfortable.

A study of the small American sects, however, reveals that they may be grouped roughly into seven main categories, according to the types of mind to which their leading principles appeal. The lines of demarcation cannot be strictly drawn, however, for here, as elsewhere, training and social pressure have operated, and since any given sect embraces several different principles there will be considerable overlapping. The categories are as follows:

1. *The Pessimistic or Adventist Sects.* These are typical groups of the disinherited, in final despair of obtaining through social processes the benefits they seek. They see no good in the world and no hope of improvement; it is rushing speedily to hell, according to the will and plan of God. The adherents of such sects magnify millenarianism and see the imminent end of the present world-order by means of a cosmic catastrophe. They have turned on the world, and they seek escape through a cataclysm which will cast down those who have been elevated, and secure to the faithful important places in a new temporal kingdom as well as eternal bliss in heaven. Adventists are the best representatives of this class, although this philosophy

[15] In *The Psychology of Religious Awakening* (pp. 115-19) I have shown by a study of 985 cases that 67 per cent of the present-day Methodists underwent no definite experience whatever, 26 per cent experienced only a slight emotional stimulus, and only 7 per cent had a definite crisis experience.

is the leading principle of the so-called Fundamentalist movement and is found in nearly all of the denominations and in many small sects.

2. *The Perfectionist Subjectivist Sects.* These seek holiness, personal perfection of life, or freedom from the temptations and "desires of the flesh." They are of the experiential type, realizing their hopes through strong emotional reactions. The early Methodists were fine examples of this type of mind, and the present-day perfectionists are nearly all offshoots of Methodism. Among these sects are the Nazarene, Holiness, and similar bodies.

3. *The Charismatic or Pentecostal Sects.* These are the left-wing of the subjectivist groups. They seek "gifts," the "spirit of prophecy," the "blessing," and spiritual enduements of various kinds. "Speaking with tongues," trances, visions, and various motor reactions characterize their worship. Examples are found in the pentecostal sects, some of the Church of God groups, and many Negro bodies.

4. *The Communistic Sects.* These groups withdraw from "the world" into colonies where they secure the social approval which is denied them elsewhere and where they engage in economic experiments. Community of goods is the common characteristic. Some of these groups have espoused free love or community of women and their rites have run into antinomian excesses. None of these sects have been able to preserve their pure communistic character over a long period; many have appeared and died, some have gradually merged with the society about them, and a few are maintaining a struggling existence. Among these religious colonies may be mentioned the Shakers, the Amana Church Society, the House of David, the Church of God and Saints of Christ, at Belleville, Virginia, and the now-defunct Llano Colony.

5. *The Legalistic or Objectivist Sects.* For want of a better name the term "legalistic" is used to designate a group of sects which stress certain rules, objective forms, observances, or "things" which can be definitely performed as essential to true religion. Frequently the distinguishing mark is the *rejection* or *denial* of some practice. The sects derive their rites or taboos from some portion of the Bible and sometimes look upon themselves as the "true church" or restorers of primitive Christianity. In this group are the foot-washing sects, those which insist upon some peculiarity of dress, as the "hook-and-eye" Mennonites, and those that cover the heads of the women, the Presbyterians who sing only the Psalms and reject the hymns, the Churches of Christ, with their antipathy to musical instruments and missionary societies, and the Primitive Baptists, who oppose Sunday schools. Included also are the sacramentarian or sacerdotal sects, which set great store by their sacraments and the "apostolic succession" of their higher clergy. Examples are the Old Catholic Churches, of which there are three in America, and the African Orthodox Church, a Negro body.

6. *The Egocentric or New Thought Sects.* These have physical comfort, personal exhilaration, and freedom from pain, disease, and ennui as their objectives. The Christian Scientists, Divine Scientists, Unity School of Christianity, and New Thought groups are examples of this type.

7. *The Esoteric or Mystic Sects.* These are devotees of the mystic. They espouse doctrines into which one needs to be initiated. They are nearly all offshoots of Hinduism and can hardly be called Christian sects. They specialize on mysteries and the occult, and their literature is scarcely understandable to the ordinary man. The best examples are the Theosophists and the Spiritualists.

CHAPTER II

PESSIMISTIC OR ADVENTIST SECTS

Aᴅᴠᴇɴᴛɪsᴍ ɪs ᴛʜᴇ ᴛʏᴘɪᴄᴀʟ ᴄᴜʟᴛ ᴏғ ᴛʜᴇ ᴅɪsɪɴʜᴇʀɪᴛᴇᴅ ᴀɴᴅ sᴜғғᴇʀɪɴɢ poor. Its peculiar world view reflects the psychology of a distressed class in despair of obtaining the benefits it seeks through the present social order and seeking escape through divine intervention and a cosmic cataclysm, which will destroy the world and the "worldly" classes and elevate "the saints" to the position they could not attain through social processes.

Adventism rests on the literal interpretation and the hope of a concrete fulfillment of Jewish and Christian apocalyptic prophecies, a literature which sprang directly from the grief of a despised and downtrodden people. Its fundamental philosophy is that of the Persian dualism, a titanic struggle between good and evil forces personified as demons and angels, the reflection in the cosmic sphere of the struggle of the oppressed with their oppressors. This philosophy was learned by the Jews during the Persian period of their history and used to bolster the flagging spirits of the people during the Hellenistic persecutions of the succeeding period. It was taken over and identically used by the early Christians when the historical situation was exactly duplicated by the persecution of the Roman emperors.

The Adventist World View. Adventism has developed a world view with a complete theological, sociological, and eschatological system. Its central feature is the second coming of Christ to establish his millennial reign. Its adherents are divided into two schools, the point of difference being the chronology of Christ's return with reference to the thousand-year period or millennium of Rev. 20:1-6. Postmillenarians do not expect human ills to be corrected by a cataclysm, but by the gradual spread of the Christian gospel until it controls the world and thus brings about ideal conditions, after which will come the return of Christ, the resurrection, judgment, and final end of all things. The social program of postmillenarians is justified by reference to the parables of the leaven, mustard seed, grain growing gradually, and other passages in which Jesus clearly teaches the social nature and developmental processes of realizing his ideal kingdom.

The premillenarians, in whose ranks are found nearly all persons who take adventism seriously, find no ground for hope in the social process. They are profoundly pessimistic. Society has been morally deteriorating since the days of Adam and the downward trend must continue until Christ comes to set things right by a cosmic catastrophe. Hence moral badness and social evils like wars, famines, plagues, and similar phenomena have always been regarded as tokens of the approaching end of time and have been followed by recrudescences of fervent millennial hopes. The doctrine inevitably operates to prevent efforts for social betterment on the part of those whose dearest dreams are set on the second advent. One finds little or no social consciousness among them. It is no part of the church's duty to reform and redeem the social order. Its function is to prepare a "true church," a comparatively small body of saints, for membership in the coming kingdom.

When affairs have reached the necessary state of badness, Christ will come with a shout, not indeed to the world but to the "upper air" immediately above the world. Here he will pause and snatch up to his side the "true church," including many who have died and are to be raised in "the first resurrection" for the occasion. Here the whole company will remain for seven years, more or less, enjoying what is technically known among adventists as "the rapture."

While Christ and his saints are floating about in the air strange and terrible things will transpire upon the earth, which will be given over to diabolical forces. The Jews will return to Palestine. Antichrist will appear, establish his capital at Babylon, which will be restored miraculously for the occasion, and devastate the world. Awful agonies and tribulations will fall upon men and the earth will be filled with woe and confusion. Suddenly Christ and "the true church" will descend from "the rapture" in the midst of flames, shoutings, and trumpet blasts. Antichrist and his capital, Babylon, will be destroyed. Satan will be captured, chained, and consigned to the lower regions; with him will go "the beast" and "the false prophet." All the hosts of evil will be destroyed. Christ will sit upon a temporal throne in Jerusalem and the millennial reign will begin, which will be glorious beyond description.

At the end of the millennium Satan will be released to wage war upon Christ and the saints. He will command a host of demons too numerous to count. But in the ensuing battle his cohorts will be overthrown and burned with fire from heaven. Once more Satan will be thrown into a pit of fire, this time to undergo eternal torment. After this consummation the ungodly dead will be raised up to be judged and sentenced to the eternal fires. Then the earth will be burned and Christ and the saints will rise to heaven and eternal bliss. Though differences of opinion prevail in premillenarian ranks concerning the details of the scheme, this is in general the world view of the group.[1]

The Jewish Background. Though the central idea of Adventism is the second coming of Jesus Christ, its background is Jewish. Certain allied conceptions do indeed root far back in history and were prevalent among many nations of antiquity. The Babylonians, for example, as well as many others, made struggle the fundamental cosmic principle; in the Babylonian creation epic the world itself was the result of the titanic struggle between the great god Marduk and the female deity Tiamat. The existence of demons, their malign influence and activity, the intrinsically evil nature of the world, an impending catastrophe—these and other notions which appear in Adventism were found among numerous peoples other than the Hebrews.[2] Indeed that branch of the Semitic stock kept its early religion relatively free from such ideas; they appeared only when manifold tribulations forced the Jews to abandon all hopes of attaining greatness through social processes and to fall back on divine intervention.

The apocalypticism from which Adventism sprang was a product of Jewish suffering. It does not appear in pre-exilic literature. Facing the captivity, the Jews dreamed of a "day of Yahweh" when God would intervene to cast down their enemies, but this idea was scorned by the prophets, who urged repentance and reform as the course of safety. But when the blow fell the people turned on the world and looked for divine intervention on their behalf. Ezekiel initiated the apocalyptic literary style, damning his enemies and glorifying the Jews under strange figures unintelligible to their oppressors but understandable to the initiated. There were to be some terrible calamities and then they would be rescued and restored to Zion.[3] In similar vein the great prophet of the exile, Deutero-Isaiah, pictured the glorious journey homeward over a miraculously prepared highway and the wonders of the new Jerusalem, built by God himself, and the temple in which God would dwell in person.[4] After the return the Jews imbibed the dualism of

---

[1] See Blackstone, *Jesus Is Coming*. This favorite volume has been circulated by hundreds of thousands and translated into twenty-five languages. See also *The Fundamentalist Publications*; Loughborough, *The Great Second Advent Movement*; Silver, *The Lord's Return*; and the *Millennial Dawn* books of the late "pastor" Russell. For critical accounts see Case, *The Millennial Hope*; McCown, *The Promise of His Coming*; Sheldon, *Studies in Recent Adventism*; Campbell, *The Second Coming of Christ*; Eaton, *The Millennial Dawn Heresy*; Mains, *Premillennialism*.

[2] For specific data on these Gentile ideas see Case, *The Millennial Hope*, ch. i; Clark, *The Origin and Development of Millennial Ideas* (unpublished MS in Temple University library), ch. i; Hastings, *Encyclopedia of Religion and Ethics*, arts. "Eschatology" and "Demons and Spirits." See also Paton, *Spiritism and the Cult of the Dead in Antiquity*; Kennedy, *St. Paul's Conception of the Last Things*; Kennedy, *St. Paul and the Mystery Religions*; Fowler, *The Religious Experience of the Roman Peoples*; Willoughby, *Pagan Regeneration*; Angus, *The Religious Quests of the Graeco-Roman World*; Sheldon, *The Mystery Religions and the New Testament*.

[3] For example, see Ezek. 38–39.

[4] Isa. 40:3, 4; 54:11, 12; 65:25.

their Persian overlords and thereafter angels and demons figured in their apocalyptic writings.

Apocalyptic flared forth again in the Greek period when Antiochus Epiphanes undertook to hasten the Hellenizing process, already well under way, by forcibly extirpating Judaism; he set up an altar to Zeus—"the abomination of desolation" in the temple and forced the Jews to offer swine's flesh to pagan deities. It was the most serious crisis the people ever faced, and when persecution became intense the apocalyptic book of Daniel appeared. Under the usual strange figures the Jews were bidden to resist unto the utmost and depend upon God, who would save them as he had saved others from the fiery furnace and the lion's den. The prophet depicted the various enemy nations under the form of strange beasts, a horn on the head of one representing Antiochus. The horn persecuted the saints until destroyed by God and a host of angels, after which "one like a son of man" established a glorious Jewish kingdom.

Here began the system of date-setting which has marked the progress of millennial speculation. Twice the writer announced that the end would come in three and one-half years and once he placed it twenty-three hundred days after December 25, 168 B.C. In the ninth chapter he reworked Jeremiah's prophecy that Jerusalem's desolation would continue seventy years; the prophet could not have been mistaken, hence his seventy years were not really seventy years, but seven times seventy, "seven weeks of years, or 490 years.[5] Here also appeared other familiar earmarks of millennialism—the final outburst of wickedness, war of the demons against the saints, resurrection of dead saints, deliverance by a messianic prince, rout of the demons, the glorious golden age to come, the cataclysmic end of the world. None of these events ever occurred, but in the next period of suffering the same ideas flourished again.[6]

The Early Christian Background. The early Christians were a despised and disinherited sect; for three centuries they had little surcease from hatred and persecution. Moreover, the first Christians were all Jews, and not one of them had any thought of separating from Judaism. They were concerned only with putting Christ into the old faith, and that faith was surcharged with apocalyptic Messianism. Involved in their acceptance of Jesus as the Messiah was the necessity that he would fulfill the traditional hopes. But he did not fulfill them during his earthly career, hence he must do so later. A second advent, unknown to Jewish Messianism, thus became a necessity. As historical circumstances were reproduced, and persecution fell upon the

---

[5] For modern critical interpretations of Daniel see the various scholarly introductions and commentaries, especially Peters, *Daniel* in the *International Critical Commentary* series, and Case, *op. cit.*, pp. 80-86.

[6] Jewish speculations after Daniel are found in the apocryphal literature, which see. Also see Clark (MS), *op. cit.*, and Case, *op. cit.*, ch. ii.

church, the familiar conceptions were revived; angels, demons, cosmic struggle, suffering, warfare, and the imminent and cataclysmic end of the world all figured in early Christian theology.

In the first years of his career Paul, the earliest Christian writer, seemed convinced that Christ would return during his own lifetime. In his first Thessalonian letter, evidently written to correct an impression the converts had gained to the effect that the parousia would soon occur, and which had given rise to perplexity and questioning when some had died before the expected event, Paul refers to the dead as "they" and to those who will remain to the end as "we." [7] He points out that the dead will be at no disadvantage, as they will be raised to meet, with the living, the Lord in the air. In the second letter to the same group he explains the delay in Christ's appearance by the statement that there must first be a great apostasy or "falling away" and the coming of the "man of sin" mentioned in Daniel.[8] After this the apostle does not lay so much stress on the second coming; he mentions the event in II Corinthians, Romans, and Philippians,[9] but in his old age and imprisonment he has abandoned all hope of being present alive at the return, remarking that the time of his departure is at hand and he will be saved in a heavenly kingdom.[10] Similar references appear in other New Testament letters,[11] but when the late second Petrine epistle was written, and the first persecution, which had originated in Jerusalem, had passed, the people were doubting the whole scheme of the second coming,[12] which doubts are used by the author as proofs of the preliminary apostasy.

The Synoptic Gospels are dominated by a wholly different idea—namely, that the ideal kingdom is a social order will be realized by a process of gradual growth. This is made particularly clear in the parables of the leaven, the mustard seed, and the growing corn. But in certain sections of these Gospels there is another conception, quite frankly derived from Jewish apocalyptic and varying fundamentally from the main drift of synoptic teaching in that it pictures a kingdom to be realized by a cosmic upheaval. There are four of these apocalyptic passages; all are recorded by each author and there are differences and discrepancies in the various stories.[13] They

---

[7] I Thess. 4:15-17.

[8] II Thess. 2:1-12; 3:1-12; Dan. 5:20, 23; 7:25; 8:23-25; 11:30-45.

[9] II Cor. 5:6-10; Rom. 14:8; Phil. 1:23, 24; 3:20.

[10] II Tim. 4:6-8, 18.

[11] I Pet. 1:16-21; 2:1-3; 3:8-10; Jas. 5:7-9; Jude 3-23.

[12] II Pet. 1:16-21; 2:1-3; 3:8-10. For detailed discussions of the eschatological teachings in all the New Testament epistles see the various volumes of *The International Critical Commentary*; Case, *The Millennial Hope*; Hastings, *Encyclopedia of Religion and Ethics*, article, "Demons and Spirits" (Christian); Terry, *Biblical Apocalyptics*; Matthews, *The Messianic Hope in the New Testament*; Kennedy, *St. Paul's Conceptions of the Last Things*; Kennedy, *St. Paul and the Mystery Religions*; Beet, *The Last Things*; Moffatt, *Introduction to the Literature of the New Testament*.

[13] The passages are: (1) Matt. 10:1-23; Mark 6:7-11; Luke 9:1-5; (2) Matt. 16:27, 28; Mark 8:38; Luke 9:26, 27; (3) Matt. 24; Mark 13; Luke 21; (4) Matt. 26:64; Mark 14:62; Luke 22:69.

embody the usual apocalyptic notions and repeatedly affirm that persons then living would witness the parousia and its concomitant events. The Roman yoke was becoming more irksome, and in "the great eschatological discourse" of Matt. 24, Mark 13, and Luke 21, the materials relating to the destruction of the temple by the Roman armies and the end of the world are so confusingly interwoven that the most careful scholarship experiences difficulty in disentangling them.[14]

Modern Adventism leans most heavily upon a literal interpretation of the Jewish-Christian apocalypse of Revelation. This strange book, in purpose, occasion, and style, is similar to the book of Daniel. It was written to strengthen the Christians and to predict the overthrow of their enemies during the terrible persecutions of Domitian, who attempted the extirpation of Christianity by demanding participation in the Caesarcult. Every feature of millennialism is exhibited: the struggle between demons and angels, the imminent end, the final outburst of wickedness, the personal return and thousand-year reign of Christ, the doom of God's enemies, the imprisonment, subsequent release, and final damnation of Satan, the depredations of antichrist, the eternal bliss of the faithful. There is here no social kingdom to be progressively realized, as in the Gospels; the world is ruled by demons and their cohorts, and there is no escape save by means of a cosmic catastrophe. The time is at hand; the slight delay is to permit a few more Christians to win the martyr's crown. The Roman power, which Paul had declared to be "ordained of God," is pictured as a beast devastating the church, the functionary who enforces the worship of the emperor is the false prophet serving the beast, the city of Rome is a harlot drunken with blood, a terrible antichrist, whose number is 666, is about to appear. But in due time Messiah and his armies will come to overthrow all these and to usher in the millennial reign and the strange events that follow it.[15]

Thus again did the disinherited of the earth turn upon the world and find their hope of release in a cosmic cataclysm. They employed the only vehicle possible under the circumstances. That these apocalyptic dreams were never fulfilled goes without saying. Rome was not destroyed. Nero did not return, nor did any similar antichrist appear. The millennium was

[14] This has been attempted by Wendt and others. Using Mark's account for his analysis, Wendt finds the authentic teaching of Jesus in 13:1-6; 9:10-13, 21-23, 28, 29, 32-36; the apocalypse is preserved in verses 7, 8, 14-20, 24-27, 30-31. See Wendt, *The Teaching of Jesus.*

[15] For detailed interpretation and critical study of the apocalypse see Charles, *The Revelation of St. John* (2 vols.); Beckwirth, *The Apocalypse of John;* Case, *The Book of Revelation;* Case, *The Millennial Hope;* Matthews, *The Messianic Hope in the New Testament;* Moffatt, *Introduction to the Literature of the New Testament;* Calkins, *The Social Message of the Book of Revelation;* Dean, *The Book of Revelation;* Port, *The Messages of the Apocalyptical Writers;* Ramsay, *The Letters to the Seven Churches;* and the articles in Cheyne, *Encyclopedia Biblica.* Hastings, *Dictionary of the Bible,* and Hastings, *Encyclopedia of Religion and Ethics.* For the literalist premillenarian interpretation see Gaebelein, *Revelation.*

not established nor did the world order come to an end. The persecution of Christianity ceased, but at the command of the very power which this book was written to denounce, and Christianity became the official religion of the very empire which the apocalyptist expected to be overthrown. Nevertheless this document has exercised a powerful influence in history, and its figures are still expected by millions to be literally fulfilled at an early date.

Adventism in the Early Church. It would have been surprising had the ideas which surcharged late Jewish and early Christian thinking not been carried over into the theology of the church. As a matter of fact these notions were nearly universal until the time of Origen. The Revelation of Saint John the Divine was not the only Christian apocalyptic. Other books of a similar nature were produced in the second century and may be read today in collections of Christian apocrypha.[16] The early fathers wrote in more sober vein, but many of them entertained lively millennial hopes. They repeated the ideas of Daniel and Revelation and engaged in fanciful speculation on the identity of the two slain prophets and the beast, the date of the advent, and similar themes.[17]

Millennial views began to be discounted at an early date also. The Gnostics, regarding matter as wholly evil, rejected the whole scheme. Origen, by his system of allegorical interpretation, dealt a body blow to millennialism, sternly scoring the literalism of its advocates.[18] Dionysius of Alexandria quotes certain others as rejecting the authenticity of Revelation.[19] Finally the great Augustine "lays the ghost of millenarianism so effectively that for centuries thereafter the subject is practically ignored." [20] By his time Christianity had conquered the empire and become its legal religion. Overnight, as it were, the sect of the disinherited had graduated into a church of the well-placed, supported by and itself in turn supporting the ruling order. Thus the taproot of apocalypticism and millennialism was cut. Adventism again became the religion of sects which the church flung off. Hopes revived as the end of the first Christian millennium approached and various preachers announced the impending end immediately prior to A.D. 1000, but their views had slight influence on a comfortable and well-placed church.

Resurgence of Adventism. In due time the wealth, moral laxness, and social prestige of the church brought into operation the familiar process of

[16] These may be read in Donehoo, *Apocryphal and Legendary Life of Christ; Excluded Books of the New Testament,* edited by Lightfoot, *et al.*

[17] This was true of the Didache, Ignatius of Antioch, Polycarp, Papias, Justin Martyr, Irenaeus, Tertullian, Hippolytus, Commodian, Lactantius, Methodius, and many others. See their writings. Also Case, *The Millennial Hope,* ch. iv, who gives a summary of such teachings.

[18] *De Prin,* ii, iii.

[19] Eusebius, *History,* vii.

[20] Case, *op. cit.,* p. 179; Augustine, *City of God,* xx.

revolt, and numerous heretical sects appeared in all parts of Christendom. Many of these espoused millenarian views. Among these sects began the practice, which passed on to the age of the Reformation and has continued until the present, of identifying the pope with the antichrist or beast of Revelation.[21] Periods of unusual stress, attended by wars and other calamities, always bred a swarm of apocalyptic ideas and prophecies of the impending end of time; this was true of the Reformation, the Peasants' Revolt, the English, French, and American Revolutions, the American Civil War, and the two World Wars.

The poor set their hopes on the Reformation, only to find themselves disappointed when Luther turned against them and issued his pamphlet *Against the Thieving and Murderous Hordes of Peasants.* Then the Anabaptists, Mennonites, and similar sects, came forward with the familiar millenarian tenets. In similar manner the Millenarians, Fifth Monarchy Men, Quakers, and others, revolted against the Commonwealth and the reforms of Cromwell.[22] The religious wars in Germany brought forth the Bohemian Brethren and the millenarian teachings of Ezekiel Meth. The persecution of the Huguenots in France inspired the works of Professor Jurieu of Sedan and Serarius in Holland. In England the revolution was responsible for the teachings of Poiret, Joseph Mede, Jane Lead, and Thomas Burnet.[23]

Many interpreters have so deciphered the symbols of Daniel and Revelation as to fix definite dates for the second advent. The years 500 and 1000 have already been mentioned. Militz of Kromeriz, a precursor of Huss, set the end between 1365 and 1367; during the Hussite Wars the Bohemians expected the parousia to occur immediately. The Bohemian Taborites selected five cities to be spared from the general conflagration, multitudes flocking thither and establishing communistic orders. The Anabaptists expected the event to occur in connection with the Peasants' War of 1525; following this revolt Melchoir Hofmann announced himself as one of the two witnesses of Rev. 11:3, took possession of Münster, at the head of a band of fanatics, and set up "New Zion" therein until the movement was suppressed by force. Alsted, in Germany, named 1694, and the French theologian Jurieu chose 1689. The Fifth Monarchy Men attempted in 1657 and 1661 to set up the throne of "King Jesus" by arms. A girl of the German Ronsdorf sect experienced a series of visions and announced that the advent would occur in 1730; she was the mother of Zion and woman clothed with the sun of Rev. 12:1; she and her husband were the two slain

[21] Hagenbach, *History of Doctrines,* II, 119.
[22] Niebuhr, *op. cit.,* ch. ii.
[23] Schaff-Herzog, *Encyclopedia of Religious Knowledge,* art. "Millenarianism."

witnesses, and one of their children was to be the savior of the world.[24]

Date-setting continued through the nineteenth century. The German theologian Bengel fixed upon 1836. The theosophist Schönherr was certain that Napoleon was the antichrist and Königsberg the doomed city of Rev. 17:9 ff. In 1826 Christoph Hoffmann undertook to rebuild the temple in Jerusalem for Christ's occupancy. The Irvingites of England and Scotland announced 1835, 1838, 1864, and 1866.[25] Mother Ann Lee and her Shakers were so sure the end was at hand that they abolished matrimony, following Paul's advice to the Corinthians.[26] The Plymouth Brethren specified no exact date, but their historian declared that "if anyone had told the first Brethren that three quarters of a century might elapse and the Church be still on earth, the answer would probably have been a smile, partly of pity, partly of disapproval, wholly of incredulity." [27] William Miller, founder of the modern Adventist sects, declared in 1844 that he had the names and addresses of three thousand preachers who were proclaiming the imminence of the end.[28]

In 1881 Claas Epp, a leader of the Mennonite Brethren (Bruedergemeinde) in Russia, announced himself as one of the two witnesses, and prepared to meet Elijah in the skies and with him proceed to heaven. Christ was to appear on March 8, 1889, the date being fixed by an old wallclock on which the hands pointed to 89. When 1889 passed without any cosmic happening, Epp was informed in a vision that the clock leaned slightly, and when stood erect the hands pointed to 91; hence the correct advent date was 1891. Epp finally claimed to be a son of Christ, a fourth person of the Godhead, and adopted a baptismal formula of Father, Sons, and Holy Ghost.[29] Another Russian sect, called the Dukhobors, settled in Canada in 1899. In the fall of 1902 nearly sixteen hundred of these fared forth, without shoes or food, and in some cases entirely nude, to meet the returned Lord in some Canadian village. Winter fell, and the fanatics endured indescribable suffering until they were rounded up by the mounted police, and in spite of stubborn resistance shipped back to their homes. The same fiasco has been repeated at various times.[30]

It has been said that more than a hundred speculators predicted that the advent would occur within the decade following the end of the American Civil War.[31] The Mormons went to Utah to await the return of Christ.

[24] Case, op. cit., pp. 187 f.
[25] Ibid., pp. 197 f.; Miller, History and Doctrine of Irvingism, ch. ii.
[26] Case, op. cit., p. 196.
[27] Neatby, A History of the Plymouth Brethren, p. 339.
[28] Loughborough, The Great Second Advent Movement, p. 105.
[29] Smith, The Mennonites, A Brief History, pp. 176, 177.
[30] Ferguson, The Confusion of Tongues, pp. 120-25. For a history of the Dukhobors see Maude, A Peculiar People, the Dukhobors.
[31] Baxter, The Great Crisis at the Period of 1867 to 1875.

Cunninghame named 1839 or a period near that date.[32] The famous William Miller named 1843 and then 1844. Elliott and Cumming looked for the end in 1866.[33] Brewer and Decker predicted 1867, an anonymous pamphlet published in 1871 argued for 1873,[34] and Seiss favored 1870.[35] "Pastor" Russell taught that the millennium began in 1873, the apostles were raised in 1878, and the end would come in 1914. Guinness was certain that earthly affairs could not endure beyond 1923.[36]

At the present time many small sects which have emerged from evangelical Protestantism in the United States adhere to some form of premillenarianism. Forty or more sects, with a combined membership of over a million, report it as one of the central ideas in their doctrinal statements; this group includes the sects bearing the Adventist label and which are the offshoots of the Millerite agitation near the middle of the nineteenth century, most of the Holiness sects, and many others. Including the Fundamentalists who have not left their denominations, there are probably three or four million persons who accept the millenarian scheme.[37]

The Millerite Movement. William Miller was a farmer of Low Hampton, New York, a Baptist licentiate and an ardent student of the Bible, especially the "chronological portions" of the apocalyptic literature. He became convinced that many events had been predicted to occur within a specified time and had always transpired according to the chronology; this was true of the flood (120 years), Abraham's sojourn (400 years), the wilderness sojourn (40 years), the duration of the exile (70 years), and other happenings.[38] This led him to study the various passages in Daniel and Revelation wherein chronology figures. Relying on such scriptural passages as Num. 14:34 and Ezek. 4:6, he assumed, as many others have done, that a biblical day really meant a year, and on that basis proceeded to make some computations. The seventy weeks of Dan. 9:24 he took to be 490 years, and he believed that this exact period elapsed between the date of the prophecy and the coming of Messiah. Similarly the "time, times, and the dividing of time" of Dan. 7:25 and 12:7 (repeated in Rev. 11:2, 3; 12:6, 14; 13:5) meant three and one-half years, or 42 months, or 1,260 days, and therefore 1,260 years. Miller identified the "little horn" of Dan. 7

---

[32] Cunninghame, *The Scientific Chronology of the Year 1839.*

[33] Elliott, *Horae Apocalyptical,* vol. iv; Cumming, *The End or the Proximate Signs of the Close of the Dispensation,* pp. 72, 73.

[34] Sheldon, *op. cit.,* pp. 41, 42.

[35] Seiss, *The Last Things,* p. 269.

[36] Guinness, *The Approaching End of the Age,* pp. 472-87. See also Case, *op. cit.,* pp. 187-204.

[37] The Adventist bodies are the Advent Christian, Seventh Day Adventist, Church of God (Adventist), Life and Advent Union, Churches of God in Christ Jesus, and Primitive Advent Christian.

[38] Olsen, *Origin and Progress of Seventh-Day Adventists,* p. 111.

with the papacy, and calculated that the popes were supreme from the year 538, when the Ostrogoths were defeated, until 1798, when Pius VI was carried as a prisoner to France, the "little horn" being thus overthrown, a period of exactly 1,260 years.

Following up this line of study, Miller turned his attention to the prophecy in Dan. 8:13-14: "Then I heard one saint speaking, and another saint said unto that certain saint which spake, How long shall be the vision concerning the daily sacrifice, and the transgression of desolation, to give both the sanctuary and the host to be trodden under foot? And he said unto me, Unto two thousand and three hundred days; then shall the sanctuary be cleansed." The 490 years (seventy weeks) of Dan. 9:24 constituted the first part of the 2,300 years (days) of this scripture; the period began with "the going forth of the commandment to restore and to build Jerusalem" (Dan. 9:25), which Miller identified with the commandment of Artaxerxes issued in 457 B.C., and mentioned in the seventh chapter of Ezra. By taking this date as his starting point and adding 2,300 years, Miller reached the conclusion that "the cleansing of the sanctuary" would take place between March 21, 1843, and March 21, 1844. His reasoning was reinforced by the assertion that 69 weeks or 483 years (Dan. 9:25) from 457 B.C. witnessed the baptism of Jesus in A.D. 27.[39] The "cleansing of the sanctuary" was supposed to be the personal return of Christ to purge the world, and Miller went forth to preach his gospel

that in about twenty-five years from that time (1818) all the affairs of our present state would be wound up; that all its pride and power, pomp and vanity, wickedness and oppression, would come to an end; and that, in the place of the kingdoms of this world, the peaceful and long-desired kingdom of the Messiah would be established under the whole heaven.[40]

Miller began to lecture in support of his theories in 1831, and carried on a vigorous propaganda. Crowds became interested and many converts were made among preachers and members of the various denominations. Enthusiasm gathered momentum and a dozen or more newspapers were published to spread abroad the adventist message.[41] Various churches looked with a certain degree of favor on the movement in its early stages, and many orthodox pulpits were opened to its advocates. At its height in 1844 the believers in the Miller doctrine numbered fifty thousand.[42]

[39] See Loughborough, *The Great Second Advent Movement*, p. 110. As a matter of fact the restoration of Jerusalem in 9:25 was to be in sixty-nine weeks instead of seventy, while the anointing of the most Holy of 9:24 was to be after seventy weeks instead of sixty-nine.

[40] White, *Sketches of the Christian Life and Public Labors of William Miller*, pp. 57-58.

[41] Mention is made of many of these in Olsen, *op. cit.*, chs. iv and v. Miller said he received sixteen different Adventist publications in one week.

[42] *Ibid.*, p. 160.

When the last day of the predicted year passed without untoward happening, there was dismay in the ranks of the Adventists. Miller stated his great disappointment in letters and a message to his followers.

I confess my error and acknowledge my disappointment; yet I still believe that the day of the Lord is near, even at the door; and I exhort you, my brethren, to be watchful, and not let that day come upon you unawares.[43]

At a camp meeting at Exeter, New Hampshire, in the late summer of 1844, when those present were in utter dejection, one John Couch announced that the end was to be in *the seventh month* of the then current Jewish year. His argument was thus summarized:

That as the seventy prophetic weeks are the first 490 years of the 2,300, and as the first seven weeks of the seventy mark the time of the work of restoring and building Jerusalem in troublous times, the great period must commence with the commencement of the work of restoring and building, which did not commence in the spring, on the first month, when Ezra started from Babylon, but after he had reached Jerusalem, in the autumn, probably on the seventh month. "For upon the first day of the first month began he to go up from Babylon, and on the first day of the fifth month came he to Jerusalem." (Ezra 7:9.) This would give more than two months for necessary preparations for the work of restoring and building to commence on the seventh month, immediately after the great day of atonement. That as the words of the angel to the prophet Daniel—"In the midst of the week he shall cause the sacrifice and the oblation to cease"—mean that in the middle of the last week of the seventy, Christ should be crucified; and as he was crucified in the spring, that prophetic week of seven years must commence and close in the fall. Consequently the seventy weeks commenced and closed in the fall, and therefore the 2,300 days terminate in the fall.[44]

According to this reasoning the Lord's return would eventuate on October 22, 1844. The old enthusiasm flared up again, running higher and higher through the summer of that year. As the day approached Adventist papers published their "last" editions and gave them away free, since funds would no longer be needed. Men planted no crops, gave away their money, discharged their employees, settled their accounts, and made all preparations for the climactic "midnight cry"—"Behold, the bridegroom cometh; go ye out to meet him." [45] On the appointed day they gathered in their churches in assured anticipation. The scoffers were on hand to mock and jeer. At one place, in Paris, Maine, two of the rowdies donned

[43] White, *op. cit.*, pp. 279-81, 282, 283.
[44] *Ibid.*, pp. 161, 162.
[45] Olsen, *op. cit.*, pp. 156, 157.

ascension robes, climbed to the roof of the church, sang sacred songs, and otherwise mocked the waiting Adventists within.[46]

When the sun went down on October 22, 1844, bringing to a close the "tenth day of the seventh month," most of the believers fell away and renounced their faith. Such provision as was possible was speedily made for those who would suffer deprivation during the approaching winter because of their excess of zeal. The leaders made a restudy of the prophecies, but could find nothing wrong in their chronological calculations, and Adventists believe them correct to this day. Acknowledgment of their error was promptly and frankly made; the Adventists confessed themselves unable to understand it and insisted that the "tarrying" of the Lord would be brief.

Rallying of the Adventists. The more thoughtful among the Adventists were still convinced that their chronological calculations in the light of prophecy were accurate, and further study failed to reveal any error. They knew there was "no mistake in reckoning the 2,300 days"; yet the date passed and "the Lord did not come, neither was the earth cleansed by fire." [47] The question then became: What exactly did happen on the date in question?

One day an Adventist, Hiram Edson, of Port Gibson, New York, was praying behind shocks of corn in a field when "the Spirit of God came upon him in such a powerful manner that he was almost smitten to the earth, and with it came an impression, 'The sanctuary to be cleansed is in heaven.' " [48] At that time all believed that the "sanctuary" was the earth. Edson communicated his impression to O. R. L. Crozier, and a new study of the Scripture was undertaken. They discovered a text in Heb. 8:1-2, to the effect that Christ, as a high priest, "is set on the right hand of the throne of the Majesty in the heavens; *a minister of the sanctuary,* and of the true tabernacle, which the Lord pitched, and not man." So there was a sanctuary in heaven! Taking the ancient priesthood as the prototype of Christ, they believed that at the end of the 2,300 days, or on October 22, 1844, he entered the heavenly sanctuary to cleanse it, as the high priest entered the earthly sanctuary once each year to make reconciliation for the sins of the people. His work is to make an "investigative judgment" of the sins of the earth, and when this work has been completed he will return to earth and execute judgment according to the results of this investigation.[49]

[46] Loughborough, *op. cit.,* pp. 180, 181. Many writers state that the Adventists also wore ascension robes but this has always been denied by the believers themselves.

[47] Loughborough, *op. cit.,* p. 192.

[48] *Ibid.,* p. 193.

[49] *Ibid.,* pp. 190-93; Olsen, *op. cit.,* pp. 177-81.

Crozier published the results of his studies and his exposition of "the sanctuary question" in the *Day Star,* published in Canandaigua, New York, early in 1846. His theory was accepted by the remnant of the Adventists and became the rallying cry of the movement. The doctrine prevails among Adventists to this day. They believe

that Christ, our great High Priest (see Heb. 8:1-2), upon his ascension to heaven entered the *holy place* of the heavenly sanctuary, and that in 1844 he entered the *most holy* place, there to cleanse it by blotting out the sins of all those who have accepted the sacrifice he made on Calvary. They learned that the great antitypical day of atonement began at the time they had supposed Christ was to appear. Furthermore, they discovered that when Christ finishes his work in the sanctuary, he will come to visit judgment upon the earth, an event, of course, still future.[50]

By this time the Adventists had become a separate sect. As previously mentioned, Miller's doctrine was at first received with complacency by ministers and laymen of the denominations and his followers did not sever their ecclesiastical connections. In some instances favorable resolutions were adopted; in others no especial objections were offered when ministers openly espoused Millerite views.[51] In 1843, however, a Methodist conference, meeting in Bath, Maine, denounced the movement and later expelled one of its Adventist ministers, L. F. Stockman, on a charge of heresy for holding and "disseminating doctrines contrary to our articles of religion." [52] This was followed by an appeal to all the Adventists to cut loose from the unfriendly denominations.[53]

Withdrawing or excluded from the churches of which they had been members, the Adventists formed congregations of their own in various places; in many instances they perfected no formal organization, deeming the time remaining before the Lord's return too short, or sometimes holding that an organization was sinful.[54] On April 29, 1845, they assembled in conference at Albany, New York, for the purpose of defining their views and planning for the future. Miller was present and under his chairmanship a committee drew up a statement of faith which was adopted by the whole body. A congregational form of organization was agreed upon, camp meetings were eliminated, a system of Sunday-school and Bible instruction was outlined, and the further circulation of Adventist literature was enjoined.[55] At the conclusion of this meeting Miller issued an

[50] Baker, *Beliefs and Work of Seventh Day Adventists,* pp. 9-11. The italics are inserted.
[51] Olsen, *op. cit.,* pp. 143, 144.
[52] *Ibid.,* p. 145.
[53] *Ibid.,* pp. 145-47.
[54] *Census of Religious Bodies,* 1926, II, 4.
[55] Olsen, *op. cit.,* pp. 162, 163.

address to the faithful.[56] The declaration of belief then adopted embodied the views of Miller regarding the imminent second advent and premillennial reign of Christ as well as other points of doctrine.

For ten years after the Albany conference the loose organization formed at that time included the whole body of Adventists except those who observed the seventh day instead of Sunday as the true Sabbath. In 1858 another conference was held at Boston at which the body adopted the name of American Millennial Association. A few years later the name of Evangelical Adventist was chosen. The sect published a periodical called at various dates *Signs of the Times, Advent Herald, Messiah's Herald,* and *Herald of the Coming One.* By schisms and otherwise the Evangelical Adventists gradually dwindled. In 1906 the census reported 18 organizations, 16 churches, 481 members, 8 ministers, 9 Sunday schools, and property worth $27,050. By 1916 only a few scattering churches in Pennsylvania remained, and by 1926 the sect had disappeared from the records.[57]

The Adventist Prophetess. The progress of the Adventist movement was accelerated by the visions of Mrs. Ellen G. White (nee Harmon), who is the virtual founder of and whose inspiration is acknowledged by the Seventh Day Adventists. The young Miss Harmon was converted in an Adventist meeting in 1842 and began immediately to have dreams which she regarded as of divine significance. In 1844, soon after the passing of "the time," and when the Adventists were in despondency, she saw in a trance the Adventists on a path traveling straight to heaven. The believers accepted this vision as divine assurance and took courage, and from that date the girl was accepted as a prophetess. For more than seventy years, until her death in 1915, Mrs. White (she married Elder James White in 1846) was an outstanding Adventist leader, and through her visions contributed to the movement a mass of instruction which the faithful received as next to the Bible in spiritual authority.[58]

Mrs. White's visions were received in a state of trance; after an experience of rapture and shouting she swooned, then regained her strength and in an entranced condition repeated her visions. Loughborough, an eyewitness, declared that while in that condition, at one time for six hours, *she did not breathe,* though her pulse was normal and she possessed superhuman strength; he cites other witnesses, and even medical authority, to that effect.

Mrs. White was responsible for the acceptance of "the third angel's

[56] Wellcome, *op. cit.,* pp. 420-27. Olsen, *op. cit.,* pp. 163, 164.

[57] *Census of Religious Bodies,* 1926. II, 5, 6.

[58] It is not necessary to repeat her teachings and visions here. Her writings are published by the Seventh Day Adventist publishing houses. See especially her *Early Writings of Ellen G. White.* See also Loughborough, *op. cit.,* ch. xiii, and Olsen, *op. cit.,* ch. vi *et seq.*

message" or the observance of Saturday as the Sabbath. In a vision of "the heavenly sanctuary" she saw two angels standing by the ark; Jesus raised its cover, revealing the tables of stone on which the ten commandments were written, the fourth being surrounded by a halo of light. An angel declared, "When the foundations of the earth were laid, then was also laid the foundation of the Sabbath." Saturday was thereafter the Sabbath for the most numerous company of believers.

Internal Dissensions. Internal dissensions about points of doctrine soon arose to disturb the peace and eventually to split the Adventists. Among the questions about which controversy raged may be mentioned the Sabbath, the state of the dead and the nature of immortality, the inspiration of Mrs. White, the propriety of manual labor, and the "open and shut door." The first three controversies brought about the formation of separate sects and will be considered later.

It has already been pointed out that on the approach of "the time" many Adventists sold or gave away their possessions and disentangled themselves from all temporal pursuits in anticipation of the end. After October 22, 1844, many were reluctant to resume their occupations, believing as they did that their chronology was accurate and the end near at hand. This reluctance developed into a doctrine, first proclaimed publicly by Joseph Turner in Maine in the spring of 1845; he and his followers "took the ground that we were in the great Sabbath—that the six thousand years had ended—consequently no Adventist should perform any more manual labor. To do so would surely, in their estimation, result in their final destruction." [59] The idea spread through Maine, Massachusetts, and other states, giving much trouble to the more responsible leaders and became the burden of some of Mrs. White's visions. One Elder Stephens, of Woodstock, Maine, refused to work or to eat food cooked by unbelievers until his derangement drove him to suicide.[60] In and near Boston another group adopted the slogan, "Sell that ye have, and give alms"; "they said they were in the jubilee, that the land should rest, and that the poor must be supported without labor." [61] The dissension over this point subsided in due course and caused no lasting schism.

Joseph Turner was also the leader of the "shut door" faction, which held that only the then existing Adventists could be saved. Playing on the parable of the ten virgins, he announced that the bridegroom (Christ) really came in 1843, "the marriage then took place, the virgins (Adventists) went in with him to the marriage, *the door was shut,* and none inside could be lost and none outside (non-Adventists) could after that be

[59] Loughborough, *op. cit.,* p. 220.
[60] *Ibid.,* pp. 239, 240.
[61] *Ibid.,* pp. 240, 241.

saved." [62] For a time all the Adventists were united in this belief.[63] Believing there was no further possibility of salvation for sinners, this group opposed evangelistic activity and the further preaching of the advent doctrine as useless. In due time, however, the main body rejected this error; they held that the door was shut to persons who had heard the advent message and rejected it, but remained open to those who had not received the light or who came to years of accountability after 1844.[64]

THE SEVENTH DAY ADVENTIST denomination is the largest church to grow out of the work of William Miller. It is an evangelical and orthodox group and accepts the principles of Protestant theology, being distinctive only in the doctrine of the second advent, in observing Saturday as the scriptural Sabbath, and in acknowledging the inspiration of Mrs. White. It began in the fraternization of Adventists with the Seventh Day Baptists. In 1844 a member of the latter body, Mrs. Rachel Preston, visited her daughter Mrs. Cyrus Farnsworth, an Adventist, in Washington, New Hampshire. Under her influence the forty members of the Adventist church near Washington, including its minister, Frederick Wheeler, adopted the seventh day as their Sabbath. This original church is still standing in good repair three miles south of Washington.[65]

This group bases its Sabbatarian doctrine on the Genesis account of creation, the Ten Commandments, and many other Old Testament references to the Sabbath. They cite further support in "the third angel's message" of Rev. 14:9-12, a passage which has become the real basis of the main body of doctrine held by the sect.

Adventists find three messages in this chapter. The first is "Fear God, and give glory to him; for the hour of his judgment is come." This was proclaimed in the preaching of the advent doctrine in 1843-44. The second is "Babylon is fallen, is fallen, that great city, because she made all nations drink of the wine of the wrath of her fornication." This was sounded when the Adventists withdrew from the denominations in 1844-45. The third is a warning against the worship of "the beast" and his image and contains the words "Here is the patience of the saints: here are they that keep the commandments of God, and the faith of Jesus." This enjoins the observance of Saturday as a part of "the commandments of God," of which the fourth commandment is a part.[66] An interpretation of Dan. 7:25, in which "the little horn" is represented as "changing times and laws," was used to the same end; "the little horn" is the papacy, which

---

[62] *Ibid.*, pp. 220, 221.

[63] *Ibid.*, pp. 221, 224, 226. Loughborough cites several contemporary authorities, including Mrs. White, to this effect.

[64] *Ibid.*, 226. See Loughborough, ch. xiv, on the "shut door question."

[65] Olsen, *op. cit.*, pp. 183-84.

[66] *Ibid.*, p. 186.

changed the sacred day from the original Saturday to Sunday. All this was confirmed by Mrs. White.

These Adventists believe that a large number of biblical prophecies indicate the end of time, and that all of these have been fulfilled save one. That one relates to the formation of a "remnant church," the proclamation of a "special message," the making ready of "a prepared people," and the preaching of "the gospel of the kingdom" to the whole world.[67] This "gospel of the kingdom" is that of the imminent second advent of Jesus Christ,[68] and the "prepared people" are the Seventh Day Adventists.[69] They are therefore possessed of a strong conviction that when their distinctive message has been preached all over the world, and a sufficiently large body of believers has accepted it, the Parousia will occur and time will be at an end.

Seventh Day Adventists baptize by immersion. They teach that man is by nature mortal and that immortality is conferred on the redeemed, realizable at the time of the second advent; death is an unconscious sleep until the first resurrection, when Christ returns, and the second resurrection when the wicked are raised and destroyed at the end of the millennium. At the first resurrection the saved ascend to heaven with Jesus, after which the earth is desolate and uninhabited, the prison of Satan. When Satan and the wicked are destroyed after the thousand years, the holy city will descend from heaven and the world will be the eternal home of the redeemed. Many groups believe that the eternal life of the saved will be spent in heaven and that the earth will be destroyed. But Seventh Day Adventists hold that the saved will be taken to heaven at the first resurrection, and will later be returned to the world, where eternity will be spent.

The polity of the Seventh Day Adventists is a modified congregationalism. Churches are united to form local conferences or missions, which meet biennially, and these in turn compose union conferences or missions with quadrennial sessions. Over all is a quadrennial general conference. Extensive publishing, medical, missionary, and other connectional activities are administered by secretaries, under a general conference committee. This denomination leads all American churches in per capita giving, in spite of the relatively low economic status of its constituency.

There are approximately 2,500 Seventh Day Adventist churches with 210,000 members in this country, and the body claims twice as many members in other lands.

The history of the ADVENT CHRISTIAN CHURCH goes back nearly a

[67] Shuler, *Is the End Near?* pp. 45, 46, 80, 110.
[68] *Ibid.*, p. 80.
[69] *Ibid.*, pp. 111-13.

century. Among the Adventists remaining in the original body after the departure of those who accepted "the third angel's message," arose a party, headed by Jonathan Cummins, which rejected the theory of "the heavenly sanctuary." This group held that Miller's calculations had been erroneous by ten years and that the 1,335 days of Daniel would end in 1854. They further differed from the majority in holding that the dead are unconscious, man is mortal, and immortality is bestowed on the faithful at the resurrection; this denied the conscious state of the dead and eternal punishment. A schism resulted.

When the Cummins party were disappointed in 1854, the dispute over the state of the dead prevented reunion. A conference of Adventists was held at Boston on June 5, 1855, but the Cummins group refused to join it and held a conference of their own on the same day. At Worcester, Massachusetts, on November 6, 1861, they organized as a denomination, and took the name of Adventist Christian Association or Advent Christian Church.

The sect differs from other Adventists only on the doctrinal point above indicated. With reference to the second coming, the Advent Christians hold it to be imminent, but decline to specify a definite date therefor.[70] The body has slightly more than four hundred churches, and its membership is about thirty thousand.

The CHURCH OF GOD (ADVENTIST) was organized in 1865 by Elder Gilbert Cranmer and others. It observes Saturday as the Sabbath and has advertised a reward of $10,000 for a Scripture citation authorizing any other day.[71] It further holds to the unconscious state of the dead and offers a $500 reward for a contrary proof-text.[72] The sect differs from the Seventh Day Adventists mainly in its refusal to acknowledge the divine inspiration of Mrs. White.

Among its other tenets are beliefs in the inspiration of the name "Church of God," the absolute destruction of sinners, and that the righteous will be rewarded in this earth and never be permanently removed.[73] In other respects it adheres to the typical Adventist theories.

The fortunes of this church have been largely bound up with its newspaper, first established in 1863 as the *Hope of Israel,* and now called the *Bible Advocate.* The publishing house and headquarters of the sect are at Stanberry, Missouri. There are about forty-five churches and around five thousand members.

The CHURCH OF GOD (SEVENTH DAY), which has been grouped with

[70] *Census of Religious Bodies,* 1936, II, 15.
[71] Leaflet, *New Testament Sabbath.*
[72] Leaflet, *Where Are the Dead?*
[73] A. N. Dugger, *What The Church of God Believes, and Why.*

the Holiness and Pentecostal churches as the Church of God (Salem, West Virginia), is an Adventist body which arose from a schism in the Church of God (Adventist) in 1933. Preliminary to establishing world headquarters in Jerusalem, Elder A. N. Dugger, leader of the Church of God (Adventist), went to Palestine, and on his return dissension arose over matters of church government, which Dugger insisted should conform more closely to the biblical pattern. He was deposed by a majority of the general conference, whereupon he went to Salem, West Virginia, and formed the Church of God (Seventh Day). The sect established a periodical called the *Bible Advocate,* the name of the paper so long published by the parent body.

The officers of this church were chosen by drawing names from a hat, Dugger insisting that the Bible knew nothing of elections after the democratic fashion. These are twelve apostles, seventy evangelists, and seven elders or business committeemen. Although Elder Dugger's name was not drawn, he remained the leader of the sect. In addition to its apostolic form of government, the body claims to adhere closely to the primitive pattern by observing the seventh day as the Sabbath, washing feet, and perpetuating the law of the "clean and unclean," especially in prohibiting the eating of pork. It retains the customary Adventist doctrines, and displays considerable emotional enthusiasm in its meetings. It claims thirty-nine churches and around twelve hundred members.

The PRIMITIVE ADVENT CHRISTIAN CHURCH is a very small body which was formed by bringing together a few congregations of the Advent Christian Church in West Virginia. All its members are in that state and such headquarters as it has (a secretary or statistical officer) are at Sissonville. There are a dozen congregations with a total membership of about five hundred. Its tenets follow the regular Adventist pattern.

The CHURCH OF GOD (OREGON, ILLINOIS) is another Adventist body. Since several groups regard the name "Church of God" as the only scriptural appellation, it is customary to distinguish between them by including in the name of the group the headquarters or name of the founder or principal leader. This is true not only of this Adventist group but also of several Mormon, Pentecostal, and Holiness churches.

The Church of God having its headquarters at Oregon, Illinois, was formerly known as the Church of God in Jesus Christ. As such it was organized at Philadelphia in 1888. It grew out of an amalgamation in that year of several independent Adventist congregations which had existed under such names as the Church of the Blessed Hope, Brethren of the Abrahamic Faith, Restitutionists, Restitution Church, Church of God, and Age to Come Adventists.[74] The body has about eighty churches and

[74] *Census of Religious Bodies,* 1936, II, 46.

five thousand members. While claiming, as many do, to "have no creed but the Bible," it has applied its own interpretations thereto and set forth a statement of beliefs which is virtually a creed. It observes Sunday. Its advent doctrine does not differ materially from that of the kindred bodies. The coming messianic kingdom will be established at Jerusalem and all mankind will be ruled therefrom; the Jews will be the most favored nation on earth, each "saint" will be given a position of trust and honor under Christ, and the wicked will be put to death.

The LIFE AND ADVENT UNION was formed at Wilbraham, Massachusetts, in 1848 by John T. Walsh, who preached that there is no resurrection for the wicked. The sect hold a peculiar view of the millennium—that it has already occurred. The present is a period of waiting for Christ's return, which is imminent and signs of which are visible on every hand; when the second advent comes to pass, the earth will be purified by fire and will become the eternal abode of the righteous. This is the smallest body of the Adventist group, having only six churches and three hundred members.[75]

JEHOVAH'S WITNESSES, the most vehement and spectacular, and also the most vigorous propagandists of all the Adventists, are the followers of the late "Pastor" Charles Taze Russell. Formerly known as the International Bible Students' Association, they are now called "Jehovah's Witnesses." The group did not, however, grow out of the Millerite movement, and is not usually listed among the churches technically called Adventists. It is not a denomination, and has no churches or ministry; it is, indeed, hostile to all churches, Catholic and Protestant alike. The movement was created and controlled by Russell, who was a haberdasher of Allegheny, Pennsylvania, and at his death the mantle fell on one Judge J. F. Rutherford, who in turn was succeeded by Nathan H. Knorr. Its propagandists travel from city to city, preaching in public halls, and attracting attention by assurances that "there is no hell" and that "millions now living will never die." During both World Wars they encountered opposition and violence because of their refusal to salute the flag and their pacifism.

The Witnesses operate a publishing house in Brooklyn, New York, and from its presses pours an amazing stream of books, periodicals, and pamphlets. These are sold on the streets and peddled from door to door by a large number of devotees. These agents also carry phonograph records, on which the sect's message has been transcribed, and which are played in homes into which they are invited.

It was claimed that Russell's "explanatory writings on the Bible are far more extensive than the combined writings of St. Paul, St. John, Arius, Waldo, Wycliffe, and Martin Luther—the six messengers of the Church who preceded him" and "that the place next to St. Paul in the gallery of

[75] *Ibid.*, II, 41.

fame as expounder of the Gospel of the Great Master will be occupied by Charles Taze Russell." [76] It was claimed that he was the angel referred to in Ezek. 9:1-11, as the seventh messenger of the Church.[77] His books were circulated by millions; it was reported that at the time of his death over thirteen million copies of six leading titles had been distributed. Russell's followers assert that his *Divine Plan of the Ages,* wherein the author sets forth his famous "Millennial Dawn" doctrine, has been translated into thirty-five languages and has enjoyed a circulation greater than any book save the Bible. The seven volumes of *Studies in the Scriptures* have also been widely distributed.

The Witnesses make the millennium the center of everything religious. Until that event transpires not even evangelistic work can be undertaken with hope of success; the present time is to be used for the gathering of a "little flock," the conversion of the world being attempted only after the return of Christ. If it be asked what chance this scheme affords those who die before the second coming, the answer is somewhat original: death means total annihilation and there are no souls waiting anywhere for a resurrection, but after the parousia all the dead will be *re-created* and brought back to earth for a second probationary period, and a thousand-year evangelistic campaign will be carried on among them.[78]

This doctrine of a second probation, or "another chance for the sinner," has been objected to on the ground that it tends to encourage wickedness. Russell agreed, holding that the more wicked men are in this life the more likely they will accept the second chance, having profited by the "experience of sin." In case they never repent they will be asphyxiated in the lake of fire and finally exterminated without suffering. Those who repent in the millennial probation will have "eternal life"; this differs from the immortality of "the little flock" in that while the latter is a state of inherent life the former must be sustained by eating food.

Russell repudiated the Trinity. No mention is made of the Holy Spirit. Christ was a created spirit and only a perfect man. After his crucifixion he ceased to be human and became again a spirit. He did not rise from the tomb; the disposition of his body is not known, though it probably was *dissolved into gases* or was supernaturally slipped away and is being *preserved as a corpse* until God chooses to produce it.[79]

According to Russell the parousia has already occurred and we are now

---

[76] Preface to Russell's *Sermons.*

[77] *The Watch Tower and Herald of Christ's Presence,* May, 1925.

[78] Eaton estimates that the total number thus raised or re-created would exceed 252,000,000,000,000 and that the earth would be covered so thickly that all could not sit down at the same time! *The Millennial Dawn Heresy,* pp. 120, 121. In his computation Eaton estimates the age of the race to be only sixty centuries.

[79] *The Divine Plan of the Ages,* II, 129.

in the millennium. Christ returned to the "upper air" in the second advent in 1874. Four years later, in the spring of 1878, all the holy apostles and the members of "the little flock" who had died were raised to meet the Lord and are now floating about in the air. At that time also God finally rejected the existing churches. The pope is identified as the antichrist or representative of the devil, and Protestant divines are included in the same category.[80]

The "pastor" announced that the consummation of all things would take place in 1914; he figured seven "prophetic times" of 360 years each, a total of 2,520 years, from the removal of Zedekiah in 606 B.C. It was later suggested that as Ezekiel was dumb for a year, five months, and twenty-six days, a similar period after the dumbness of Russell in death might witness the end. At any time now the final battle may take place, hence "millions now living will never die." Though more lurid in detail than usually portrayed, the picture of events attending the last struggle between Christ and his enemies and the winding up of earthly affairs is typically apocalyptic.

The FORT WAYNE GOSPEL TEMPLE is a fundamentalist and premillenarian group. It stresses its interdenominational character, but has for all practical purposes become an independent sect, centering in the Fort Wayne Gospel Temple, Fort Wayne, Indiana. It has no connection with the pentecostal movement but is an evangelistic radio center which operates a church and a missionary training school, and publishes a periodical called the *World-Wide Christian Conservative*. The movement was founded by B. E. Rediger, a Mennonite, and his successors in the leadership were Methodists and Baptists. A related organization under a separate incorporation is the World Christian Crusade, a foreign missionary enterprise which has sent missionaries to Cuba, Haiti, the Dominican Republic, and Sumatra. It has around one hundred workers in these fields and has developed fifty congregations in Haiti.

Adventist Exegesis. Inasmuch as Adventist exegesis departs widely from the canons of modern critical scholarship, light may be thrown on the psychology and theology of Adventism by citing some illustrations of its manner of interpreting the Scriptural passages on which it rests. In general, the Adventists, like the other fundamentalist sects, repudiate "higher criticism" and decline to accept its findings. One finds little or no reference to the historical situation which produced a given literature or the problems to which it was addressed. The "proof-text" method is employed, and phrases and sentences are frequently taken from the context and used to support ideas which doubtless never occurred to the original writer. Scriptural pas-

[80] Rutherford, *Deliverance*, pp. 208, 216.

sages which, according to the concensus of modern scholarship, have no relation to the subject in hand, are used to prove Adventist theories.

Blackstone, for example, makes the statement that "Moses, David, Isaiah, Jeremiah, Daniel, Zechariah, all the prophets and apostles were believers in the second advent of Christ." [81] As proof he cites sentences from Deuteronomy (33:2), the Psalms (102:16), and other books of an alleged messianic character. Modern scholarship, on the other hand, holds that Moses, David, and some of the other personages mentioned, did not write the passages attributed to them, and that Jewish messianism, while expecting a deliverer, had no idea of a *second advent* of that hero. Even if the passages cited are messianic, which many scholars would not admit, they have no reference to a second coming.[82]

Sometimes the plain meaning of language is exactly reversed. One Adventist writer declares in italics: *"There is not a single instance in which it is asserted that the Lord Jesus would return during the lifetime of the generation then living. . . . The Holy Spirit never permitted one single New Testament writer to teach that he would so return."* [83] Yet Matthew, the other two Synoptists concurring, reports Jesus as saying that "there be *some standing here,* which shall not taste of death" before the parousia (Matt. 16:27-28; Mark 9:1; Luke 9:27). Each of the Synoptic writers declares that "this generation shall not pass away" before the apocalyptic event. (Matt. 24:34; Mark 13:30; Luke 21:32.) Matthew and Mark report the plain assertion to the high priest that *"ye shall see"* the event. In speaking of the second coming Paul said that "we which are alive and remain" will join those who have already died in meeting the Lord in the air. (I Thess. 4:15-17.)[84] Since these hopes were not realized the theory of inspiration held by Adventists forces them to explain away the fact that certain New Testament writers and early Christians expected the world order to end immediately.[85]

Since the Reformation period it has been a common practice to identify the pope or Roman Catholic Church with the dread personage who is to devastate the world immediately preceding the end. The papacy is the

[81] *Jesus Is Coming,* p. 16. The passages used in proof are Deut. 33:2; Ps. 102:16; Isa. 59:20; 60:1; Jer. 23:5-6; Dan. 7:13; Zech. 14:4-5. While some of these may refer to a messiah, not one of them relates to a *second* advent.

[82] Many such prophecies referred not to an individual but to the nation or a godly group within the nation. See, for example, the "servant" prophecies in Isaiah as discussed by Smith, *Book of the Twelve Prophets,* and Gray and Driver in the *International Critical Commentary.*

[83] Shuler, *Is the End Near?* pp. 20, 22.

[84] The Adventist writer says that Paul was speaking in the name of the corporate body of Christians of all ages. Any ordinary reader would certainly conclude that the writers expected some persons then living to witness the event in question, and most scholars agree. The Adventist says they hoped and expected that Christ might return, but were not permitted to say so. *Ibid.,* p. 22.

[85] See such authorities as Moffatt, McNeille, Allen, Gould, Plummer, Frame, Charles, Matthews, etc.

"man of sin," "son of perdition," and "mystery of iniquity" mentioned in II Thess. 2:3-10.[86] The Church of Rome is the "little horn" of Dan. 7:8, according to Seventh Day Adventists, because in changing the Sabbath from the seventh to the first day it fulfilled the prophecy that the horn should "change times and laws" (Dan. 7:25).[87] The method by which critical scholars find one evidence that the "666" or "beast" of Rev. 13:18 is Nero *Redivivus*, the computation of the numeral value of letters in certain words, has been used to show that antichrist is the pope of Rome. It is pointed out that the sum 666 is found in *Vicarus Filii Dei*, which appears on the papal crown, *Saturnia*, the Chaldean name of Italy, *Romüth*, the Hebrew name of Romulus, and *Lateinos*.[88] Those writers who do not regard the pope as antichrist [89] indulge in equally peculiar exegesis. Gaebelein, for example, thus interprets Rev. 13:18:

Seven is the complete perfect number; six is incomplete and is man's number. Here we have three times six. It is humanity fallen, filled with pride, defying God. The number 666 signifies man's day and man's defiance of God under Satan's power in its culmination.[90]

Nearly every calamitous event and notorious personage in history has been fitted into the elaborate scheme of prophetic interpretation. Modern European nations fulfill the prophecy in the ten toes of Nebuchadnezzar's metallic image (Dan. 2:31-35); Caesar, Cleopatra, Mohammed, Napoleon, the Turks, the Crimean War, and the World Wars are all found in the eleventh chapter of Daniel; Mussolini in 1929 fulfilled Rev. 18:7; "the eighth head was Atheistic France in 1792; the red dragon released from the Pit unseated the Woman (Papacy) and now she has been seated on the water (people) ever since." (Rev. 17.)[91] Many persons saw the fulfillment of millennial prophecies in World War I. It was pointed out that the Kaiser literally fulfilled Zech. 11:15-17; his left arm was "clean dried up," his right eye was "utterly darkened," he did not "heal that that is broken" or "visit those that be cut off" because his Turkish alliance prevented the return of the Jews to Palestine.[92]

[86] Shuler, *op. cit.*, p. 31; *The Great Controversy Between Christ and Satan*, p. 356.

[87] Shuler, *op. cit.*, p. 29; Baker, *op. cit.*, p. 76.

[88] *Our Time in Bible Prophecy*, pp. 45, 46; *The Number of the Beast 666* (Church of God Publishing House, Stanberry, Missouri).

[89] Blackstone, for example, *op. cit.*, ch. xii, holds antichrist is some terrible figure yet to come, but does not try to identify him.

[90] *Revelation*, p. 84.

[91] C. V. Tenney, leaflet, *God's Outline of Human History*.

[92] Dugger, *The Battle of Armageddon*, pp. 44-46. Numerous booklets and leaflets of the Adventists set forth these and similar interpretations of history. See the publications of the Church of God Publishing House, Stanberry, Missouri, especially Ward, *Babylon*; Dugger, *Desolation of the*

Though most of these writers will not now set definite dates,[93] they explain from Scripture the disappointments of past ages and prove the certainty of the end in the present age. The arguments and interpretations are numerous and involved, but nearly all center around contemporary events as the fulfillment of prophecy. Most of the "signs of the end" have been accomplished. The darkening of the sun and moon and falling of the stars (Matt. 24:29; Mark 13:24-25) occurred on May 19 and 20, 1780, and November 13, 1833. The emergence of the United States as a nation fulfilled Rev. 13:5, 10, 11.[94] Shuler devotes two chapters to descriptions of modern inventions, the speed of trains, steamships, and airplanes, telegraphic and radio communication, and similar matters—all in fulfillment of the prophecy that in the last days "many shall run to and fro, and knowledge shall be increased." (Dan. 12:4.)[95] Automobiles with headlights are the chariots that "shall rage in the streets" and "seem like torches" mentioned by Nahum (2:4), and drawbridges fulfill his statement that "the gates of the rivers shall be opened" (2:6).[96] Writers see in wars and famines, religious apathy, apostasy, social problems and disturbances, and the spread of foreign missionary work, certain signs of the imminent end.[97] One sign remains— the preaching of the Adventist message all over the world and the gathering of "a prepared people" to welcome the returning Lord (Matt. 24:14; Rev. 14:6, 15-18), and as this movement is well under way the long-awaited second appearance of Jesus may eventuate at any moment.[98]

Earth; The Four World Empires; The Battle of Armageddon, The Seal of God and Mark of the Beast; The Signs of Our Times; Goodenough, The Restitution of the First Dominion; Dodd, Gentile Times Ending Now; The Return of the Jew and Jerusalem; Our Time in Bible Prophecy. None of these are in agreement with critical scholarship. The Zechariah passages in which Dugger finds references to the Kaiser came from the Greek period when the Jews were suffering under Ptolemy IV (Philopator). The prophet refers to the coming punishment of Ptolemy in words borrowed from Ezek. 32:21-22, which originally referred to God's punishment of Pharaoh. See Mitchel on "Zechariah" in the International Critical Commentary, How on "Zechariah" in A New Commentary on the Holy Scriptures, ed. by Bishop Gore et al.; Dummelow in The One-Volume Bible Commentary.

[93] This is not true of all, however. C. N. Wisner of Richmond, Virginia, expected the end in 1933. He justified his hope by reference to a great many thirty-third verses of Scripture, verses with thirty-three words, series of words with thirty-three letters, etc. See his circular New Jerusalem Is Coming Down in the 1933d Year. Charles G. Long of Pasadena, California, declared that the end would come during the seventh month of 1945. See his book Treasures of Truth.

[94] Shuler, op. cit., Ch. VI.

[95] Ibid., chs. vii, viii.

[96] Dugger, Our Time in Bible Prophecy, pp. 7, 8. The Nahum prophecy refers to Nineveh and its dynasty, as is plainly stated in the text. The chariots represent the Medes who destroyed the city, and the gates of the waters that shall dissolve the palace refer to the sluices of the moats that protected the palace of Nineveh's king. Read the more correct translation of Moffatt. See Wade on "Nahum" in A New Commentary on the Holy Scripture, and the authorities there cited; also Dummelow, The One-Volume Bible Commentary, and other critical works.

[97] Baker gives a catalogue of such signs with references to Scriptural predictions fulfilled thereby, op. cit., p. 79.

[98] Shuler, op. cit., ch. xii.

CHAPTER III

PERFECTIONIST OR SUBJECTIVIST SECTS

THE CENTRAL ELEMENT IN ALL RELIGION AFTER IT EMERGES FROM primitive forms is the fact of sin, and its main quest is to secure release therefrom. Not only does it seek to prevent the commission of sinful acts, but it aims also to eliminate the desires from which such acts spring. There has been a long dispute as to whether this is possible. Many groups have held that man cannot wholly refrain from wrongdoing or ever be entirely free from temptation and the various perverse subjective reactions. Others hold that moral perfection in one's daily walk and spiritual holiness, the total eradication of sinful desires and deplorable psychological states, is entirely possible and should be the goal and hope of all Christians. The latter are the Perfectionist sects, which will be discussed in the present chapter.

Theologically sin is subsumed under two ideas or definitions which are related as effect and cause. In the first place, there is sin as wrong action; it is any known violation of the moral law or any conscious refraction of the will of God.

In the second place, there is Sin—spelled with a capital S—which is not an act but a subjective state; this kind of sin has ever been regarded as of greater importance than "sins of commission." It is original sin, natural depravity, birth sin, an impairment or fault of human nature; "it is the corruption of the nature of every man, that naturally is engendered of the offspring of Adam, whereby man is very far gone from original righteousness, and of his own nature inclined to evil, and that continually." [1] Christian theology has discoursed at great length upon this subject, its doctrines ranging from the total depravity of the school of Augustine to the milder statements of Pelagianism. [2] All influential

---

[1] Methodist Article of Religion, "Of Original or Birth Sin."

[2] For the most extreme statement of this doctrine in modern creeds see the Westminster Confession and the Larger and Shorter Catechisms of Presbyterianism. For discussions of the doctrine of original sin see Clark, *The Psychology of Religious Awakening*, ch. iv, the church histories of Schaff, Hurst, Dryer, and others, the histories of doctrine by Hagenbach, Harnack, Shedd, Shelton, and others, and the standard works on systematic theology.

creeds and theologies agree that there is such a thing or fact as sin in the generic, apart from and the cause of actual sin, that it is native to man and that freedom therefrom is the *summum bonum* of the religious life.

The Philosophy of Perfectionism. The underlying principle of perfectionism is that of natural depravity and the impotence of the individual to help himself, morally and spiritually. These ideas are unknown to psychology, but have been fundamental in most theologies. Man is "a mass of corruption" and his salvation must come from outside himself. In attaining that ideal three steps are usually recognized. Justification secures remission of sins; it is divine forgiveness, conditioned on repentance in evangelical thinking, and does little or nothing to man's nature. Regeneration is an inner work, usually accompanying but distinct from justification, which purifies the life and purges it of the original taint. But there still remains "sin in the regenerate"; men are still tempted, evil desires remain, and depravity still manifests itself. So there must be sanctification, which completes the work of regeneration and frees man entirely from inbred sin. Evangelical theology has never been very clear as to the exact relation between regeneration and sanctification or just why two works are necessary to accomplish the end in view. Some theologians, while retaining the two names, think the two works are simultaneously accomplished by the same experience. Most perfectionists, however, definitely separate the two in time, and teach that sanctification is achieved by an experience subsequent to regeneration.

Roman Catholic theologians, in practice if not in theory, have definitely toned down the element of helplessness which is the life breath of evangelical perfectionism. Man is naturally depraved and doomed, but this condition is corrected instantly by baptism. After baptismal regeneration, such sanctification or perfection as is possible has a large human element. It must be attained, if at all, by monastic asceticism, mystical contemplation, the rigid observance of rules of conduct or the performance of acts of charity.

Not so in evangelical perfectionist thinking. The experience is secured in only one way—by the direct operation of the Holy Spirit, manifested in the believer by a definite emotional reaction. Sometimes these emotional spasms run into strange channels, inducing trances, speaking in unknown tongues, prophecy, and "gifts," and even antinomian immorality. It is this emotional perfectionism that will be discussed.[3]

Perfectionism in History. In the New Testament the duty and hope of attaining perfection is never defined, but is set forth in metaphors and

---

[3] For discussions of the philosophic aspects of the subject see Warfield, *Perfectionism* (2 vols.). This Calvinistic theologian, opposed to the doctrine, finds that both rationalism and mysticism hold perfectionist tendencies.

theological terms. The Gospels and apostolic writings hold before the believer the hope of being "perfect, even as your Father who is in heaven is perfect." [4] In Patristic writings the doctrine is stated in scriptural terminology and connotes for the most part freedom from actual sins; the doctrine of original sin had not then been formulated.[5] The Gnostics held that perfection was attained by the spiritual or pneumatics, the highest of the three types of personalities. The Pelagians, denying depravity as an inherited taint, believed in a naturalistic perfection attained by man's own efforts seconded by original grace, a position condemned at the Council of Carthage in A.D. 418. Augustine, the father of total depravity, reacted so powerfully against Pelagianism that he denied the practical possibility of perfection in this life, save perhaps in the case of the Blessed Virgin, though he admitted theoretically that divine grace might bring it about.

In the Middle Ages Thomas Aquinas, father of Roman Catholic theology, taught that perfection might be attained by "works" on the part of the clergy practicing monastic asceticism, thus giving the monastic mystics a practical monopoly on the experience. The Catholic position is that the state may be attained by works of charity; by "works of supererogation" it is possible for the charitable believer to surpass the demands of the moral law and lay up an extra supply of goodness which may be drawn upon by the church in behalf of others.

Intense and vital perfectionism, however, was found mainly among revolting sects, heretical parties, and fanatics. These have always held that the state is attained by abnormal effusions of the Holy Spirit upon elect souls; it is an experimental and emotional process entirely, careful ordering of conduct having little or no influence in the process of attainment. To this day the theory finds most favor among those who discount human ability and are predisposed to strong emotional experiences. The ecstatic excesses which have been so much in evidence among perfectionists down to the present, allegedly a reproduction of the experience of the apostles on the day of Pentecost, mentioned by Paul as appearing among his converts and even being indulged in by himself,[6] became a sectarian mark in Montanism, which sprang from the prophetess Maximilla and her successor Montanus, in the second century; these heretics insisted on the imminent

[4] Matt. 5:48. Numerous passages holding up the ideal of perfection may be found by reference to any concordance. It is not deemed necessary to review here the New Testament doctrine. Discussions will be found in the various volumes on holiness and Christian perfection. See especially "Perfection (Christian)" in Hastings, *Encyclopedia of Religion and Ethics*, and Wesley, *A Plain Account of Christian Perfection* and *Brief Thoughts on Christian Perfection*.

[5] It is found in Clement of Rome (*Ad. Cor.*, 49), Polycarp (*Ad. Phil.*, 3), Ignatius (*Ad. Eph.*, 14; *Ad. Smyrn.*, 11), Irenaeus (*Adv. Her.*, V, VI, 1), Clement of Alexandria (*Strom.*, IV, 21; VII, 14), Jerome (*Dial. against the Pelagians*, III, 4) and others.

[6] I Cor. 12:10; cf. 14:18.

end of the world, stressed the dynamic presence and influence of the Paraclete, and indulged in orgies of ecstasy, uttering their "prophecies" while in the ecstatic state. In the following century the Novatianists regarded themselves as the *teleioi* or perfecti, possessors of an unusual gift of the Spirit, and therefore a group superior to the general body of credentes or believers.[7]

In the Middle Ages appeared the numerous sects of the Fraticelli, or Little Brothers of the Free Spirit. They rejected the church as apostate and regarded themselves as the spirituals, on the ground of definite outpourings of the Holy Spirit. With them may be said to have begun the antinomianism which has frequently characterized perfectionism; by reason of their spiritual enduements they were above or beyond the obligations of the moral law and are said to have indulged in excesses of an immoral nature.[8] During the same period there was a swarm of New Manichean sects, the Bogomiles, Euchites, Cathari, Bulgari, Albigenses, and several others. They usually preached a gross dualism, embraced orgiastic elements, received outpourings of the Spirit, refrained from sexual exercises, and were a scandal to their more orthodox contemporaries.[9]

The churches of the Reformation, Lutheran and Calvinistic alike, discounted Christian perfection. Immediately a revolt brought forth the Anabaptists, Mennonites, and other sects on the continent, which espoused the doctrine on grounds of direct spiritual experience, along with marked adventist views. In England a similar revolt resulted in the appearance of such sects as the Quakers with their "inner light" experiences, and the Shakers with their extreme emotional reactions. Here again perfectionism combined with fervent chiliastic hopes; indeed, perfectionism and millenarianism have nearly always shown a distinct affinity.

In the early American revival period perfectionism exerted a wide influence, in most cases taking the form of a sane doctrine of Christian holiness but occasionally running into wild excesses and antinomianism. Charles G. Finney was an exponent of the theory, though he refused to be called a perfectionist because of the bad associations of the term. The Oberlin theology was akin to that of the early Methodist holiness preachers. Finney experienced a profoundly emotional conversion in 1818, and then in 1843 he underwent a "fresh baptism of the Spirit," corresponding in all details to the Methodist "second blessing" or "entire sanctification." Even after his first experience, which he called justification, he remarked, "So far as I

---

[7] See Hastings, *op. cit.*, "Perfection," "Novation."

[8] See the standard church histories and articles on the Fraticelli in the *Catholic Encyclopedia* and Schaff-Herzog, *Encyclopedia of Religious Knowledge*, also Hastings, *op. cit.*

[9] See Schaff-Herzog, *op. cit.*, "New Manicheans," and literature there cited as well as church histories.

could see, I was in a state in which I did not sin." [10] But the outpouring of 1843 possessed a purifying and exhilarating finality which did not characterize his conversion. From that time, save for a period of illness in 1860, he says "a religious freedom, a religious buoyancy and delight in God, and in his word, a steadiness of faith, a Christian liberty and overflowing love have been abiding." [11] As is true of nearly all holiness preachers, Finney showed marked hostility toward luxury, personal adornment, theatergoing, secret societies, and other "worldly" practices. "Opposition to secret societies," says Gaddis, "became almost an obsession with the Oberlinites." [12]

Wesleyan Perfectionism. The doctrine of holiness loomed large in the teaching of John Wesley, running like a thread through his *Journal*, sermons, tracts, letters, and the minutes of his conferences with his preachers. He never claimed the state for himself, but was always preaching it and "going on" to it. The vivid experience in Aldersgate Street, London, when he "felt his heart strangely warmed," was a typical holiness experience, though he never so denominated it. The details of Wesley's doctrine of Christian perfection need no discussion here. They are, indeed, in dispute, for Wesley's ideas were variable and points set forth in his treatise on the subject seem contradicted by ideas expounded in his sermon on "Sin in Believers" and other teachings. Nevertheless, Wesleyan perfectionism has exerted the most far-reaching influence of any type of the doctrine ever presented; and while it has not remained vital in Methodism, it has persisted in numerous smaller bodies. In fact, most of the groups that today inculcate holiness are offshoots of the Wesleyan movement. These draw their tenets from Wesley's *A Plain Account of Christian Perfection* and *Brief Thoughts on Christian Perfection*. Briefly summarized, the doctrine therein set forth contains the following features:

1. Christian perfection is the product of faith and means freedom from all sin, both outward and inner, including "evil thoughts and tempers," though it does not insure against such human frailties as ignorance, mistakes, temptations, and the common infirmities of the flesh.

2. It is not the same as, nor does it ever accompany, justification, but is always subsequent thereto. "We do not know a single instance, in any place, of a person's receiving, in one and the same moment, remissions of sins, the abiding witness of the Spirit, and a new, a clean heart," Wesley wrote.

3. It is always an instantaneous experience, though there may be gradual growth both previous and subsequent thereto. Wesley's statements to this

[10] Finney, *Memoirs*, p. 23.

[11] *Ibid.*, p. 381.

[12] Gaddis, *Christian Perfectionism in America*, manuscript in the library of the University of Chicago, p. 329.

effect are explicit, though his exact meaning is not entirely clear.

4. It may be at the moment of death, as Calvinists claimed; but Wesley combats this idea and holds that it might be attained long before death. While exhorting all persons to "press on" to the ideal, he seems to concede that the experience is relatively rare among Christians.

5. Once obtained, the blessing may be lost, in which case there is no insuperable obstacle to securing it again.[13]

Wesley's doctrine encountered much opposition from Calvinists, the clergy of the Church of England, and others.[14] He had considerable trouble with persons who used his doctrine as the basis of wild enthusiasm, antinomian excesses, and millenarian notions.[15] The split between the Wesleys and the Calvinistic party led by George Whitefield and others revolved about perfectionism as well as the Arminian principle.

Perfectionism in American Methodism. This doctrine was brought over into American Methodism. Ministers entering the itinerancy were told that they were "to save as many souls as you can; to bring as many sinners as you possibly can to Repentance, and with all your power to build them up in that holiness without which they cannot see the Lord." [16] At the organization of the Methodist Church it was declared that "the purpose of God in raising up the people called Methodists" was "to spread Christian holiness over these lands," and this became and remains the honored motto of American Methodism. Furthermore, ministers were, and still are, required to return affirmative answers to three questions: "Are you going on to perfection? Do you expect to be made perfect in love in this life? Are you earnestly striving after it?" [17] Many, perhaps most, of the early preachers proclaimed the doctrine in season and out of season, and many professed the experience for themselves, though Gaddis is struck with the alleged fact that among the leaders with heavy administrative duties "there was manifested the maximum of aspiration with the minimum of profession." [18] Asbury was in doubt as to his own state, but was ever seeking to attain perfect love. But there can be no doubt about the official doctrine; Wesley's tracts on the subject were printed in the early *Disciplines,* beginning with 1789, and in 1808 the restrictive rule was passed which forbade changes

[13] See Wesley's, *A Plain Account of Christian Perfection* in *Works, Miscellaneous,* II, 483-531. See also his *Brief Thoughts on Christian Perfection, Ibid.,* pp. 531-34. The reader should bear in mind the word of caution above uttered. It is not contended that this is Wesley's last or fullest thought on the subject, but only that these points became the basis of the most vital Wesleyan holiness doctrine. For Wesley's most mature opinion see Lee, *John Wesley and Modern Religion.*

[14] He mentions some of this in his *Plain Account.*

[15] *Plain Account,* sections 20-22; Wesley, *A Short History of Methodism,* in *Works, Miscellaneous,* I, 246-48.

[16] *Discipline,* 1787, p. 22.

[17] *Ibid.,* pp. 13, 14. The requirement still remains in the quadrennial *Disciplines.*

[18] *Op. cit.,* p. 243.

in the then existing standards of doctrine. This rule still remains, and since many Methodists believe that Wesley's *Notes and Sermons,* as well as the Articles of Religion, are parts of the "standards of doctrine," [19] it may be contended that perfectionism is official in Methodism today.

It was largely this doctrine, in contradistinction to the sterner Calvinism, which gave Methodism its power in the frontier regions of the West, where Presbyterianism was so largely helpless except as it toned down its severe determinism. The Cumberland Presbyterians succeeded where the Old School Calvinists failed, largely because the former rejected fatalistic predestinarianism. At the same time, and largely for a similar reason, Methodism was relatively impotent in New England, where the population was religiously sophisticated, where Puritanism was entrenched, and where lingered memories of the perfectionistic vagaries of Noyes and his New Haven and New York compatriots.[20]

But though perfectionism lingered on in the official doctrines of American Methodism, where it is still imbedded, it did not long remain as a vital tenet, and The Methodist Church cannot in any real sense be classed today among the perfectionist denominations. The decline began early in the nineteenth century, due, according to Gaddis, to (1) the increasingly autocratic character of the episcopacy; (2) the decline of the class meeting; (3) the abandonment of camp-meeting revivalism; (4) the passing of the frontier itinerancy; and (5) general environmental circumstances.[21] In 1835 an article in the *Christian Advocate and Journal* deplored the fact that "Christian holiness is at the present time so little talked of and so little enjoyed in the Methodist Church." [22] In 1840 the bishops called attention to the fact that the doctrine was "a leading feature of early Methodism," and continued that "it is not enough to have this doctrine in our standard," thus evidencing their knowledge of its decline as a vital force.[23]

In 1870 the bishops of the Methodist Episcopal Church, South, in their quadrennial address, deplored the low spiritual state of the people and pleaded for "an increase of inward, genuine, scriptural holiness." They feared that "the doctrine of perfect love," "a prominent theme in the discourses of our fathers," was being "overlooked and neglected." "Nothing is so much needed at the present time, throughout all these lands," continued the bishops, "as a general and powerful revival of scriptural holi-

---

[19] On this point see Tigert, *The Doctrines of the Methodist Episcopal Church in America* and *Constitutional History of American Episcopal Methodism;* also Gaddis, Appendix F., *op. cit.*, pp. 555-57.

[20] Gaddis, *op. cit.*, p. 262.

[21] *Op. cit.*, p. 384.

[22] May 8, 1835.

[23] *General Conference Journal*, 1840, p. 161.

ness." [24] But twenty-four years later, when this advice seemed to be heeded, and a holiness movement was sweeping over the country and through the church, giving much trouble to the staid leaders, there was a different tone in the Episcopal Address. In 1894 the bishops pointed out that Methodism had ever taught the privilege of entire sanctification, though few had attained the experience; "let the doctrine still be proclaimed, and the experience still be testified." Then followed a virtual denunciation and repudiation of the "party with holiness as a watchword," and the holiness associations, meetings, preachers, and evangelists. The bishops were seeking to bring under control the perfectionist advocates who, true to form, were finding themselves uncomfortable in the complacent congregations which in their sophistication had outgrown the doctrine dear to the heart of the naïve and ardent rural enthusiasts. The bishops deplored the tendency to "separate themselves from the body of ministers and disciples," and pointed out that "the responsibility of appointing and directing religious services belongs to the preacher in charge." They warned against unauthorized holiness meetings and even went so far as to suggest legislation against "such interference."

Vital holiness was passing out of Methodist faith and practice. Finally, all traces of the doctrine were carefully eliminated from the songs of the church in the hymnal published in 1935. For example, in Charles Wesley's great hymn, "Love Divine, All Loves Excelling," which has appeared in all the hymn books since 1747, a line in the second stanza reading "Let us find *that second* rest" was altered by the hymnal commission to "Let us find *the promised* rest." Nothing was allowed to remain that might remind Methodists that their church had ever endorsed a *second* work of grace!

All this is interesting as showing the beginnings of a new sect, and in the customary manner. With perfectionism definitely eliminated from Methodism, there began first an agitation for its reinstatement, and then withdrawals and schisms on the part of the poor and lowly into congenial groups.

Between 1792 and 1860 there were five schisms, all in protest against the episcopacy and favoring a return to early Wesleyan standards.

Every sect which has risen as a schism from Methodist ranks or has drawn most of its members from the Methodist constituency (with the exception of the Methodist Episcopal Church, South, and certain of the colored churches) has democratized its government; and nearly all have returned wholeheartedly to perfectionism at the same time.[25]

There are twenty-three bodies in the country bearing the Methodist name,

[24] *General Conference Journal*, 1870, pp. 164, 165.
[25] Gaddis, *op. cit.*, pp. 388, 389.

nine of which are Negro churches. The Colored Methodist Episcopal Church was set up by the Methodist Episcopal Church, South, in 1870 and the Primitive Methodist Church was imported from England in 1829. All the others represent schisms or withdrawals from some of the other Methodist bodies.

There are about a dozen groups which may be termed quasi-Methodist sects. These are, and profess to be, Wesleyan in doctrine; their organizers were for the most part Methodists, and they drew their original members mainly from the Methodist constituency. In addition to all these, there are about two dozen sects which do not bear the Methodist name and did not arise under direct Methodist auspices, but which owe their existence to the Methodist genius. All espouse the sanctification doctrine promulgated by the early Methodist preachers. Thus Methodism is directly or indirectly responsible for over fifty of the existing American sects. These have a combined membership of nearly ten million persons. All may be called perfectionists so far as their official doctrines are concerned, and at least thirty of them still make sanctification one of their central principles.

In addition to these perfectionist sects there are many Negro groups which should be included in the same category. Some are avowedly perfectionist and the others are such to all intents and purposes. In fact, one would not be far amiss in including most of the colored groups of the nation in that classification, for in their emotional reactions and their tendency to "gifts," "blessings," "prophecies," and various spiritual enduements they aspire to and obtain experiences which characterize the most thoroughgoing perfectionists.

Characteristics of the Perfectionist Sects. The perfectionist sects are nearly all alike, although there are some differences between them. Certain features are common to those that still adhere to their original pattern.[26]

1. They espouse sanctification of the "second blessing" type. The experience is subsequent to justification or conversion. It is an emotional experience which is attributed to the direct operation of the Holy Spirit in the heart of the believer, the effect of which is to eradicate natural depravity or inborn sin.

2. Spirit guidance is prominent. The believers seek inner impressions and feelings and rely upon the same in many affairs of life. Among the more radical groups the guidance of the spirit is sought in visions, "gifts," and various spiritual enduements which are not infrequently orgiastic in character; these are the pentecostal churches discussed in the chapter on charismatic sects.

3. The sectarian spirit is seen in an exaggeration of their own importance

[26] It will, of course, be understood that there are variations from the norm in the beliefs and practices of the various bodies, though this is a true general picture.

or acceptability to God, and a corresponding disparagement of other denominations, especially the large and prosperous. Over and over again one hears the charge that the large denominations and their ministers have forsaken the true faith and are corrupt; some extremists find in this alleged corruption the fulfillment of prophecies and even refer to the great churches as antichrist. As for themselves, they are frequently regarded as the "true church"; often they deny that they are sects, and propose to unite all "true Christians" into one body, which is invariably their own. These characteristics are not peculiar to the perfectionist groups, however.

4. They are usually fundamentalist in character and sometimes oppose modern scholarship as "modernism." They hold to the verbal inspiration and literal interpretation of the Bible. Though many of them maintain schools, they are quite suspicious of learning and there is usually an important "but" in their advocacy of education.

5. Many of these sects employ the believers' meeting technique and rely upon the revival as the principal method of winning converts. Practically all maintain Sunday schools, but use them for teaching the Bible and their own tenets; the aim of modern religious education in securing Christian character and religious experience by the developmental process is opposed. They hold to a kind of disciplinary theory of training; the words of the Bible, faithfully taught, will in some way be used by the Holy Spirit to bring about the experience without which one cannot become a true Christian.

6. These sects adhere to the older theology. Original sin, of course, is necessary to their main doctrine of sanctification; this is held to be the result of Adam's fall. Otherworldly ideas are prominent, and a heaven for the faithful and eternal punishment for the wicked are featured. The same is true of nearly all the elements of the older theology.

7. Practically all the perfectionist sects are premillenarian. Though this is not always featured as a central doctrine, and not all the sects magnify the imminence of the parousia and the Adventist cosmology, the premillenarian scheme is found in the tenets of most of the small bodies being considered.

8. Most of them inculcate the puritan morality. There is usually opposition to "worldliness" in all its forms. Specifically they decry the use of tobacco and intoxicating beverages, such amusements as dancing and theatergoing, wearing of gold and costly apparel, reading of novels and "light" literature, and similar practices. Many of them oppose membership in secret societies.

Methodist Divisions. Numerous divisions have rent the Methodist body, and these have resulted in twenty independent Methodist denominations and as many others which, under other names, stemmed from Methodist sources, drew Methodist members into their folds, and adopted essentially Methodist doctrine. The issues of slavery and race figured in a few of these divisions, but for the most part they grew out of the neglect of holiness and the power of the episcopacy, and the reforms made by the new bodies were on these points.

The earliest schism was in 1792, when James O'Kelley led a large group out of the Methodist Episcopal Church when the conference rejected a motion which would have given the pastors the right to appeal from the episcopal appointments. This group was known as Republican Methodists, but they joined with dissident Baptists, Presbyterians, and Disciples to form the Christian Church, which united with the Congregational Church in 1931.

The Methodist Protestant Church came into being in 1830, following the refusal of the General Conference of 1828 to admit laymen to all the conferences of the church. This denomination adopted sanctification but did not specify that the experience was necessarily subsequent to justification.

In 1844 the general conference voluntarily provided for the division of the church into two branches. The immediate occasion was a stalemate over slavery, but the deeper issues involved the right of the general conference to depose or set aside by simple vote a bishop who had violated no law of the church and against whom no charges were brought, and the power of the general conference to determine the constitutionality of its own actions. Churches and conferences in the South and Southwest were organized into the Methodist Episcopal Church, South, which became the fourth largest Protestant body in the United States, with seventeen thousand churches and three million members. Sanctification or holiness was not among its doctrines.

In 1939 unification of the Methodist Episcopal Church, the Methodist Episcopal Church, South, and the Methodist Protestant Church was brought about by a reorganization which brought into existence the largest Protestant denomination—The Methodist Church, which has 40,000 churches and 8,500,000 members in the United States, and around 5,000 churches and 1,000,000 members in its foreign fields. The reorganized body printed the Methodist Protestant article on sanctification in the *Discipline* in connection with the historic Articles of Religion, which had remained unchanged in the other two uniting bodies, but the article was not adopted as official in the new denomination.

As is not unusual in such cases, a small group in South Carolina declined to enter the united church. Forbidden to use the name of the Methodist Episcopal Church, South, a few rural churches organized the SOUTHERN METHODIST CHURCH on a congregationalist basis, and some churches were formed in Georgia and Tennessee. This sect is fundamentalist in nature and has about a dozen small congregations with several hundred members.

Small Methodist Sects. One of the earliest schisms in Methodism occurred in 1814 and resulted in the REFORMED METHODIST CHURCH. It was so small that it goes unnoticed in many Methodist histories. It involved only fourteen persons, led by unordained laymen, mostly local preachers and exhorters, the most prominent being Elijah and James Bailey, Ezra Amadon, Ebenezer Davis, Caleb Whiting, and William Lake. These were opposed to the episcopal form of government, which they held to be destructive of "true Christian humility" and scriptural holiness. Their petitions failing to secure redress of grievances, they withdrew and organized the Reformed Methodist Church at Readsboro, Vermont, on January 6, 1814.

This group first attempted a communistic experiment on a farm between Bennington, Vermont, and Hoosick, New York, but the project failed and the people scattered. Their evangelistic zeal resulted in the establishment of several congregations, and within thirty years the sect had three thousand members, seventy-five preachers, and six conferences. By this time other Methodist groups, especially the Wesleyan Methodist Church, had arisen on similar platforms and attracted many Reformed members. There has been a gradual falling away, only about ten churches and four hundred members remaining at the present time. The group is "distinctively Methodist, following the teachings of their founder, John Wesley." Its outstanding principles are entire sanctification, the imminent return of Jesus Christ and the end of the world, and the healing of disease by prayer.[27]

The PRIMITIVE METHODIST CHURCH is an importation to the United States from the "camp meeting" Methodists of England. In 1810 the spectacular wilderness evangelist Lorenzo Dow, who was denied entrance to the conferences of this country, went to England and attempted to introduce the camp meeting to the British. Though denounced by the Wesleyan conferences as "highly improper in England and likely to be productive of mischief," the chief convert Hugh Bourne persisted in holding such meetings, and was expelled for his "insufferable contumacy." In 1812 the converts of the movement organized as the Primitive Methodist Church. Outdemocratizing the already democratic Wesleyans by admitting to the conference two laymen for each preacher, and professing a return to the perfectionism and evangelism of John Wesley, the Primitives outstripped in growth all other English Methodist bodies save the original Wesleyan.[28]

In July, 1829, Primitive Methodist missionaries came to the United States, following members who had emigrated to these shores. Bourne himself came in 1844. The sect in this country has in general followed the democratic polity and, officially at least, adhered to the holiness doctrine of

[27] *Census of Religious Bodies*, 1936, II, 1170-71.
[28] Petty, *History of the Primitive Methodist Connexion.*

the early English group; pastors are invited by the churches annually, first, second, and third choices being made, and the conference merely ratifies, "except for grave reasons," the appointment of the man who accepts. The sect has never been large but has grown steadily, from less than 4,800 members in 1890 to 12,000 at the present time. There are eighty-five churches, over half of which are in Pennsylvania, the others being thinly scattered over seven near-by states. In common with the larger Methodist bodies, Primitive Methodism preserves perfectionism in its creed but has largely abandoned it in practice.[29]

The defection of the WESLEYAN METHODIST CHURCH from the Methodist Episcopal Church in 1843 grew out of the abolition controversy, coupled with dissatisfaction over the episcopacy and the current state of Methodist piety. The revolting group was made up of abolitionists under the leadership of Orange Scott, J. Horton, L. R. Sunderland, L. C. Matlock, and others, who agitated for emancipation of the slaves, publishing a paper, the *True Wesleyan*. In 1843 they withdrew in a body, taking with them twenty-two ministers and six thousand members.

The sect prospered until after the Civil War, when large numbers, deeming the main cause of the schism to have been eliminated, returned to the original body. Questions of polity, practice, and doctrine, however, have preserved the denomination as a separate entity, and of late years there has been a slow growth. The Wesleyan Methodist Church (or Connection) has around 800 churches and 30,000 members. It has preserved the doctrine of perfection.[30]

The FREE METHODIST CHURCH separated from the Methodist Episcopal Church in 1860 after ten years of agitation on the subject of perfectionism and the practices common thereto, with which was combined complaints against the arbitrary exercise of power. As in the case of the Wesleyan schism, this defection occurred in the territory which had witnessed the revivalism of Finney and the vagaries of Noyes and his perfectionist contemporaries. Headed by B. T. Roberts and other members of the Genesee Conference, a considerable group protested worldly practices, decline of sanctification, membership in secret societies, admission of unconverted persons, departure from primitive simplicity, renting of pews, indulging in questionable amusements, choir singing, building of costly churches and similar practices. In 1858 Roberts and Joseph McCreary were expelled from the conference for contumacy and alleged immoral and unchristian conduct; four other ministers were then expelled and two were "located" or

---

[29] Gaddis, *op. cit.*, p. 432, quotes the secretary of the denomination as saying that "our ministers are not obligated to preach it; few of them do."

[30] See the various histories of American Methodism; Gaddis MS, *op. cit.*, p. 418; Schaff-Herzog, *op. cit.*, "Methodists," IV, 4; *Census of Religious Bodies*, 1926, II, 947-54.

retired from the itinerant ranks for expressing sympathy with Roberts and McCreary. When the general conference refused to allow the appeal of Roberts and the others, the Free Methodist Church was organized at a convention in Pekin, New York, in 1860. It has twelve hundred churches with approximately fifty thousand members.[31]

The HOLINESS METHODIST CHURCH came into existence in 1900 when certain rural preachers in North Carolina "became intensely interested in local conditions," and at a meeting held in Union Chapel Church, Robeson County, organized the sect. Thus without previous antecedents of note there came into being the "Lumbee Mission Conference of the Holiness Methodist Church," the name later being changed to "Lumbee River Annual Conference of the Holiness Methodist Church." It is a tiny sect with three circuits, eight congregations, and six hundred members. The body is a typical rural holiness group.

The CONGREGATIONAL METHODIST CHURCH originated in a secession from the Methodist Episcopal Church, South, in Georgia, in 1852, the bone of contention being the episcopacy. The sect is congregational in form and has 275 churches and 16,000 members.

Another sect in Georgia and Florida is known as the NEW CONGREGATIONAL METHODIST CHURCH. It originated in a revolt on the part of certain rural congregations when the Georgia Conference of the Methodist Episcopal Church, South, in 1881, unable to support all its mission circuits, decided to consolidate several small rural churches. Some of the churches concerned formed an independent body, rejecting the episcopacy and connectional assessments, and adding foot washing to the customary Methodist practices. This sect has twenty-five churches and fifteen hundred members.

A small group called the APOSTOLIC METHODIST CHURCH is endeavoring to secure a foothold in Florida. It originated in the agitation of E. H. Crowson and his father, F. L. Crowson, against alleged heresy and defection from Wesleyan fundamentals on the part of the Florida Conference of the Methodist Episcopal Church, South. In 1931 E. H. Crowson was "located" or deposed from the itinerant ministry for "unacceptability." Two years later F. L. Crowson was tried on charges and suspended for one year, at the end of which period he withdrew from the conference. The Apostolic Methodist Church was organized by E. H. Crowson and a few others at Loughman, Florida, in 1932. A rather elaborate *Discipline* has been published, in which are set forth grievances against episcopal autocracy and the neglect of holiness. The sect is congregational in polity and teaches

---

[31] Hogue, *History of the Free Methodist Church* (2 vols.); Bowen, *History of the Origin of the Free Methodist Church*; McCreary, *The Free Methodist Church*; Schaff-Herzog, *op. cit.*, "Methodists," IV, 5; Gaddis MS, *op. cit.*, pp. 427-30; *Census of Religious Bodies*, 1926, II, 976-84.

premillenarianism and holiness of the "second blessing" type. It has but one or two congregations and only a handful of members.[32]

The HOLINESS METHODISTS is a small holiness body in North Carolina. It grew out of a defection from the Wesleyan Methodist Church (or Connection) and was organized at Forest City, North Carolina, in 1913 by the Rev. H. C. Sisk and four other members. It has four churches and six hundred members.

The REFORMED NEW CONGREGATIONAL METHODIST CHURCH is another small sect of eight churches and three hundred members. It was organized in Illinois, in 1916, by a mission minister and an evangelist of the Congregational Methodist Church, with which body it is in agreement. The sect opposes divorce, secret societies, and adornment in matters of dress.

American Methodism did not escape the fundamentalist vs. modernist controversy, though disputes revolving around dogma and methods of interpretation caused relatively little trouble among the people who had no distinctive doctrines of their own and had always been more interested in man's spiritual state than in the correctness of his opinions. Their family quarrels were nearly all about sanctification and matters of church administration; in a few cases conservatives published dissenting newspapers which, though they originally stressed alleged abuses of power or maladministration of polity, usually ran eventually to doctrinal matters also. In the North appeared the *Methodist,* and in the South the *Southern Methodist* flourished briefly and died. On the West coast a later publication, the *Methodist Challenge,* was launched by the noted conservative pastor Dr. Bob Shuler, of Trinity Methodist Church in Los Angeles. The protestants pointed to the undue influence of modernism in theological seminaries, Sunday-school literature, newspapers, courses of study for ministers, leading pulpits, and general councils of Methodism, and they called names and cited chapter and verse in support of their accusations. The conservatives charged that there was widespread disbelief in the inspiration of the Bible, the virgin birth of Christ, the fall of man, the scriptural account of creation, miracles, the atonement, personal salvation, the bodily resurrection of Jesus, and similar doctrines that had always been regarded as among the fundamentals of the faith.

Only one actual schism, however, sprang directly from these discussions—the EVANGELICAL METHODIST CHURCH. On May 9, 1946, a number of ministers and laymen met at Memphis, Tennessee, and organized this group, with half a dozen preachers and congregations. The new church declared itself to be essentially Methodist in doctrine, denounced modernism, embraced the fundamentalist position, and set up a congregational

[32] E. H. Crowson, "Secretary of the General Assembly," in a letter to me, refused information about churches and members.

form of government, "with enough supervision to make it connectional." When its first annual conference met at Chattanooga, in December, 1947, it was announced that the number of preachers and members had been doubled, a mission in Mexico had been started and a thousand members had been secured there, and the "Mission of the Andes" in Colombia had been taken over. Six months later forty preachers and about fifty churches were reported in this country. An unsuccessful attempt by a Methodist bishop and district superintendent to invoke the law of the church to prevent Dr. Shuler, who did not join the new church, from holding a revival at Abilene, Texas, in the church of Dr. J. H. Hamblen, the chairman of the Evangelical Methodist Church, was used by the group to illustrate the lengths to which the "modernists" might go to prevent the preaching of the old-time evangelistic gospel.

Negro Methodist Sects. There are approximately 17,000 Negro Methodist churches in the United States, having around 1,800,000 members. Of these, 3,000 churches and 325,000 members are found in the Central (Negro) Jurisdiction of The Methodist Church, and the others are in nine different independent denominations which adhere to the Methodist doctrine and polity. These, with the Negro Baptists, which have nearly seven million members and are organized in two conventions, account for 90 per cent of all the Negro church members in the country. Negroes have shown an understandable reluctance to attach themselves to interracial or predominantly white denominations. Only the Methodist and Roman Catholic churches retain sizeable groups in their own bodies. The United States census reports that nearly 94 per cent of all Negro church members are found in exclusively Negro denominations. The fact that most American Negroes are Baptists is probably due largely to the congregational polity among Baptists which facilitates complete independence.

Negroes were found in many of the early churches formed by Methodists in this country. As their numbers increased they drew apart into separate congregations of their own, ministered to by white pastors or unordained Negro preachers. The absence of Negro ministers who could qualify for holy orders, the reluctance of Methodist authorities to ordain Negroes, and the grievances of Negroes at what they regarded as discrimination against them in the course of time led these congregations to become independent and to associate themselves with others in what became separate denominations. Such is the historical background of the three earliest Negro Methodist bodies.

The AFRICAN METHODIST EPISCOPAL CHURCH is the largest. In 1787 a group of Negro Methodists in Philadelphia withdrew from a white congregation and built a chapel. Their ministry was supplied by ordination of the Protestant Episcopal Church, but in 1799 Bishop Asbury ordained

Richard Allen. The group remained under white superintendency until 1814, and in 1816 Allen led in the formation of the African Methodist Episcopal Church. It now has more than 7,000 congregations and around 900,000 members.

THE AFRICAN METHODIST EPISCOPAL ZION CHURCH is the second largest. A Negro group from the John Street Church in New York organized a separate congregation in 1796, and in 1800 the Zion Church was erected and incorporated under the name of the African Methodist Episcopal Church. The white body provided an unordained ministry until 1820, and an independent general conference was convened in 1821. The name of the chapel was added to the title and the African Methodist Episcopal Zion Church came into being. This denomination has approximately 2,500 churches and 525,000 members. This church placed the doctrine of holiness in its creed.

The UNION AMERICAN METHODIST EPISCOPAL CHURCH grew out of a separation of Negro members from the Asbury Church at Wilmington, Delaware, in 1805. The group had a white preacher, but in 1813 an unordained Negro preacher, Peter Spencer, led a movement which resulted in the formation of a denomination under the name of the Union Church of Africans. There was a division in 1850 over the question of lay representation in the conferences, and from this emerged the Union American Methodist Episcopal Church, which now has seventy churches and nearly ten thousand members.

THE AFRICAN UNION METHODIST PROTESTANT CHURCH goes back to 1866, when the African Union Church united with the First Colored Methodist Protestant Church, a body which had arisen from Methodist Protestant sources. The name of the united church became officially the African Union First Colored Methodist Protestant Church of America or Elsewhere, but it is ordinarily called the African Union Methodist Protestant Church. It has thirty-seven congregations and two thousand members.

There is also an independent COLORED METHODIST PROTESTANT CHURCH, consisting of one congregation with about two hundred members, which is the remnant of a group which organized in Maryland in 1840.

The COLORED METHODIST EPISCOPAL CHURCH is a denomination of 4,000 churches and 380,000 members, which was set up in 1870 by the Methodist Episcopal Church, South, at the request of its Negro members. Through the evangelistic work of the Plantation Missions, under the direction of William Capers of South Carolina, the Methodist churches in the South prior to the War between the States had built up a Negro membership of 207,000 and had 327 white preachers ministering to the slaves. As a result of the war, reconstruction, and the activity of the Northern branch of the church and the independent Negro denominations, the number dwindled rapidly, and both the white and Negro members in the Southern church deemed separation to be advisable. The Colored Methodist Episcopal Church was a sister denomination of, and received material aid from, the Methodist Episcopal Church, South, and the relationship was preserved in the unification of the three large Methodist bodies in 1939.

The REFORMED ZION UNION APOSTOLIC CHURCH dates from 1869, when Negro Methodists in Virginia organized the Zion Union Apostolic Church. Five years later dissension arose over a change in the constitution, which permitted the president to become the bishop with life tenure, and this almost destroyed the church. A reorganization of the scattered congregations and members was effected in 1882, and the name was changed to the Reformed Zion Union Apostolic Church. The sect has about thirty churches and three thousand members.

The REFORMED METHODIST UNION EPISCOPAL CHURCH was organized in 1885 by a group of ministers and members who withdrew from the African Methodist Episcopal Church because of differences with reference to the election of ministerial delegates to the general conference. Originally a nonepiscopal body, it adopted episcopacy in 1896, and in 1899 its first bishop was consecrated by a bishop of the Reformed Episcopal Church. The sect has sixty-five churches and three thousand members.

The INDEPENDENT AFRICAN METHODIST EPISCOPAL CHURCH goes back to 1897, when a group of eight ministers of the African Methodist Episcopal Church at Jacksonville, Florida, became involved in disputes with the presiding elders of that body. They withdrew and organized the Independent African Methodist Episcopal Church, which now has a dozen churches and one thousand members.

German Perfectionist Sects. The United Brethren differ little from the Methodists; in fact, they owe their separate existence to Bishop Asbury's reluctance to sanction preaching in the German language. Philip Otterbein and Asbury were co-workers and fellow spirits, proclaiming similar messages of holiness. Otterbein and Martin Boehm, a Mennonite preacher, both experienced deeply emotional spiritual awakenings, and together evangelized among the Germans. There appears to have been no thought of organizing an independent church. Meetings of the evangelists, however, revealed the need of an organization to conserve the results secured; and since the converts did not find their spiritual needs met in the English-speaking Methodist services, the UNITED BRETHREN IN CHRIST was organized in 1800, Otterbein and Boehm being elected bishops.

The EVANGELICAL CHURCH was more definitely Methodist in origin than the United Brethren. Jacob Albright, the founder, originally a Lutheran, joined the Methodist Church as the result of a definite conversion experience. The first conference was known as the Newly-Formed Methodist

Conference, and the believers were referred to as Albright Methodists or German Albright Methodists. Here again the refusal of Asbury to permit preaching in the German language thrust a large group out of the Methodist fold. An organization was formed in 1803, and at the first conference, in 1807, Albright was elected bishop. The name Evangelical Association was taken in 1816.

Albright and his Evangelicals were aggressively perfectionist and none preached the doctrine more assiduously. By 1855 the group had definitely classed merely "justified" or "partly sanctified" persons with sinners and the lost. The controversies with reference to the doctrine tended to cast it entirely on the dogmatic plane, to its detriment as a vital tenet. Though the perfectionists won and perfectionism was made doctrinally supreme, a decline set in soon after the Civil War, with the result that the idea largely became a theoretical matter.[33]

The controversy over sanctification was not settled when the perfectionists secured the supremacy of their doctrine. Rival holiness groups developed, and there was a disruption in 1891, when two fifths of the whole membership withdrew and formed, in 1894, the UNITED EVANGELICAL CHURCH. The differences concerned matters of polity and administration mainly. According to Gaddis, "there were proportionately about as many perfectionists in the two-fifths group which seceded as in the three-fifths group of conservatives remaining under the old name." [34]

The UNITED CHRISTIAN CHURCH stems back to 1864, when a number of members left the United Brethren in Christ as the result of a controversy growing out of alleged departures from the original positions. The malcontents were opposed to secret societies, bearing arms, and infant baptism; they worshiped in homes, barns, and groves until they secured a church building in 1868. The name of United Christian Church was adopted in 1878. This is a small and conservative body, with only fifteen churches and six hundred members. In addition to the prohibitions mentioned the sect practices foot washing. Sanctification is defined as a rebirth by which men are "separated in their acts, words, and thoughts from sin." [35]

The UNITED BRETHREN IN CHRIST (OLD CONSTITUTION) arose from a schism in the ranks of the United Brethren in 1889, when a new constitution was adopted. Many conservatives refused to accept the new instrument and withdrew, thus originating the United Brethren in Christ (Old Constitution). This group holds more steadfastly to the older pietistic and

[33] See Gaddis, *op. cit.*, pp. 404-9, for a discussion of this whole development. Gaddis cites the Evangelical historian Schwab and Bishop Spreng to the effect that vitally the doctrine of entire sanctification has lost much of its power in the church.

[34] *Op. cit.*, p. 407.

[35] *Census of Religious Bodies*, 1936, II, 1643.

perfectionist traditions, rejects membership in secret societies, is strict in the matter of temperance, and refuses to participate in war. It holds to the old constitution adopted in 1841. The body has 250 churches with 15,000 members and has steadily declined since its inception.

In 1946 the EVANGELICAL-UNITED BRETHREN CHURCH grew out of a union perfected between the Church of the United Brethren in Christ and the Evangelical Church. The united body reports a total membership of nearly 750,000 and 5,000 local congregations.

The EVANGELICAL CONGREGATIONAL CHURCH dates from 1922, when schism was to a large degree healed and the Evangelical Association and the United Evangelical Church reunited under the name of the Evangelical Church. But the East Pennsylvania Conference of the United group refused to acquiesce in the merger and organized the Evangelical Congregational Church on a democratic basis. Doctrinally the two present bodies were not far apart. The Evangelical Congregational now has 160 churches and 25,000 members.

The APOSTOLIC CHRISTIAN CHURCH (NAZAREAN) was introduced about 1850 by the Rev. S. H. Froehlich, who came to the United States from Switzerland, and by evangelistic labors established a number of churches among the German and Swiss immigrants in the Middle West, into which were drawn many Mennonite believers. The doctrine of entire sanctification, presented in the customary way, is a tenet of this group. There are about thirty churches and the reported membership is about sixteen hundred.

The APOSTOLIC CHRISTIAN CHURCH OF AMERICA is a similar body which originated in the preaching of Benedict Weyeneth among the German and Swiss immigrants in this country after 1847, the date of the founder's arrival here. Its main doctrine is that of entire sanctification, and it adopts a pacifist attitude towards war. It is loosely organized, but available data give it around fifty-five congregations and six thousand members.

The MENNONITE BRETHREN IN CHRIST dates its origin in 1853, when a number of Pennsylvania Mennonites began revival meetings. These were so successful that in 1858 they organized a conference under the name of Evangelical Mennonites. A few years later a Canadian Mennonite preacher was converted and sanctified by evangelists of the Evangelical Association. His introduction of prayer and class meetings caused him and his followers to be disowned by the main body of Mennonites. They took the name of Reformed Mennonites, in 1874, and on being joined the next year by a small group that had organized as New Mennonites the joint body became the United Mennonites. In 1879 this group merged with the Evangelical Mennonites, the designation then becoming Evangelical United Mennonites. In 1883 they were joined by a group which had seceded from the River

Brethren, and the Mennonite Brethren in Christ came thus into being.

In all this history the Methodist influence appeared; the historian of the body definitely traces its perfectionist doctrine back to Wesleyan sources —the preaching of Free Methodists, United Brethren, and Evangelicals.[36] These Mennonites are avowed exponents of the Wesleyan "second blessing" holiness experience, and display the typical early Methodist emotionalism in their meetings. Their polity is also cast in the Methodist mold, though democratic. In 1878 they established a holiness paper, the *Gospel Banner*, and began holding camp meetings, the first ever held by Mennonites.[37] This sect practices divine healing by prayer, laying on of hands and anointing with oil, expects the imminent return of Christ, and prohibits the use of tobacco, alcoholic beverages, and other forms of "worldliness." It has around one hundred churches and nearly eight thousand members.

Religious Society of Friends. If the Quakers are not perfectionists they are at least subjectivists. They are so well known and have so little of the sectarian spirit that no lengthy description of the people who in their meetings "speak when the Spirit moves them" is needed. They have never been numerous but their influence has been, and is now, out of all proportion to their numbers.

The Friends are the followers of the doctrines expounded by George Fox in England near the middle of the seventeenth century. They came to America as early as 1656, but were promptly arrested and shipped away. Eight more arrived two days later, and they continued to come until persecution ended around 1725. Their most notable success, as even school children know, was the founding of Pennsylvania by William Penn in 1682.

In matters of doctrine the Quakers stress the "inner light" or the immediate influence of the Holy Spirit, and do not employ outward ordinances such as baptism and the Holy Communion. Their meetinghouses are usually plain and their worship is simple. For a long time most of the churches did not have ordained or professional ministers, and in their services all who felt an inward prompting to do so were permitted to speak, and this is still the practice in the typical "Quaker meeting." In the earlier period the Quakers dressed in a plain garb that was distinctive, and used the pronouns "thee" and "thou" in conversation. The people have always been known as opponents of war and have consistently refused to bear arms. The Friends Service Committee, a relief organization which operates on funds raised mainly from other denominations and non-Quakers, received the Nobel Peace Prize in 1947.

The RELIGIOUS SOCIETY OF FRIENDS (GENERAL CONFERENCE) stemmed

[36] Huffman, *History of the Mennonite Brethren in Christ Church*, p. 163.
[37] *Ibid.*, p. 149.

from disagreement among the Friends, caused largely by the prevalence of modern thought and the evangelical spirit. This occurred in 1827 and involved the doctrines of Elias Hicks, a liberal who taught that God's spirit alone was sufficient guidance for every man, and whose followers were called Hicksites and accused of Unitarian leadings. The Hicksite groups did not adopt a definite theology but they represent the liberal arm of Quakerism.

The second separation, resulting in the RELIGIOUS SOCIETY OF FRIENDS (CONSERVATIVE), was in 1845 and was led by John Wilbur, hence the designation of Wilburites. It was a conservative movement in protest against the teachings and evangelical attitude of Joseph John Gurney, an English Quaker, who urged the importance of Bible study and higher education and stressed the authority of the Scriptures. The favorable attention given to Gurney in this country led Wilbur and his followers to fear that the Friends were departing from their original faith. Groups favoring the principles of Gurney also withdrew in 1854. The PRIMITIVE FRIENDS came into being in 1861 as the result of a secession from the Wilburites of a small group which adopted a still more conservative attitude and desired to maintain "the ancient testimonies of the society." The Primitives are quite small.

The other Quaker bodies, which are commonly regarded as the Orthodox, are grouped in five Yearly Meetings, as their conferences are called, formed on a geographical basis, and one confederation of about ten Yearly Meetings, known as the RELIGIOUS SOCIETY OF FRIENDS (FIVE YEARS MEETING). There are about 115,000 members in all the denominations.

The National Holiness Movement. At the close of the Civil War, as at the close of all great conflicts, including both World Wars, there swept over the country a wave of immorality, secularism, and religious indifference. The spirit naturally affected the churches, bringing about what many believed to be a lowered moral tone, compromise with "the world," weakening of the insistence on definite religious experience as a condition of membership, with the consequent influx of unconverted persons into the fold, and a general decline of vital piety and holiness of life. As a result, by the familiar process of sectarian psychology, the humbler Christians with emotional temperaments and perfectionist leanings began to feel uneasy, to protest against the abandonment of earlier practices, and to seek wherever it might be found the experience of perfect love.

This movement was almost exclusively a Methodist phenomenon, led by Methodists, and appealing mainly to Methodists; this was but natural in view of the practical monopoly held by Methodism at that time on the perfectionist tradition, including the revival, class meeting, and testimony technique which has always been the strongest support of holiness. Soon those who professed or were "groaning after" sanctification began to seek companionship with other congenial souls, drawing apart into "bands," establishing holiness periodicals, and sponsoring holiness camp meetings. The great denominations became alarmed and endeavored to bring the movement under control, making verbal gestures to the doctrine of entire sanctification but showing no sign of returning to it as a vital experience.[38] Controversy and mutual recriminations ensued, and the holiness people became more and more alienated from the churches. The small "bands" and groups declared independence in large numbers and in every part of the country. Later these began to drift together and form holiness denominations; the Church of the Nazarene and the Pilgrim Holiness Church are examples of sects formed by the amalgamation of several independent and previously unrelated "bands" of sanctificationists. Thus the postwar situation bred a swarm of "second blessing" sects, all having the common features of perfectionist groups.

The National Holiness Movement assumed large proportions in 1867, when the first general holiness camp meeting was held at Vineland, New Jersey. While professing to be interdenominational in character, this camp meeting was essentially a Methodist institution. Its success caused others to spring up, the Methodists giving them cordial support in the early period before the holiness movement was in definite competition with the churches.[39] A "National Camp Meeting Association for the Promotion of Holiness" was formed under Methodist leadership, and then a "Holiness Union" appeared. Periodicals began to appear,[40] some of which flourish to this day. Then came holiness colleges,[41] many of which also survive. Within thirty years after the launching of the National Holiness Movement on a nation-wide scale the perfectionists had largely withdrawn from the Methodist and other churches and set up housekeeping for themselves, with the cult and all the propaganda agencies of well-organized sects. The movement made large inroads on Methodism, drawing off multitudes of members in towns and rural districts, as indeed perfectionist and "pentecostal" groups continue to do, and finally eliminated from the large Methodist bodies the last vestiges of vital "second blessing" holiness or entire sanctifi-

[38] See, for example, the address of the Bishops of the Methodist Episcopal Church, South, in 1894, previously mentioned.

[39] Gaddis, op. cit., p. 444, cites the Round Lake camp meeting in the Troy (N. Y.) Methodist Episcopal Conference as attracting President Grant and bishops and other outstanding leaders from every branch of American Methodism.

[40] The Guide to Holiness, said to be the "original holiness journal of America," began in 1842. In the postwar period appeared the Christian Witness and Advocate of Bible Holiness, Banner of Holiness, Texas Holiness Advocate, Herald of Holiness, Pentecostal Herald, and others.

[41] Among these may be mentioned Asbury, Trevecca, Texas Holiness, Illinois Holiness, Pentecostal, Northwest Holiness, Taylor, Oklahoma Holiness, and Alma Colleges. There were, and are, many others, including numerous "Bible Schools."

cation.[42] All the sects later mentioned in this chapter, and many others mentioned elsewhere, are products of the National Holiness Movement.

The CHURCH OF THE NAZARENE, the largest of the sects emerging from the National Holiness Movement, has approximately 3,000 churches and 200,000 members and is represented in all the states. Its history is somewhat complicated.[43] It is the product of several mergers among holiness groups and associations of the East, South, and West; one of its aims is to bring together all such groups into one large denomination and it has a permanent committee to negotiate such mergers.

In 1894 three "Pentecostal Tabernacles" sprang up in Brooklyn, New York, representatives of which formed in the following year the Association of Pentecostal Churches of America. About the same time a similar movement developed in New England, resulting in the Central Evangelical Holiness Association, which in 1896 merged with the New York Association.

In the West, Rev. Phineas F. Breeze organized the First Church of the Nazarene at Los Angeles in 1895. The previous year R. L. Harris launched the First Church of Christ at Milan, Tennessee. In 1898 the Holiness Church was organized in Texas, and in the same state the Independent Church of Christ came into being in 1900. These two Texas groups united in 1904 to form the Holiness Church of Christ. In 1898 the Rev. J. O. McClurkan and others called a meeting of Tennessee holiness people at Nashville, and there organized the Pentecostal Alliance, later known as the Pentecostal Mission.

In 1907 there was perfected at Chicago a union of the Association of Pentecostal Churches of America and the Church of the Nazarene. The body thus resulting was called the Pentecostal Church of the Nazarene. One year later the union was joined by the Holiness Church of Christ, and the Pentecostal Mission adhered in 1915. During the latter year the affiliation of the Pentecostal Church of Scotland was brought about. In 1919 the word "Pentecostal" was dropped from the name and the body became the Church of the Nazarene.

This is to all intents and purposes a Methodist sect. Its ministers and members originally were nearly all drawn from the Methodist fold. Five of the first seven general superintendents had formerly been Methodist preachers, and the other two had been closely identified with Methodism and had obtained their holiness views from that church.[44] The Nazarene polity is Methodistic, its *Manual* being little more than a rewritten and modified

[42] The world is full of holiness literature, each of the many sects having its histories, periodicals, and pamphlets. See especially Jernigan, *Pioneer Days of the Holiness Movement in the Southwest;* Chapman, *History of the Church of the Nazarene;* Gaddis MS, *op. cit.,* ch. xi, and the literature of the various sects, cited hereinunder.

[43] See Chapman, *History of the Church of the Nazarene.*

[44] *Year Book of the Church of the Nazarene,* 1925, p. 9.

Methodist *Discipline*. The sect makes no attempt to conceal its borrowings from Methodism; on the contrary it claims the heritage and avows that it is a reversion to original Wesleyanism.

To advance perfectionism was the sole excuse for the existence of this sect. It wrote the doctrine in its Articles of Faith and requires that all ministers and local church officials shall have undergone the experience of sanctification. The Nazarene tenet minimizes the developmental aspect of holiness and enlarges upon the direct operation of the Holy Ghost. A distinction is made between the "perfect heart," which comes from the instantaneous "second blessing," and the "perfect character," which is the result of growth in grace. "It is one thing to have the heart all yielded to God and occupied by him," declared the general assembly, somewhat obscurely, "it is quite another thing to have the entire character, in every detail, harmonize with His Spirit, and the life become 'conformable to His image.'" This seems to be an attempt to distinguish between the emotional reaction so highly valued as bringing sanctification and the living of a morally blameless life.

The Nazarenes, as Gaddis remarks, are a sort of "right wing" [45] among holiness advocates. They discountenance the "tongue talking" which marks the radical "Pentecostal" groups; it was to avoid confusion at this point that the word "Pentecostal" was eliminated from the denominational name. Divine healing through prayer is believed in, though not to the exclusion of medical agencies.

In spite of all these doctrines and practices, however, there are signs that vital perfectionism is already on the decline in the Church of the Nazarene. Gaddis attributes this to the tendency to ape The Methodist Church in polity, superintendence, centralization of authority, complexity of organization, attention to statistics, striving for bigness, and similar details. [46] Thus are being lost the freedom, spontaneity, and democracy so essential to the perfectionist spirit. Already there have been revolts within the body; as early as 1917 one rebellious group in Pasadena, California, withdrew into the Pilgrim Holiness Church. The Nazarene schools especially have been embarrassed by the holiness label, and all of them have elided the designation from their names; Texas Holiness University changed to Peniel College, Illinois Holiness University to Olivet College, Pentecostal Institute to Eastern Nazarene College, Oklahoma Holiness College to Bethany-Peniel College, Northwest Holiness College to Northwest Nazarene College. Not one institution of the denomination now exposes its doctrinal character in its name. Such straws indicate the blowing of the wind in the inevitable direction taken by the large Methodist bodies, and show the Church of

[45] Gaddis, *op. cit.*, p. 509.
[46] *Ibid.*, pp. 507, 508.

the Nazarene in danger of drifting away from vital and into merely formal, verbal, or dogmatic perfectionism.

The PILGRIM HOLINESS CHURCH, dates from 1897, when the Rev. Martin W. Knapp, a Methodist minister, gathered a dozen people in his home at Cincinnati and organized the International Apostolic Holiness Union. This action he deemed necessary because, in his opinion, Methodism had deserted the Wesleyan landmarks of holiness, divine healing, and premillenarianism. The purpose was to form an interdenominational union which would react helpfully upon the churches, but inevitably the union itself became an independent sect. As in the case of the Nazarenes, this body grew by the adherence of similar groups. The Holiness Christian Church, which originated in a Pennsylvania holiness revival in 1882, joined in 1919, and the name became the International Christian Church. The Pentecostal Rescue Mission of Binghamton, New York, followed in 1922. The same year witnessed the adherence of the Pilgrim Church, a schism from the Nazarenes in Pasadena, California, which occurred in 1917, and the adoption of the present name. Then came the Pentecostal Brethren in Christ, a small group of holiness people in Ohio, in 1924, the Peoples' Mission Church of Colorado Springs in 1925, and the accession of small groups of malcontents from the Church of the Nazarene and other sources. In this manner the Pilgrim Holiness Church built up a membership of 25,000 with 700 churches in half the states.

The Pilgrims are in every noticeable respects a replica of the Nazarenes. The doctrines, polity, practices, and attitudes are essentially identical. The Pilgrims themselves feel that there is a difference but are not definite in pointing it out: they are "considered more radical" while the Nazarenes are more "conservative." The only distinctions between the two bodies are those of degree. The Pilgrims have not evolved so far as their compatriots, the Nazarenes, and hence cling to the common tenets and practices with somewhat greater zeal. The former group, being younger, is closer to the sources of its inspiration and remembers more clearly the conditions against which its protests were made. More obscure, it remains more definitely the possession of the disinherited. It is the smaller body, and its local units are smaller, hence it must continue the struggle for existence and is able to use the class meeting and revival to better advantage. "The Nazarene denomination has evolved from the state in which the Pilgrim denomination finds itself today." [47]

The CHRISTIAN AND MISSIONARY ALLIANCE was organized in 1887 by A. B. Simpson, a Presbyterian quasi-perfectionist of New York when he withdrew from his ecclesiastical connections to become an independent

[47] *Ibid.*, p. 512.

evangelist. While professing to have no creed, it adopts the customary fundamentalist positions, especially with reference to the inspiration of the Bible, premillenarianism, and Spirit baptism. Some preachers of ability have been attracted to the body by its fervent evangelical character. It prefers not to be known as a denomination but rather as an evangelistic and missionary movement; however, it has the full denominational organization and is entirely independent of all other bodies, though it is in fellowship with all that are sympathetic with its pronounced fundamentalist views, and it regards the other churches with a tolerance unusual among sects of this character. Its main work is the evangelization of neglected groups and the promotion of foreign missionary enterprises. The sect is found in about forty of the states and has over 400 congregations with nearly 40,000 members.

Evangelistic Associations. Under this category the *Census of Religious Bodies* classifies eleven small perfectionist sects. Some of these are of the extremist order and are discussed elsewhere. Others are more conservative and deserve mention in connection with the groups being considered here.

The MISSIONARY BANDS OF THE WORLD are a small group of three hundred persons and five societies in Indiana, Illinois, and Michigan. They are offshoots of the Free Methodist Church. In 1885 a minister of that denomination, the Rev. Vivian A. Dake, formed among his young people a society for fellowship and missionary recruiting, which he called a Pentecost Band. Other groups were formed and these became so self-conscious and so intent upon fellowship and holiness that they declared independence under the name Pentecost Bands of the World. In 1925 the present name was adopted. There is nothing distinctive about this little company, which is patterned after Methodism of a congregational type. Its peculiar interest is missionary work.

The tiny CHURCH OF DANIEL'S BAND has 4 churches and 125 members in Michigan and has declined rapidly since the census of 1916. It was organized in 1893 at Marine City, Michigan. It is distinctly Methodistic, the band idea being derived from the old class meeting. It is one of the numerous offshoots which have sought to revive primitive Wesleyanism and to inculcate Christian perfection.

The METROPOLITAN CHURCH ASSOCIATION was organized in 1894, when a revival broke out in the Metropolitan Methodist Church, located in a congested area of Chicago among the poorer classes, as a result of which the congregation attempted a return to primitive Wesleyan holiness. Groups were formed among the poor, enthusiasm ran high in the meetings, and a wider range of evangelism and missionary work was undertaken. Under the popular name of The Burning Bush, adopted as suggestive of its enthusiastic character, the movement spread through several states.

It now has a following of a thousand members grouped in fourteen societies and is known as the Metropolitan Church Association.

This company of perfectionists adopted a quasi-communism and the "faith" principle. Members are supposed to possess nothing which can be sold and the proceeds applied to evangelistic work. Ministers receive no salaries, nor do they solicit any gifts. All money received from any source goes into the treasury and is distributed for the various causes of the association.

The HEPHZIBAH FAITH MISSIONARY ASSOCIATION, like many other holiness sects, claims that it is not a denomination but a group which "advocates the establishing of independent non-sectarian full-salvation, local churches and missions." [48] It was formed at Glenwood, Iowa, in 1892 by the merging of several small congregations without definite denominational affiliations. It differs little from the other holiness sects, save perhaps in more definitely magnifying the work of the Holy Spirit in the matter of emotional reactions. The ministers are unsalaried and engage in other occupations for their livelihoods. The sect has twenty churches with four hundred members.

The CHRISTIAN CONGREGATION, organized at Kokomo, Indiana, in 1887, has seven congregations with 1,250 members. It is essentially Congregational in doctrine and polity. Its original idea was to draw out of the "sectarian churches" a "spiritual" element which would preserve holiness in life and simplicity in organization, and it has held aloof from other perfectionist groups, declining to enter into any of the mergers effected by bodies of a similar nature. It seems to differ in no way from many of the groups already described, though its members seem to feel that they stand for something distinctive. It has adherents in rural areas of Indiana and Texas, and its colportage service is carried on from the latter state.

The MISSIONARY CHURCH ASSOCIATION is somewhat similar in character to the Christian Congregation. It was organized at Berne, Indiana, in 1898, by a group of premillenarian perfectionists and now has forty-five churches and five thousand members. Its extreme positions alone differentiate it from bodies of a similar nature.

The PILLAR OF FIRE is an extremely interesting quasi-Methodist sect. It owes its existence to the zeal and labors of Mrs. Alma White, its founder, bishop, and controlling personality. Born in Kentucky, where she came under the influence of Methodist holiness preachers, she went west in early womanhood and married a Methodist pastor in Colorado. From his pulpit she exhorted and preached holiness views, at last branching out and establishing missions and preaching at camp meetings. This brought her into

---

[48] *The Work of the Hephzibah Faith Missionary Association* (pamphlet).

conflict with the church authorities, and she cut herself loose from all ecclesiastical moorings and founded a sect of her own. She organized first in 1901 in Denver as the Pentecostal Union and the name was changed in 1917 to the Pillar of Fire.

Mrs. White sought a revival of primitive Wesleyanism and a reversion to the "true" early church. The Pillar of Fire has the Methodist polity; Mrs. White herself was the first bishop, and her two sons were associated with her in a leadership which was practically a dictatorship. Strongly fundamentalist and insisting on the plenary inspiration and literal interpretation of Scripture, the sect opposes all forms of intellectual modernism. An intense devotion to "second blessing" holiness and premillenarianism with its usual concomitants characterizes it. Mrs. White warmly supported the Ku Klux Klan and published three books defending it as an agency of God raised up in fulfillment of prophecies.

The Pillar of Fire has forty-five churches, half of which are in New York and Pennsylvania, with four thousand members. At Zarephath, near Bound Brook, New Jersey, the sect has a college, academy, training school, publishing plant, radio station, and a large camp meeting tabernacle. Other schools are operated at Denver, Cincinnati, Los Angeles, and Jacksonville and there is a school and a publishing house in London.[49]

The PENIEL MISSIONS center largely in California and other Pacific states, a fertile field for cults and isms of various kinds. Unlike most groups of a similar character, these are urban bodies; employing the customary mission technique, they specialize in winning the masses on city streets. Spirit guidance is prominent, and sanctification and sinlessness are the goals of endeavor. The leaders of these missions have displayed remarkable energy in soul-saving.

The founder of the Peniel Missions was T. P. Ferguson. In early life he was influenced by the preaching of Finney, and he experienced sanctification in 1880 under the ministry of some holiness evangelists of the pentecostal order.

The intense zeal of Ferguson in seeking "the lost" throws light upon the practices of the Peniel Missions. During one evangelistic trip to Oregon it was said of Ferguson that "if he led one soul into the blessing of holiness, he led a thousand."[50] His travail for souls is described by his wife:

He would drop on his knees beside a chair. . . . Pretty soon I would see the perspiration starting on his forehead, then he would slip down on the carpet and laugh and cry. He talked real reverent love talk to the Lord, and laughter, tears,

---

[49] A good survey of the Pillar of Fire movement is found in Mrs. White's *Looking Back from Beulah*. She has written another autobiography in several volumes. The sect has issued a large number of books and pamphlets.

[50] Mrs. Ferguson, *The Love Slave*, p. 20. The very title of this work is suggestive.

and praises would all mingle together in the presence of the King. . . . Then up and out to the battle again—invincible . . . and such a glory face.[51]

On occasions when an obstinate person would leave the meeting he would be told that the door would be open and the evangelist praying until he returned—"and the fellow always came back, . . . occasionally on the run and bawling."[52] When Ferguson's health began to fail he refused to desist. "Maybe I will get a soul," he replied to all words of caution. And when he did "get a soul," "he would caper all around our little sitting room like a boy, crowing over me, 'I got my soul, I got my soul!' "[53]

The Peniel Missions have not reported any statistics. They stand for orthodoxy of a conservative type. Spontaneity and the direction of the Holy Spirit are features of their services, which are frequently marked by enthusiasm.

Churches of God. Several sects bear the name "Church of God," with or without some other distinguishing word. Many of these are of the "pentecostal" group and will be discussed in the next chapter. A few will be mentioned at this point, however, because they are less extreme than the typical pentecostal bodies and do not stress speaking in unknown tongues.

The CHURCH OF GOD (ANDERSON, INDIANA) is a conservative holiness body and the second largest of those not included in the pentecostal category. It has around fifteen hundred churches and ninety thousand members.

The body originated in a secession from the General Eldership of the Church of God, or Winebrenner movement, in 1880, under the leadership of Daniel S. Warner. The issues were the doctrine of sanctification as a second work of grace, which the Winebrennarians rejected, and the nature of the church. The seceding group espoused holiness and regarded the name "Church of God" as the only scriptural designation covering the total body of Christians.

This Church of God does not regard itself as a denomination but as a movement within the church universal to restore Christian unity on a scriptural basis. It does not keep membership lists, but believes that all Christians are by virtue of their faith and experience members of the true church of God.

The doctrine of sanctification is interpreted conservatively, especially with reference to its concomitants. Speaking with tongues has never characterized this church, but on the contrary has been strongly opposed.

[51] *Ibid.*, pp. 27, 28.
[52] *Ibid.*, p. 30.
[53] *Ibid.*, pp. 30, 31. See also Gaddis, *op. cit.*, pp. 499-503.

The personal return of Christ is accepted, but it is held that the advent has no connection with a millennial reign. The body adopts a liberal attitude with reference to co-operative movements, religious education, and general church procedure. Immersion and foot washing are practiced and the polity is congregational. This church maintains headquarters, a publishing house, and an educational institution at Anderson, Indiana.

The CHURCH OF GOD (APOSTOLIC) has fifty churches and three thousand members. It is one of several bodies that thinks it has "recovered the true Church" and "got back to a scriptural, apostolic basis." Sanctification and the direct operation of the Holy Spirit are essentials, and foot washing is indulged in. The fundamentalist theology and opposition to the customary forms of worldliness are prominent. The sect sprang out of the holiness movement in Kentucky in 1897, when it was organized as the Christian Faith Band Church at Danville by Thomas J. Cox. In 1915 the name was changed to the Church of God (Apostolic), but owing to objections within the fold this name was not inserted in the charter until 1919.

THE CHURCH OF GOD AS ORGANIZED BY CHRIST has perfectionist traditions, but it opposes sanctification as a climactic second work of grace and "second work holyites." Among the elements which encounter the opposition of this sect are "denominationalism, churchianity, or sectism," union meetings or any form of denominational co-operation, tobacco, secret societies, war or the use of force, going to law, church schools, Sunday schools, revivals, emotional demonstrations such as shouting and talking in unknown tongues, all forms of worldliness such as theaters, amusements, fine clothing, and jewelry, "human traditions," creeds, and "a hireling ministry." [54]

This sect came into existence in 1886 as the result of a schism from the Mennonite Brethren in Christ. It holds that it alone is the "true church," and that Christ bestows church membership and ordination to all church offices as divine gifts. It has fourteen congregations and two thousand members.

The CHURCH OF GOD IN NORTH AMERICA (GENERAL ELDERSHIP) practices sectarianism while holding the same to be antiscriptural. This sect is over a hundred years old and has 350 churches and 30,000 members in this country. It is a product of the revivalism which characterized the Methodist, Baptist and other churches, but in this case took toll of the German Reformed Church. John Winebrenner experienced a form of conversion considered strange among his group, and his revivals around Harrisburg, Pennsylvania, aroused such dissatisfaction that he was brought to trial and finally forced to sever his connection with his church.

[54] See Gaddis, *op. cit.*, p. 488. The sect has little literature, but publishes a paper called the *Gospel Teacher;* see the issue for April, 1928.

In 1825 he began organizing independent groups, known in each place simply as the Church of God. In 1830 a group of six preachers organized these groups into the General Eldership of the Church of God. In 1845 the phrase "in North America" was added to the name. This body has an Arminian theology and a Presbyterian form of government. It stresses the operation of the Holy Spirit, but its doctrine of holiness is not greatly emphasized at the present time. It is an orthodox body, considers itself not a sect but the "true church," and is extremely biblio-conscious. "Bible things, as church offices and customs, should be known by Bible names, and a Bible name should not be applied to anything not mentioned in the Bible." [55] There are three perpetually binding ordinances, baptism by immersion, the Lord's Supper, and washing of the saints' feet, the last two being observed together. This sect has a more or less elaborate set of beliefs, but insists that it has no written creed, and accepts the Bible as "the only rule of faith and practice."

Other Holiness Groups. The CHURCH OF THE GOSPEL is a small holiness sect which was organized in 1911 at Pittsfield, Massachusetts, and incorporated as the Church of God; the name was changed in 1930 to avoid confusion with other groups bearing the same name. The distinguishing principles of the body are sanctification as a second work of grace subsequent to justification, the imminent second advent of Jesus Christ, and baptism by immersion. It traces its origin to Methodist sources and claims adherence to early Wesleyan principles. There are only four or five churches and the total membership is less than one hundred, but it carries on an active propaganda by means of tracts, called the "Narrow Way Tracts."

The CHRISTIAN NATION CHURCH is a group of five congregations with around one hundred members which has been operating since 1892, when eight young men at Mount Victory, Ohio, began personal evangelistic work in that region. They were called "equality evangelists." Little was accomplished, but at a reassembling of the workers with others at Marion, Ohio, in 1895, a plan of government was prepared and in 1896 the group was incorporated as a church. It is a second-blessing holiness, but not a pentecostal sect, extremely conservative and intolerant of other churches; "absolute rejection of other evangelical societies" is a condition of membership. There is opposition to adornments in attire, clubs and lodges, remarriage after divorce, marriage between the saved and unsaved, church festivals and entertainments, slang and jesting, tobacco and snuff. It teaches that there is a fourfold gospel: justification, entire sanctification, divine healing, and the second coming of Christ; it holds to sanctification

[55] *Census of Religious Bodies,* 1936, II, 478-85.

but believes that "the evidence of having received this experience is not the manifestation of any certain 'gift of the Spirit.' " [56]

The KODESH CHURCH OF IMMANUEL is a second-blessing holiness group which was founded at Philadelphia in 1929 by the Rev. Frank Russell Killingsworth. The original members were dissidents who withdrew from the African Methodist Episcopal Zion Church. It teaches entire sanctification as a supernatural work of grace subsequent to regeneration, but discounts speaking in unknown tongues, foot washing, and gifts of an extreme nature. There are nine churches and around six hundred members.

The CHURCHES OF CHRIST IN CHRISTIAN UNION OF OHIO is a small body of believers in the doctrine of sanctification subsequent to regeneration, which separated from the parent Council of Christian Union Churches. The schism was the result of a controversy over the holiness principle; this was brought to a head when the council, meeting at Marshall, Ohio, in 1909, decided against the second-blessing group. The minority withdrew and formed a separate denomination in the same year. It is a fundamentalist sect, distinguished from the parent body and others of a similar nature only by its emphasis on the nature and manner of the sanctification experience. There are around one hundred congregations with approximately six thousand members.

The OXFORD GROUP MOVEMENT, which may be included under the general category of perfectionism, was started about 1908 by Dr. Frank N. D. Buchman, a Lutheran minister in Pennsylvania. It is not a separately organized sect but a movement which seeks to regenerate both individuals and the social order by a combination of inner attitudes and objective supernatural power. It has experienced two periods of considerable influence and has displayed a rather surprising success in enlisting the collaboration of prominent persons in this and other countries.

In its first stage Buchmanism aimed at the regeneration or "change" of individuals by a process of psychological catharsis which involved meditation, prayer, Bible reading, surrender, and confession of sins to other individuals. Coming to the United States from Cambridge and Oxford, where Buchman had gone after a misunderstanding with the officials of his congregation at Overbrook, Pennsylvania, the "Groupers," as they were called, launched a nation-wide series of "house parties," at which students, and in some cases prominent and wealthy men and women, gathered to seek the "change." At one point in this stage of the movement the insistence upon "confession" caused trouble in some of the "house parties," particularly on college campuses, because the confessions were largely sexual in nature; the movement was banished from Princeton

[56] *Short History and Polity of the Christian Nation Church,* p. 24.

University after Buchman declared that 85 per cent of the students there were sexually perverted.

Following the decline of this phase of Buchmanism, it flared up again under the name of "Moral Rearmament Movement." In this second stage the emphasis shifted from individual change to social salvation, the object being to prevent the approaching World War II and secure international peace through the regeneration of people who might otherwise be responsible for war. Buchman was widely quoted as "thanking God" for Hitler and Mussolini, because if such men would "surrender to the control of God" they would be able to "solve the last bewildering problem."

The Moral Rearmament campaign created a greater furore than the Oxford Group Movement house parties. Great meetings were held in Switzerland, Sweden, New York, Washington, San Francisco, and elsewhere. Important men endorsed the idea—including President (then Senator) Truman, Henry Ford, Fiorello La Guardia, and dignitaries of many lands—and the peace plan was promoted by elaborate publications, broadcasts, and other modern techniques of propaganda. The movement rode high on the crest of a popular wave.

When the world was plunged into war in spite of Moral Rearmament, there was another resurgence of the Buchman enterprise. This took the form of a national defense program, operating under the slogan "You Can Defend America." The leader organized a Home Defense School for Morale in America, conducted victory campaigns, and fostered the presentation of a revue or pageant on the defense theme at war plants. During this period the movement received some unfavorable publicity because of its alleged attempts to secure exemption from military service for twenty-eight aliens because of their work in its morale-building campaign. With the coming of peace Buchmanism again dropped into obscurity.[57]

[57] See Van Baalen, *The Chaos of Cults*, ch. x; Bach, *They Have Found a Faith*, ch. v; and Buchman's own works, *Rising Tide, Moral Rearmament, The Rise of a New Spirit, You Can Defend America, Your Part in Winning the War, The Fight to Serve, Remaking the World.*

CHAPTER IV

CHARISMATIC OR PENTECOSTAL SECTS

THE GROUP OF SECTS HEREIN CLASSIFIED AS "CHARISMATIC" HAS AS ITS distinguishing mark the reception of charismata or "gifts" on the part of adherents. Such gifts are nearly always of a nervous or emotional character. Most American bodies which fall within the category at the present time are of the "Pentecostal" variety. They constitute the left wing of perfectionism. They flourish mainly among the ignorant and nervously unstable sections of the population, and differ from the common variety of holiness groups in the extreme degree of their emotionalism. Primitive traits and the experiences of frontier revivalism make their last stand among these groups, and one encounters "tongue talking," shouting, visions, trances, jerking, dancing, "gifts of prophecy," and various other radical motor automatisms or "blessings" as by a familiar psychological process the starved emotional natures of people less cultured escape rational control and run to extremes.

Primitive Charismata. Enduements of an emotional nature have always been highly valued in religion. The charism of particular importance in Christian history is the "gift of tongues," first mentioned in Acts 2:1-13, which gave much trouble in the Church at Corinth (I Cor. 14).[1] The glossalalia were peculiar to the Christians, but there were many parallels and precedents. Among the Hebrews the ecstatic state was assiduously cultivated and highly valued as possessing divine significance. Over and over again one encounters the phrase "The spirit of Yahweh came upon him!" Balaam's oracles were delivered in a state of ecstasy, and the same is true of Gideon (Judg. 6:34), Jephthah (Judg. 11:29), and Samson (Judg. 14:6, 19; 15:14). Similar features were exhibited by the prophets of Baal (I Kings 18:26-28), and Elijah seems to have employed the same device (II Kings 3:14-19). There were guilds of roving prophets who indulged in practices not unlike clairvoyance and used music to induce the state; madness was ascribed to the prophets as a class (II Kings 9:11).

[1] There seems to have been a difference between the two manifestations, though no discussion is in order here. See Lindsay, *The Church and Ministry in the Early Centuries*; Zeller, *The Acts of the Apostles*; and standard commentaries.

Saul came under their influence, and in frenzy he stripped off his clothing, rolled on the ground, and prophesied for a day and night, whence the surprised query, "Is Saul also among the prophets?" (I Sam. 10:5-11; 19:20-24). Even the greater prophets saw visions; the strange revelations to Ezekiel (chs. 1, 8–10, 17, 37, 40–44), Isaiah (ch. 6), who "saw" his messages, and Daniel (2:19; chs. 7-9) are cases in point.

Joseph secured his ascendancy at the court of Pharaoh because he had the power of interpreting the king's dreams after the official court soothsayers had failed (Gen. 41), and Moses secured the freedom of the Israelites from the Egyptian bondage in a successful contest with the sorcerers of the king and the exercise of supernatural powers (Exod. 5–12). In later years the prophets and kings forbade magic and witchery under pain of death, and Saul "put away those that had familiar spirits, and the wizards, out of the land," yet Saul himself consulted a witch who was able to summon gods out of the earth and call the spirits of men back from the other world (I Sam. 28).

The environment in which Christianity arose was surcharged with such phenomena. In the Greek oracles messages were uttered by priests or priestesses in a state of ecstasy, consciousness being in abeyance, and it was necessary to interpret them to the laity, as both Plutarch [2] and Heraclitus [3] testify. In his well-known *Timaeus* Plato says the art of the mantis or prophet was exercised during unconsciousness, sleep, sickness, or ecstasy, and that interpretation was necessary. In the orgies of the cult of Dionysius music, dancing, drink, and other means were employed to superinduce the ecstatic state, in which the devotees ate raw flesh, disported themselves with frenzied enthusiasm in the forests, and indulged in wild phallic excesses.[4] The ecstatic person was "in the divinity" and out of normal consciousness. Cicero makes prophecy and madness practically synonymous,[5] and declared that Cassandra spoke by means of a divinity clothed in the human body.[6] Origen quotes Celsus to the effect that both in and out of the sanctuaries persons in ecstasy uttered strange and unintelligible speech.[7] What Plato called *theomania* appeared everywhere in the Greek world; the *Bacchal* of Euripides contains a study of its more sinister aspects. Oriental cults that employed ecstasy were common in the Roman Empire and their frenzies are described by Lucretius, Catallus, and Apuleius. The various "mystery religions" specialized in the production of emotional

---

[2] *De Pythiae Oraculis.*

[3] *Sermo*, p. 79.

[4] See Willoughby, *Pagan Generation*, ch. iii; Fowler, *The Religious Experience of the Roman People*; Argus, *The Mystery Religions and Christianity*; Kennedy, *St. Paul and the Mystery Religions.*

[5] *Pro Sexto*, p. 10.

[6] *De Divinitatione*, I, 67.

[7] *Contra Celsus*, VII, 9.

states. Even Plotinus enjoyed ecstatic "initiation" four times. Psychologically such practices were akin to the Christian practice of "talking in unknown tongues."

After the flurry at Corinth the gift of tongues, while continuing here and there, seems to have been of little importance in the early church. Irenaeus notes the presence of "many brethren in the church who through the Spirit speak all kinds of languages." [8] Tertullian challenges Marcion to explain an obscure kind of speech which has appeared among the Christians,[9] and the same writer mentions utterances which must be interpreted. Justin Martyr witnesses to the presence of spiritual gifts and names seven different kinds, but the gift of tongues is not in his list.[10] Before the end of the fourth century it is certain that the strange gift had long since ceased to be exercised, since Chrysostom places it in the past and is unable to explain it. The phenomenon has, however, broken out again and again in the church.

Motor Phenomena in the Church. Students of the psychology of religion are familiar with the strange manifestations induced by strong religious feeling.[11] A high form of mystical ecstasy flourished mainly at two periods, in the fourteenth and seventeenth centuries, in both cases near the close of great intellectual and spiritual awakenings. In cruder forms it has had a continuous history among the lower and less cultured strata of the population. In the fourteenth and fifteenth centuries the Dancers or Chorizantes created much excitement in Germany. These wild enthusiasts, numbering thousands of the poor and ignorant of both sexes, danced madly in the churches and streets for hours at a time, frequently until they fell exhausted. They saw fantastic visions, leaped high in the air to get out of the flood of blood in which they imagined themselves to be wading, and indulged in many other marvelous exercises, wholly oblivious of the throngs of amazed spectators. Gifts were showered upon them, attracting many rascally imitators and thus offering a breeding ground for shocking immoralities. The priests vainly tried to exorcise the demons with which the poor fanatics were regarded as possessed; in some places

[8] *Against Heresies,* I, 531.

[9] *Against Marcion,* III, 445-46.

[10] *Dialogue with Trypho,* I, 240, 243, 244.

[11] Considerations of space forbid discussion of mysticism, which is really a part of the present subject. But there is a mass of literature on the subject. See the article "Ecstasy" by Dean Inge in Hastings, *Encyclopedia of Religion and Ethics.* Also Inge, *Christian Mysticism;* Underhill, *Mysticism, The Mystics of the Church;* Jones, *Studies in Mystical Religion, New Studies in Mystical Religion;* Otto, *Mysticism, East and West;* Pratt, *The Religious Consciousness,* chs. xvi-xx (Pratt well describes the systematizing of the mystical experience); Herman, *The Meaning and Value of Mysticism.* Attempts are now being made to revive the practice of mysticism. See Hillyard, *Spiritual Exercises.*

St. Vitus was invoked, on account of the traditional association of the name with the disease known as chorea.[12]

In the turmoil which followed the revocation of the Edict of Nantes in France (1685) appeared the Camisards, known in England, where their movement was carried by refugees, as the French Prophets. They embraced pronounced millennial views, looked for the speedy overthrow of the papacy, and the return of Christ. The rise of a prophetess in Dauphine, and many prophets elsewhere, augmented their ardency, and ecstatic disorders became rife. They went into trances and convulsions, saw visions, uttered predictions, pointed out traitors in their own ranks, and indulged in various frenzied orgies. They called themselves "friends of God," and their camps were "camps of the Eternal." Their excesses continued until, in spite of stubborn and fanatical resistance, their leaders were exiled or murdered and "the French Reformed Church was blotted out in blood." [13]

Forty years later the extreme exercises of the "convolutionaries" startled Belgium and France. The grave of a young Jansenist clergyman, François de Paris, in the cemetery of Saint-Medard in Paris, became the scene of reputed marvelous cures. Multitudes flocked thither for healing. Strange bodily agitations seized the devotees. They fell in shakings and convulsions, threw themselves about on the ground, screamed, and assumed unusual and often unseemly postures. The cemetery was closed, but the convulsionists resorted to private houses where the phenomena continued with unabated intensity. Those seized claimed the gift of healing, their bodies became insensible to blows or wounds and various untoward exercises were indulged in. One convolutionary, called "la Salamandre," remained suspended for nine minutes over a fiery brazier, clad only in a sheet, which remained intact in the flames. Scoffers attributed these affairs to the agency of the devil, an explanation which seems to prevail among Catholics even today,[14] while the worshipers, of course, deemed themselves under the influence of the Spirit of God.

Extreme emotional disturbances, ecstasies, and bodily seizures of various sorts were common in the Wesleyan Revival of the eighteenth century in England. In Wesley's meetings, especially in and near Bristol, violent motor reactions were common among his poor and ignorant hearers. They were seized with severe pains and screamed aloud,[15] fell upon the ground in convulsions and shakings, sometimes continuing thus for hours

[12] Hauck, "Dancers," in *The New Schaff-Herzog Encyclopedia of Religious Knowledge*.

[13] Baird, *The Camisard Uprising; The Huguenots and the Revocation of the Edict of Nantes*, vol. II; Tylor, *Huguenots in the Seventeenth Century*; Smiles, *Huguenots in France after the Revocation of the Edict of Nantes*; see "Camisards" and "French Prophets," in *The New Schaff-Herzog Encyclopedia of Religious Knowledge*.

[14] See "Jansenius," in the *Catholic Encyclopedia*.

[15] Wesley's *Journal*, April 17, 1739.

at a time.[16] Sometimes the din was so great that his voice could scarcely be heard.[17]

Such phenomena made their appearance in America in connection with the first Great Awakening, which began under Jonathan Edwards at Northampton, Massachusetts, in 1734 and, sponsored by Whitefield, the Tennants, and others, swept like a contagion, as indeed it was, through all the colonies. The bodily exercises exactly duplicated those which characterized the Wesleyan movement in England. Edwards preached a stern and extreme Calvinism, the fatalism of which would not seem especially conducive to exaggerated emotionalism, yet the vividness with which he pictured the torments of eternal hell-fire, and the awful thunderings with which he depicted "sinners in the hands of an angry God"—the theme of his most notable sermon—caused many to scream aloud in terror and fall like dead men under the thrall of fearful oratory.

Some have been so overcome with a sense of the dying love of Christ to such poor, wretched, and unworthy creatures, as to weaken the body. Several persons have had so great a sense of the glory of God, and excellency of Christ, that nature and life have seemed almost to sink under it; and in all probability, if God had shewed them a little more of himself, it would have dissolved their frame.[18]

Edwards was somewhat reticent about such matters, and never describes them in such detail as does Wesley, yet the pages of his *Narrative* and his *Thoughts on the Revival of Religion* teem with the incidents. Men saw Christ on the cross with blood running from his wounds.[19] They cried aloud and fell upon the ground, sometimes a great number being so affected simultaneously.[20] Hands were clinched, the flesh became cold, persons leaped in the air "with all the might," and "it seemed to the person as if soul and body would, as it were of themselves, of necessity mount up, leave the earth, and ascend thither." [21] In overwhelming weakness men saw the flames and "the piercing all-seeing eye of God" with such vividness that the body was overcome.[22] In at least one instance a man was driven to suicide by cutting his throat, whereupon the suggestion was so powerful that multitudes in different towns were prompted to do the same; they heard voices urging them, "Cut your own throat, now is a good oppor-

[16] April 21, 25, 29; May 1, 21; June 15, 22, 24, 25; July 1, 30; August 11; October 11, 23, 25, 28, 1739.

[17] May 1, 1739. Numerous other cases will be found in Wesley's *Journal*. See, for example, May 2, 1739, and October 23, 1739.

[18] Edwards, *Narrative of Many Surprising Conversions*, pp. 46, 47.

[19] *Ibid.*, p. 54.

[20] *Thoughts on the Revival of Religion*, p. 107.

[21] *Ibid.*, pp. 130, 131.

[22] *Ibid.*, pp. 134, 135.

tunity," and "were obliged to fight with all their might to resist it." [23]

The eloquence of George Whitefield produced similar phenomena and his far-flung revivals were marked by them. So with his fellow evangelists. Some of the latter went to the utmost extremes. Jonathan Barber and James Davenport were directed by signs and wonders to become prophets, and the latter, emulating the example of the biblical Jonathan, went about with an "armor bearer." Davenport was arrested for the disturbances he caused but was adjudged *non compos mentis*, whereupon he had his followers bring their "vanities" in the shape of wigs, clothing, jewelry, and books, of which he made a great bonfire. Hugh Bryan, of South Carolina, set himself up as a prophet, led an army of armed fanatical whites and Negroes into the swamps, and sent to the legislature a twenty-page prophetic declaration. Attempting to part the waters of a river with a rod, he was nearly drowned, and the failure of this "sign" convinced him that his prophetic inspiration was not of God but emanated from "the evil Spirit, the Father of Lies." [24]

These excesses split the American church in twain. The New Lights vehemently denounced the customary order of things and the saner preachers as "an unconverted ministry." The latter replied in kind. Harvard and Yale excoriated Whitefield. Dr. Charles Chauncey, the Rev. Timothy Cutler, Presidents Holyoke of Harvard and Clapp of Yale, and others were outspoken in criticism. "Our presses are forever teeming with books and our women with bastards" [25] as a result of the stir, declared Cutler.

After him (Whitefield) came one Tennant, a monster! impudent and noisy, and told them all they were dam'd, dam'd, dam'd; this charmed them, and in the most dreadful Winter I ever saw people wallowed in the snow night and day for the benefit of his beastly brayings, and many ended their days under these fatigues. Both of them carried more money out of these parts than the poor could be thankful for.[26]

The Kentucky Revival. With the subsidence of the exciting aspects of

[23] *Narrative*, pp. 74, 75.

[24] Loud, *Evangelized America*, ch. iv.

[25] A modern novel, *God in the Cow Pen*, pictures an old-time camp meeting, with the local prostitute plying her trade in the woods adjacent. There is a relation between sex and the emotional and mystical aspects of religion that deserves a saner and more sympathetic study than it has yet received. Most mystics have been women and many were unmarried or experienced an abnormal sex life. Of the four hundred cases of stigmatization on record, over three hundred were women and all but twenty were unmarried. The language and imagery of the mystics are often extremely erotic. Madame Guyon, the Blessed Angela de Foligno, and the more modern Mlle. Vé are examples of persons in whom sexual abnormality and mysticism blended. See Cutten, *op. cit.*, Thouless, *op. cit.*, and other authorities.

[26] Loud, *op. cit.*, pp. 76-77. There is a voluminous literature on the Great Awakening. See in particular Tracy, *The Great Awakening*, and Maxson, *The Great Awakening in the Middle Colonies* and its excellent bibliography.

the first Great Awakening the American church enjoyed surcease from extreme emotional outbreaks for approximately half a century. Then the Great Awakening of the Middle West broke out at the beginning of the nineteenth century, and its nervous disorders and motor phenomena exceeded anything known in the country. This revival began in the Kentucky camp meetings, first launched by the Presbyterians but soon taken over and practically monopolized by the Methodists. The primitive frontier conditions then prevalent, the entire absence of emotional outlets and the consequent starving of the emotional natures of the frontier people, the lack of an adequate social life among the scattered settlements, and the low state of education and general culture combined to provide fertile soil for evangelism of the excitable kind.

James McGready, of terrible visage, thundering voice, and hell-fire orthodoxy, left North Carolina in 1796 upon receipt of a letter written in blood and came to Logan County, Kentucky, called "Rogues Harbor" because an actual majority of its citizenry was composed of criminals. Three years later the McGee brothers, William a Presbyterian, and John a Methodist, appeared on Red River. The famous Peter Cartwright, a Methodist, grew up in Logan County. Elder B. W. Stone, a Baptist-Campbellite, lived and preached in Bourbon County. These, with others who joined the movement, were the leaders of the revival, Cartwright becoming an outstanding figure of the movement.

In the summer of 1799 the two McGees preached on Red River. John thus relates what occurred:

William felt such a power come over him that he quit his seat and sat down on the floor of the pulpit, I suppose not knowing what he did. A power which caused me to tremble was upon me. There was a solemn weeping all over the house. At length I rose up and exhorted them to let the Lord God Omnipotent reign in their hearts, and their souls should live. Many broke the silence. The woman in the east end of the house shouted tremendously. I left the pulpit and went through the audience shouting and exhorting with all possible ecstasy and energy, and the floor was soon covered with the slain.[27]

This was the beginning of one of the most remarkable religious movements of modern history; it typed religion in the Cumberland country for a century and is still remembered and still exerts an influence in Kentucky. Barton Stone came from Bourbon County to see what it was all about.

Many, very many, fell down as men slain in battle, and continued for hours together in an apparently breathless and motionless state, sometimes for a few moments reviving and exhibiting symptoms of life by a deep groan or a piercing

[27] *Ibid.*, p. 70. The quotation is from a letter written by John McGee in 1820 to the Rev. Thomas L. Douglas, Methodist presiding elder of the Nashville, Tennessee, District.

shriek or by a prayer for mercy fervently uttered. After lying there for hours . . . they would rise, shouting deliverance.[28]

At Cane Ridge occurred one of the most amazing religious outbreaks of American history. Thousands camped on the ground until the food gave out, and by day and night the preachers exhorted under rude brush arbors erected in the primeval forests. The frenzy to which persons were wrought almost surpasses belief, though fully attested by many eyewitnesses and careful investigators. They shouted, sobbed, leaped in the air, writhed on the ground, fell like dead men and lay insensible for considerable periods, and engaged in unusual bodily contortions.

At no time was the floor less than half covered. Some lay quiet, unable to move or speak. Some talked but could not move. Some beat the floor with their heels. Some shrieking in agony bounded about like a live fish out of water. Many lay down and rolled over and over for hours at a time. Others rushed wildly about over the stumps and benches, and then plunged, shouting "Lost! Lost!" into the forest.[29]

In order to test the reality of the seizures a Rev. Mr. Lyle poured hartshorn into the nostrils of a man lying on the ground, but the person took no notice of it.[30] A minister present kept an account of the number of the "slain" and reported that three thousand, one in six, were struck down.[31]

Once started at Cane Ridge, the revival spread like a forest fire; it brooked no opposition and swept unabated through Kentucky, Tennessee, and adjoining states. The preachers rode far and wide, arbors were erected everywhere, and for fully five years the religious fervor raged unchecked. For fifty years this form of revivalism typed the religious life of the Middle West and is not without influence at the present time; Davenport saw the contortions characteristic of the Cane Ridge meeting in the Chilhowe Mountains as late as 1903.[32]

In this movement appeared certain phenomena unique among motor automatisms. One of these was the "holy laugh."[33] Another was the "barks." The votaries would fall upon "all fours," form groups, lope about and gather at the foot of a tree yelping, barking, and snapping like dogs; this exercise was called "treeing the devil."[34]

Most extreme and notable of all the paroxysms was the famous "jerks." This seizure was experienced by large numbers. The victim shook and

[28] Quoted by Tyler, *The Disciples*, American Church History Series, XII, 14.

[29] McMaster, *History of the United States*, II, 581.

[30] Lyle, *Diary*, p. 18, quoted by Davenport, *Primitive Traits in Religious Revivals*, p. 78.

[31] Davenport, *op. cit.*, p. 77.

[32] *Ibid.*, p. 79. They were quite prevalent in the Ozark Mountain country during my boyhood near the beginning of the present century.

[33] *Ibid.*, p. 81.

[34] *Ibid.*, p. 80.

jerked in every joint, the body was violently bent double, the head was thrown backward and forward and from side to side with great rapidity, the body would be thrown to the ground where it bounded about from place to place like a ball, or the feet would be affected and the victim would jump about like a frog. Peter Cartwright saw five hundred persons jerking at once, and Lorenzo Dow, in a meeting at Knoxville where the governor was present, gave the "jerks" to one hundred and fifty. A peculiar fact is that the "jerks" became a morbid contagion and passed beyond the stage of imitation until it laid hold on casual onlookers and irreligious scoffers. Ladies of fashion who visited the meetings for amusement were not immune. The collapse of such persons "excited the risibilities" of Peter Cartwright. "The first jerk or so, you would see their fine bonnets, caps, and combs fly; and so sudden would be the jerking of the head that their long loose hair would crack almost as loud as a wagoner's whip." [35] In one of Cartwright's revivals the reflexes seized a large scoffer who had a bottle of whisky in his pocket. He tried to run away but the paroxysms were too severe.

He halted among some saplings, took out his bottle of whiskey and swore he would drink the damned jerks to death. But he could not get the bottle to his mouth, though he tried hard. At this he became greatly enraged, fetched a very violent jerk, snapped his neck, fell, and soon expired, with his mouth full of cursing and bitterness.[36]

On another occasion a victim of the "jerks" seized a sapling with both hands and was thrown from his feet and whirled so violently around and around that the bark was twisted from the tree in his grasp. Cartwright declared that persons usually got relief from the "jerks" by dancing. "If they would not strive against it and pray in good earnest, the jerking would usually abate," but "the more they resisted the more they jerked." [37]

Modern Glossolalia. Of these unusual phenomena few have persisted save the glossolalia or gift of tongues. This exercise is still quite prevalent and is the distinguishing mark of several pentecostal sects, to be discussed later. This charism gains its survival power because of its place in the Bible. Many persons feel that a gift bestowed upon the early Christians is not to be denied to believers in any age; to believe otherwise seems to them a denial of "Bible religion." To persons holding such convictions a repetition of the phenomenon requires only an unstable nervous structure,

[35] Cartwright, *Autobiography*, pp. 48, 49. This interesting work by a leader of the revival movement is the best source of data on the revival phenomena.

[36] *Ibid.*, pp. 50, 51.

[37] *Ibid.*, p. 48. See the description of an almost exact phenomenon which I witnessed in a House of Prayer service, pp. 123–24.

an intense expectancy and longing, a high degree of suggestibility, and the proper setting for the operation of crowd psychology.

A description of the gift of tongues as it prevails in modern times will throw light upon its psychology. Unlike trances, visions, ecstasy, and the other accompaniments of mysticism, this is never a gift in solitude—that is, it is never bestowed as a result of solitary contemplation or individual preparation. The crowd is necessary. Masses of people must be swept by an emotional wave and the "tongue talker" catches the contagion by suggestion from the group, though, of course, not all the company are similarly affected. It is a product of the revival technique and disappears even from those who have obtained it when the excitement of the revival dies down. A person who talked with tongues in ordinary routine would be as unusual as a football "rooter" who yelled at his own fireside.

The congregation is composed of men and women from the lower ranks of culture.[38] The evangelist preaches on the gift of the Holy Spirit, stresses the possibility and priviledge of the pentecostal outpouring for present-day believers, relates experiences thereof, perhaps now and then breaks out in ecstactic jabbering of strange phrases, and points out the barrenness of those who have never been so blessed. The enduement is held out as God's supreme act of grace. Mixed with such expositions are dissertations upon the familiar and accepted themes so dear to the lowly soul—"mother, home, and heaven"—with denunciations of the conventional churches, educated preachers, worldly manners, and unbelief, usually characterized as "evolution," "higher criticism," denial of miracles, and the like. All the tricks of rhythm are employed and gradually the mass melts into what Pratt calls the "psychological crowd." For a more or less extended period this is continued before the desired effect is secured; in one instance that came under my observation such a revival continued for a dozen weeks or more before a "break" occurred; the whole community became sharply divided over the merits of the doctrines being daily proclaimed, a favorable group being thus created.

At last conditions become right. Seekers come forward in anticipation of the gift. Confessions are made. Excitement runs high. Various blessings in the form of emotional reactions are secured. Some cry out, others fall in trances or wave their hands or bodies rhythmically in near ecstasy. One feels unduly blessed and rises to testify. He begins speaking, faster and faster, words fail, there is a muttering in the throat, and the subject breaks out in a flood of words that have no meaning to ordinary individuals. The pentecostal power has fallen, the blessing has been received, hallelujahs ring out, persons crowd about the favored saint, a familiar

[38] This description is drawn from my personal experience. I have many times watched the process in revivals of the pentecostal sects.

94

hymn is struck, and a wave of emotion, perceptible even to the unbelieving onlooker, sweeps the company like an electrical charge.

The rest is easy. The actual demonstration of the Spirit's operation, the exalted position of the person who has obtained the gift, and the surcharged atmosphere all combine to brush aside doubts, opposition, and psychological obstacles and inhibitions. By the well-known process of mass suggestion and crowd psychology the contagion sweeps over others and soon many have been similarly endued. Not infrequently the preacher or some other person interprets the tongues, and messages and prophecies direct from God are thus delivered.

All this seems strange to the average person of education who has established rational control over the more primitive impulses, and to whom such experiences are made impossible by temperament or nervous stability. Nevertheless there are multitudes who indulge in such experiences and attribute their exhilaration to the direct agency of God.[39]

Psychology of the Unknown Tongue. Various psychological explanations of such phenomena have been offered. Cutten quite seriously discusses inherited memory as a possible solution of the problem, though he admits that the hypothesis "leads us into more difficulty than the original problem causes." He quotes Fairfield, however, to the effect that "abundant proofs" show that "matters impressed deep on the memory of the father present themselves to the consciousness of his posterity." [40] Such a thesis will scarcely appeal to modern psychologists, even to those who accept the transmission of acquired characteristics.

The ground is laid for the gift of tongues by the well-known methods of revival evangelism.[41] Pratt finds the explanation of successful revivalism in the laws of rhythm and crowd psychology. It is not to be supposed that evangelists know much about psychological principles in the technical sense, but by a process of trial and error many have become experts. Curiosity is subtly turned into expectancy; the advance publicity usually "plays up" previous successes, and testimony figures prominently in sermons. The successful evangelist gets *en rapport* with his audience quickly; he is always a conservative in theology and sticks to themes on which the people are agreed. He never argues, but uses repetition instead of logic, relying upon "primitive credulity," or the tendency of the mind to accept as true every uncontradicted idea continuously presented. The inhibiting influence of rival ideas in educated minds is largely lacking among the

---

[39] For discussions of modern "tongue talking" see Cutten, *The Psychological Phenomena of Christianity;* Pratt, *The Religious Consciousness;* Davenport, *Primitive Traits in Religious Revivals;* and the authorities therein cited.

[40] Cutten, *op. cit.,* p. 56, quoting Fairfield, *Ten Years with Spiritual Mediums.*

[41] No better treatment of the revival technique can be found than that of Pratt, *op. cit.,* ch. ix.

uncultured, so that inhibitions are easily broken down by that repetition which narrows the field of attention. Like-mindedness must at all costs be created. When inhibitory tendencies are eliminated and one central idea or impulse gains control of attention, then suggestibility is greatly increased. This is the essential principle of hypnotism.

The denser the throng the more successful the revival. So much the better if the people are packed closely together; evangelists always crowd them into a relatively small space, even when the room is only half filled. Just as freedom of bodily movement enhances the feeling of independence, so the loss of such freedom in a dense crowd creates a sense of helplessness which is conducive to the breaking down of inhibitions. This is not peculiar to revivals; cheer leaders know that there would be little rooting if the prospective cheerers were scattered about in a half-filled stadium. Then in the crowd one gains a sense of added power while the feeling of responsibility is weakened—"Only the crowd is responsible and the crowd is big and strong and need not fear. Hence the ordinary inhibitions of prudence and propriety are thrown off, and the individual may act as a primitive being who has not reached the stage of reflection." [42] Autosuggestion operates powerfully under such circumstances, aided and abetted by suggestion from the platform. Coe tells of an evangelist who shouted, "See them coming! See them coming!" when nobody had started forward, a premeditated and fraudulent device of suggestion.

Testimony, scripture quotation, and congregational singing are similar devices. The use of hymns is exceedingly important; most evangelists refuse to use the official hymnals of denominations and substitute small books of "gospel hymns" for the stately music of the church. All are urged to sing; this is the first action element introduced in the revival. Such singing is a powerful suggestion device.

By singing out at the top of his voice the sentiment and ideas which the revivalist desires to instill in him, each member of the audience suggests them to himself, in the technical meaning of that phrase. And he also at the same time passes on the suggestion to his neighbor. [43]

Pratt points out that "a masterpiece of autosuggestion" is found in the favorite revival hymn:

> Just as I am, without one plea,
> But that thy blood was shed for me,
> And that thou bidd'st me come to thee,
> O Lamb of God, I come, I come!

[42] *Ibid.*, p. 172.
[43] *Ibid.*, p. 176.

The verses describe exactly the feeling of sinfulness, hope, and love with which the revivalist wishes to fill the hearts of his hearers. And most important and effective of all, each verse ends with the refrain "I come, I come!" Between the singing of the verses the speaker says in low and tender tones, "Won't you come? Come now!" And then the audience sings, "I come, I come!" A more obvious case of autosuggestion could not be found.[44]

Under all these circumstances the cerebro-spinal system becomes highly excited, and the nervous energy thus generated or liberated in excess expends itself, as indeed it must in persons of low culture who lack rational control, in muscular movements. The emotions stirred in the revivals are those of fear, hate, and joy, the most powerful feelings known. Persons given to such reactions as those being discussed are nearly always the ignorant, in whom the lower brain centers and spinal ganglia are relatively strong and the rational and volitional powers residing in the higher centers of the cortex are relatively weak. Rational control is never marked in such individuals and it completely vanishes under great emotional excitement. They are reduced to something like a primitive mental and nervous condition. Impulsive feeling rules. The stimuli never reach the higher centers, but are stopped by the lower centers and shunted immediately to the muscles. In the cases of glossolalia the subject breaks out in speech which is entirely divorced from thought, resulting in the jargon of unknown tongues. Jerks and the other muscular contortions are similarly explained.[45]

Many neurologists have resorted to pathological explanations, attributing the phenomena to disease and serious derangement of the nervous system. Dr. H. I. Schou, noted Danish psychiatrist, has shown by clinical evidence the close connection between pathological melancholia and the typical sudden conversion, and he warns the clergy to "view with some skepticism and timely reserve all sudden conversions occurring after long periods of depression." It is well known that such periods, known to theology as "conviction," nearly always do precede extreme conversions. Schou describes the symptoms of the disease mentioned in almost the exact words of conversion testimonies in religious biographies.[46] Undoubtedly many ex-

---

[44] *Ibid.*, pp. 179, 180.

[45] See Davenport, *Primitive Traits in Religious Revivals,* ch. xi.

[46] Schou, *Religion and Morbid Mental States.* In this psychological discussion there is no disposition on my part to deny or obscure the divine influence and high spiritual value of the conversion experience. This has been undergone by many—perhaps most—of the greatest religious leaders of history. Even such a highly educated and emotionally controlled man as John Wesley experienced conversion following a long period of depression in which "conviction" or a sense of personal guilt was the major element.

treme religious experiences are pathological in character, but this explanation by no means covers the whole field. Nor is it necessary, for psychological laws offer a sufficient explanation of most cases without invoking pathology. The great majority of persons undergoing the experiences described are entirely normal.

American Charismatic Sects. There are in the United States about two dozen sects which make speaking with tongues prominent in their worship. There are also numerous independent churches and small groups of the same character. All may be classed as charismatic, since the experiences they stress are regarded as divine gifts. The churches of these various groups are scattered widely over the United States, all the states being represented. In all the groups which may be so classified there are at least 5,000 local churches and 250,000 members. There are also many detached and unrelated groups, especially among Negroes and the remote backwoods population, which are never reached by any cataloging agency, but which carry on the customary practices of the Pentecostal bodies. Among colored people nearly all the congregations of the ignorant indulge in shouting, trances, visions, prophecies, and all manner of ecstasy, which the devotees regard as divine charismata.

Some of these sects indulge in bizarre practices, although these are by no means representative of the Pentecostal movement. One such group figured prominently in the news in February, 1933. At Inez, Kentucky, this company indulged in a fantastic rite denominated "the death of sin." After a period of fasting, dancing, incantations, and talking in unknown tongues prolonged for nearly a week, an aged woman, Mrs. Lucinda Mills, was selected as a human sacrifice and was choked to death by her son, John H. Mills. It was said that preparations were being made to burn her body on a rude altar when officers, attracted by the uproar, invaded the shack where the rites were in progress. Three other women had been selected for similar fates. In court Mills uttered only guttural sounds, similar to the unknown tongue, while attendants held his writhing body on a cot. The six others of the group testified that the mother consented to her own sacrifice in the belief that it would in some way benefit another son, a patient in an insane asylum. All declared that while they opposed the murder, believing that "John wrongly interpreted a divine message to demonstrate 'the death of sin,' " and that " 'the death of sin' could be shown some other way," they were held by a supernatural power and were unable to intervene while the man killed his mother.[47]

More recently various "snake cults" have appeared in Virginia, Kentucky, Tennessee, and other states. Relying on the scriptural statement

[47] See Associated Press stories of the incident, February 10-11, 1933.

that the followers of Jesus "shall take up serpents" without suffering any harm (Mark 16:18; Luke 10:19) and the experience of Paul, who calmly shook off a viper which fastened itself on his hand (Acts 28:3), these cultists use poisonous reptiles in their services and regard immunity to the venomous bites as the test of faith and sign of holiness. It appears that most of them actually do withstand the bites, and the few that have died therefrom are regarded as having possessed insufficient faith.

The practices of these sects, which are known simply as holiness churches, were featured prominently in press despatches in 1945-47. Some states found it necessary to pass laws prohibiting the handling of reptiles in religious services. In 1947 the church of one sect in Virginia was raided by police on orders of the governor, and a large copperhead was clubbed to death; the leader then immersed his face in the flames of an improvised torch, apparently suffering no harm.[48]

A newspaper feature writer has described a bizarre service of one of the snake cults in Kentucky. The backwoods church was decorated with snake skins, a huge stuffed snake hung over the pulpit, on the altar was a bowl filled with snake rattles, and snake-catching tools were piled on the floor. A dozen screen-covered boxes held the reptiles. In the midst of the meeting men and women surged forward, some of them crawling along the floor like serpents, and as the rattlers were released they were seized, fondled, and kissed by the frenzied worshipers. One girl draped a serpent about her neck, and the writer declared that it struck her repeatedly in the face, and blood streamed from twenty wounds while the girl "kissed it lovingly from its skull to its buzzing rattles." According to the writer all the persons who were bitten by the snakes were back at their work the following day.[49]

Only brief mention, mainly historical, needs to be made of the present-day charismatic sects. All their characteristics have been covered by the previous discussion. They run true to the uniform type, and, save for the bizarre elements just mentioned, there are few differences between them. Theologically they are usually premillenarian and look for the imminent second coming of Christ to destroy this world order. They are literal biblicists, hold to plenary and verbal inspiration, and ascribe divine authority to their own interpretations of prophecy. Their morality is generally of the puritan type, in opposition to the jewelry, fashionable and expensive clothing, amusements, and general "worldliness" of their better-placed neighbors. The conventional churches and regular ministry are nearly always regarded as having corrupted or departed from "the faith" or "Bible religion." They regard themselves as the true church, and

[48] Associated Press story in *New York Herald Tribune*, June 23, 1947.
[49] Preece and Kraft, *Dew On Jordan*, pp. 45-49.

some of them trace their genealogy direct to the day of Pentecost. Several adopt the name Church of God or Church of Christ and feel that their mission is to preserve true religion and bring about the union of all churches and Christians.

Religious education, in the modern sense, is often discounted or opposed, as is also modern biblical and scientific learning. The preachers are usually uneducated and often unsalaried. The revival technique is exclusively employed in gaining adherents; conversion and salvation are accomplished by the direct divine agency operating through emotional channels, and the "gift of the Holy Spirit" is the highest boon bestowed upon the faithful. Divine healing is practiced by nearly all of these sects.[50]

Outpouring of the Latter Rain. Many of the Pentecostal or left-wing holiness churches now operating throughout the country grew out of what is known among them as the Latter Rain Movement, a revival characterized by baptisms of the Holy Spirit evidenced by "speaking in other tongues as the Spirit gives utterance." The modern movement began in the mountain area of East Tennessee and Western North Carolina in 1886 under the leadership of two Baptist preachers, R. G. Spurling and R. G. Spurling, Jr. In that year the elder Spurling participated in a holiness revival in Monroe County, Tennessee, and, owing to opposition from fellow Baptists, he organized an independent body called the Christian Union, which he regarded as a "reformation movement" to restore primitive Christianity and bring about the union of all denominations.

In 1892 the junior Spurling led a revival in his church at Liberty, near Turtletown, Tennessee, in which persons received Spirit baptism and spoke with tongues, as a result of which the pastor and thirty other persons were turned out of the Baptist Church. This group was invited to meet in the home of W. F. Bryant, a Methodist preacher who lived at Camp Creek, in Cherokee County, North Carolina, six miles from Liberty, on what is now called Burger Mountain. Here other conversions and baptisms accompanied by the gift of tongues occurred, and an organization was perfected under the name of the Holiness Church.

---

[50] Charismatic elements appear in the novenas, healings accomplished by the bones and relics of saints, and gifts bestowed by patron saints in the Roman Catholic Church. In every part of the world there are Catholic shrines, usually possessing some holy relic such as a bone, wherein healings and supernatural blessings are bestowed upon the worshipers. Canonization of saints is dependent upon miracles wrought by the person exalted. In many places, New Orleans for example, shrines are filled with votive offerings, plaster casts of limbs miraculously healed, crutches, and similar mementos of miracles. The New Orleans papers almost daily contain in the "personal column" paid advertisements expressing thanks to some saint for blessings received. The Catholic Penitentes of New Mexico mutilate their bodies and indulge in extreme orgies and, until the practice was recently prohibited, persons were tied, or allegedly nailed, to crosses. Among the American Indians there is a "peyote cult," in which the devotees induce ecstasy and carry on wild extravagances by the use of the deadly narcotic peyote, or mescal button, obtained from a certain species of cactus.

The Camp Creek group is regarded as the original church of the Pentecostal revival, and Burger Mountain has been purchased and made into a shrine by adherents of the movement.

This revival became of nation-wide significance under the leadership of A. J. Tomlinson, the founder and general overseer of the Church of God, who as a colporteur came upon the Camp Creek church in 1896. He decided after long reflection that this was the ideal church after the New Testament pattern, and in 1903 he united himself with it and began to preach the doctrine of holiness as a distinct work of grace subsequent to justification.

Tomlinson took charge of the movement, and in 1906 convened the first annual assembly at Camp Creek in the home of Mrs. Melissa Murphy. The second assembly, held at Union Grove, twelve miles from Tomlinson's home at Cleveland, Tennessee, in 1907, changed the name from the Holiness Church to the Church of God. It was not until the following year, however, that Tomlinson received the baptism of the Holy Spirit attested by the gift of tongues, although the experience had been prominent in the revival from the beginning. The most active era of Tomlinson's evangelistic career dated from the reception of that blessing in 1908, when headquarters for the whole movement were definitely established at Cleveland, Tennessee, and he became the general overseer.

Tomlinson promoted the revival with great vigor. He not only held revivals, made his own converts, ordained preachers and established churches, but he visited other revivals that came to his attention and incorporated their groups into his Church of God. One such revival broke out at Topeka, Kansas, under the preaching of the Rev. Charles F. Parham, and the most spectacular of all occurred in the Azusa Street Methodist Church at Los Angeles, a Negro congregation, led by the Rev. Charles Seymour, the somewhat erratic Negro pastor. People from various parts of the country visited the Azusa Street revival, and many of them received the baptism of the Spirit and became leaders in the Church of God. It was in this revival that the movement became known as the Outpouring of the Latter Rain.

During the next forty years it spread throughout the country and into foreign lands. Most of the churches raised up were the direct or indirect creations of A. J. Tomlinson. But divisions occurred in many places and the Church of God became split into numerous independent groups. This was due to the individualistic nature of the doctrines preached, the rivalry of various leaders for power, and the insistence on the part of Tomlinson that he exercised authority as general overseer by virtue of his work and divine commission.

There are today a dozen or more branches of Tomlinson's original

Church of God. Three of them operate from headquarters at Cleveland, Tennessee, another is at Chattanooga, and still another is headed by Tomlinson's son in New York. There are also numerous independent congregations which adhere to the Pentecostal doctrine but which refuse to become identified with any denominational group and often decline to keep a register of members. It is not possible to estimate the numerical strength of the Latter Rain Movement but its adherents probably run into the hundreds of thousands. Bishop Homer A. Tomlinson asserts that in many states and cities the Pentecostal churches outnumber all the others combined, and he quotes a police captain of long experience as declaring that this is true in New York city. He estimates that there are 100,000 congregations throughout the world and 24,000 in the United States, and says that his father personally signed the ministerial credentials of more than 100,000 preachers.[51]

Churches of God. The ORIGINAL CHURCH OF GOD resulted from the first schism in the Church of God. This occurred in 1917, when the pastor of the congregation in Chattanooga set up for himself and took the name of the Original Church of God. Aside from the pastor's desire for independence, the only points at issue were the tithe, which he regarded as optional and not obligatory, and the reception of divorced persons into the church, which he permitted. In common with other branches, this group traces its ancestry direct to the Spurling revival of 1886, and regards itself not as the seceding faction but as the original body. The Original Church of God has about sixty congregations and around five thousand members.

The CHURCH OF GOD (CLEVELAND, TENNESSEE) emerged from a serious schism which occurred in 1909 as the result of a controversy over the supreme power of the general overseer. Two years previously Tomlinson. The church is governed by a council of twelve elders and the a young preacher who served the Cleveland church during the overseer's absence on an evangelistic tour. These charged that the leader had never been elected to the position he held, and they furthermore took the position that the gift of tongues should not be expected or required of all church members. In 1921 the general assembly adopted a constitution which associated other leaders with the general overseer in the ruling affairs of the church. In 1922 Tomlinson made an unsuccessful attempt to secure the repeal of the constitution. He resigned his office, but later consented to serve, whereupon the supreme command was vested in a committee of

---

[51] Bishop Tomlinson, overseer of the Church of God (World Headquarters), who was associated with his father from the early days of the movement, prepared for me a lengthy manuscript covering the history and the various offshoots of the original Church of God. Much of the material herein presented has been drawn from this manuscript source.

three. The other two members so restricted Tomlinson's functions that a complete break followed.

This controversy was marked by charges and counter charges involving the use of church funds, and Tomlinson was tried and vindicated by the courts. But the church was split wide open, and the founder was cast out by a considerable group which claimed the name of the Church of God.

This body first called itself the "General Assembly of the Church of God," but in 1930 it assumed the original name. It is now known as the Church of God (Cleveland, Tennessee), and it is also called the "Elders Church of God" or the "Church of God, Elders," because of the form of government adopted after the repudiation of the leadership of A. J. Tomlinson. The church is governed by a council of twelve elders and the general overseer and his two assistants. There is also a council of elders which makes recommendations to the supreme council regarding the election of the general overseer and his assistants. The concurrence of the twelve elders is necessary for the appointment of state overseers. The doctrines of the church do not differ from those of the original Tomlinson group. The body has approximately 1,600 congregations and 65,000 members.

The (TOMLINSON) CHURCH OF GOD came into being when Tomlinson, repudiated by his own flock, gathered the remnant of faithful followers into a body which was known as the (Tomlinson) Church of God, though he insisted that his own name was no part of the name of the church but was used for purposes of identification only. He redoubled his evangelistic energy, and by 1943 he claimed two thousand congregations. Then came another schism.

At his death in 1943, A. J. Tomlinson designated his son and long-time associate, Homer A. Tomlinson, as his successor and general overseer of the (Tomlinson) Church of God. The selection was opposed by a group of state overseers, whereupon Homer A. Tomlinson placed his younger brother, M. A. Tomlinson, a printer, in charge. The state overseers and the nonministerial general overseer then combined and expelled Homer A. Tomlinson from the church.

The CHURCH OF GOD OVER WHICH M. A. TOMLINSON IS GENERAL OVERSEER thus resulted, though it is widely known as the "Tomlinson Church" or the "Overseers Church." The sect claims around two thousand churches, though the most authentic reports in 1940 indicated less than half that number of congregations, with a total membership of around eighteen thousand.

Then came the CHURCH OF GOD, WORLD HEADQUARTERS. On being cast out of his father's church by his own brother, Homer A. Tomlinson formed the Church of God, World Headquarters, with himself as bishop and general overseer, and from his headquarters at Queens Village, New York, he reorganized his father's followers and renewed his evangelistic activities. He began the erection at Red Bay, Alabama, of what he called the largest church in the world. Striving to unify the scattered forces, and practicing a friendly fellowship with numerous groups which embrace the Pentecostal doctrine but are not actually under his supervision, he claims to have more than a thousand congregations in the World Headquarters Church of God.

Other Developments. While these unhappy schisms were rending the main body of the Church of God, the fruits of A. J. Tomlinson's sowing were springing up in other pastures, as his converts and those who had come under his influence evangelized and established independent Latter Rain churches all over the country.

The Rev. Thomas Garr, who received the baptism of the Spirit and the gift of tongues in the Azusa Street revival at Los Angeles, established the GARR AUDITORIUM at Charlotte, North Carolina, and it became one of the largest churches in the city and a sect in its own right. In 1924 Pentecostal believers organized the FAITH TABERNACLE in California. Preachers of the Church of God in Arkansas were instrumental in the organization of the Assemblies of God, the largest Pentecostal sect in the country. The MOUNTAIN ASSEMBLY CHURCH OF GOD, with headquarters at Jellico, Tennessee, permitted its members to use tobacco and established forty congregations with eighteen hundred members. The CHURCH OF GOD, INCORPORATED, worked from Pulaski, Virginia, and formed two or three dozen churches. Bishop Sam Officer founded the CHURCH OF JESUS at Cleveland, Tennessee, and BISHOP POTEAT'S CHURCH OF GOD grew up in the same city. In the South the interracial BIBLE CHURCH OF GOD flourished; and the JESUS AND WATCH MISSION, the CHURCHES OF OUR LORD JESUS CHRIST OF THE APOSTOLIC FAITH, the FORWARD MOVEMENT BIBLE SCHOOL AND HEADQUARTERS, the churches of Mother Horn and Mother Robinson, and numerous Spanish, Italian, and Latin-American Churches of God sprang up in and around New York. The REMNANT CHURCH OF GOD has headquarters at Lansing, Michigan.

One interesting development was the growth of several "Jesus Only" sects, Negro, white, and biracial, which originated in the preaching of a Negro Church of God evangelist at Indianapolis, Indiana, in 1915. These reject the doctrine of the Trinity and baptize only in the name of Jesus Christ. The original Indianapolis body took the name of APOSTOLIC CHURCH OF JESUS CHRIST, and a similar sect in New York organized as the Churches of Our Lord Jesus Christ of the Apostolic Faith. Both of these are Negro denominations. One "Jesus Only" congregation occupies one of the largest church buildings in Harlem. Bishop Officer's Church of God is also a "Jesus Only" group. The movement claims three thousand congregations throughout the country.

This development has been paralleled among the Churches of God by the rise of "Father Only" groups. These also reject the trinitarian formula and baptize only in the name of the Father.

The SCHOOL OF THE PROPHETS, with headquarters at Louisville, Kentucky, claims as many as five hundred churches. These feature somewhat unique services. A member propounds a doctrine and challenges any other member to "cross" him, thus opening a free-for-all discussion which may continue for hours. This method, it is believed, will develop a unity of spirit among those who differ in points of doctrine, and thus lead to the ultimate goal of unity in both spirit and doctrine.

Other offshoots of the Latter Rain revival are the NON-DIGRESSIVE CHURCH OF GOD, the JUSTIFIED CHURCH OF GOD, the CHURCH OF GOD OF THE BIBLE, the HOLSTEIN CHURCH OF GOD, and the GLORIFIED CHURCH OF GOD. These are all independent sects with but slight divergencies from the main line of Pentecostal doctrine. The Holstein group places emphasis upon the biracial nature of all its congregations. The Glorified Church has two unique principles: (1) It insists that two persons must shout or dance together, and that one individual must not indulge in the exercises alone; and (2) the congregation will advance money to pay the debts of all new members.

The outpouring of the "latter rain" has given rise to numerous sects and independent churches among the foreign-language groups in the United States and in foreign countries. There are large Pentecostal churches in Panama, Chile, and other Latin-American countries, and followers in Italy are said to outnumber all other Protestants in that country.

Bishop Homer A. Tomlinson places the number of Spanish-speaking Pentecostal churches in the United States at about two thousand. All of these are self-supporting, many do not accept any denominational affiliation, and the total group carries on an active missionary program in Latin-American countries. They are found in New York City and in nearly every community where Spanish-speaking immigrants reside in large numbers. Among the most important are the CHURCH OF GOD, which occupies a former Jewish synagogue in East Harlem, LA CASA DE DIOS at Jamaica, New York, the LATIN-AMERICAN COUNCIL OF CHURCHES, and the SPANISH CHRISTIAN CHURCHES with headquarters in New York City. The growth of this movement among the Spanish-speaking people is largely due to the evangelistic work of the Rev. Francisco Olazabal, who was a Methodist preacher of some prominence in Mexico and California before he entered the Church of God.

The Italian Churches of God in the United States number around two thousand according to Bishop Tomlinson's figures. Most of these are quite small groups which meet in little chapels, "store-front" churches, and private rooms, though some of them are very large. A few are affiliated with the general council of the ITALIAN PENTECOSTAL ASSEMBLIES OF GOD, which grew out of a Pentecostal revival in Chicago. A still larger number are listed among the UNORGANIZED ITALIAN CHRISTIAN CHURCHES OF NORTH AMERICA, a nonsectarian and nondenominational Pentecostal federation which permits its member churches to retain their autonomy. This was formed in Chicago in 1907 by the Rev. Louis Francescon, its senior elder and missionary. In 1936 the general council reported 16 churches and 1,600 members, and the unorganized body reported 104 churches with 9,600 members. No later figures are available. Many will not countenance a congregational organization and refuse to keep a list of members.

The "latter rain" has fallen among nearly every other language group in America, according to Bishop Tomlinson, who mentions fifteen nationalities, other than Latin Americans and Italians, among which there are churches of the Pentecostal faith and practice. None of these are the result of missionary work, but all are of an indigenous nature, autonomous and self-supporting, and maintain contacts with their fellow immigrants here and their fellow countrymen in their native lands. The whole Pentecostal movement abroad is the result of the evangelism of expatriates who experienced Spirit baptism and received the gift of tongues in America and returned to spread the message among their own people.

The ASSEMBLIES OF GOD, GENERAL COUNCIL, is the largest Pentecostal body in the United States, with 5,000 local churches and a total membership of 240,000 persons. Its denominational form emerged from a union of Pentecostal churches which had been established in Arkansas and adjoining states by certain evangelists of the Church of God. In 1914 a group of pastors of such independent churches called a meeting at Hot Springs and perfected an organization of about a hundred congregations, which was incorporated in Arkansas in the same year. In 1916 the headquarters were established at Springfield, Missouri, and the sect was incorporated under the name of the General Council of the Assemblies of God.

While stressing the sanctification of believers and the baptism of the Spirit attested by speaking in other tongues, this sect is unique among holiness groups in eliminating from its doctrinal statement the idea of a second work of grace subsequent to justification and in accepting the progressive nature of sanctification. It preaches the puritan type of morality, including condemnation of worldliness and immodesty and extravagance in dress. Divine healing is prominent, as is the ever-present expectation of the end of the world, with the customary interpretation of prophecy to that effect.

"We are 'fundamentalists' to a man!" declares a spokesman. "The only difference that we have with other fundamentalists is concerning 'the evidence of the Baptism of the Holy Ghost!' " It is declared that the sect "is in no wise affected by liberalism." Though Sunday-school work is stressed, it is insisted that the aim of religious education is that all "should be born again of the Spirit and also filled with the Spirit of God," the experiences being two distinct "works of grace." In order that no misconception may be entertained as to the charismatic character of the sect it is officially declared:

This Council considers it a serious disagreement with the Fundamentals for any minister among us to teach contrary to our distinctive testimony that the baptism of the Holy Spirit is regularly accompanied by the initial physical sign of speaking in other tongues as the Spirit of God gives the utterance, and that we consider it inconsistent and unscriptural for any minister to hold credentials with us who attacks as error our distinctive testimony.[52]

The PENTECOSTAL HOLINESS CHURCH was formed in 1898 when representatives of a number of holiness associations, as a result of a revival movement in the South and West, met at Anderson, South Carolina, and organized the Fire-Baptized Holiness Church. In 1899 a similar group met at Clinton, North Carolina, and resolved themselves into the Pentecostal Holiness Church. These two bodies came together in 1911, at Falcon, North Carolina, and effected a merger under the name of the younger group.

Between this sect and the other Pentecostal bodies already mentioned there are two slight points of divergence: (1) This group is somewhat more tolerant of other churches, though its adherents are not comfortable therein because they prefer "more joyous demonstrations" and greater "fervor of spirit" in worship, and it is not quite so certain that it alone represents primitive Christianity and constitutes the true church; and (2) its polity is less democratic, being modeled after the pattern of episcopal Methodism, kinship to which is freely admitted. In other respects it is a typical Pentecostal charismatic sect. It insists on three distinct works of grace, the crowning experience being the baptism of the Spirit attested by speaking in other tongues. It is sympathetic to medical science and endorses "simple remedies," but prefers divine healing as "the more excellent way." Ardent millennial hopes are entertained. Typical also is its strict moral discipline and opposition to worldliness. In 1946 this sect reported 786

[52] Letter from J. R. Evans, general secretary.

churches, 26,251 members, 8,043 saved, 3,179 sanctified, and 1,724 baptized with the Holy Spirit.

The CONGREGATIONAL HOLINESS CHURCH dates from 1921. The strict superintendence involved in the Methodist polity caused uneasiness among persons whose fundamental principle was spontaneity and Spirit guidance. A schism occurred in 1921, when a group desiring greater freedom withdrew and set up for themselves under the name of the Congregational Holiness Church. This sect practices washing of feet, and places slang under the ban along with secret societies and other forms of worldliness, but in all other respects, save in polity, which is thoroughly democratic and congregational, it is an exact replica of the parent body. It has 70 churches and a membership of around 2,500.

Other Pentecostal Churches. There are several other Pentecostal churches or assemblies in the country, some of which owe their existence to the Latter Rain Movement, and all of which adhere to similar teachings and practices. All believe in Spirit baptism attested by the gift of tongues.

The UNITED PENTECOSTAL CHURCH, organized in 1945, was a union of two "latter rain" bodies, the Pentecostal Assemblies of Jesus Christ, and the Pentecostal Church, Incorporated, the new group taking the name of the United Pentecostal Church, and establishing headquarters in St. Louis. The Pentecostal Assemblies of Jesus Christ traced its ancestry through the Topeka and Los Angeles revivals back to the day of Pentecost,[53] but it actually resulted from a merger of some small Pentecostal groups that did not enter the General Council of the Assemblies of God. The Pentecostal Church, Incorporated, was formed in 1924 from a company of people who withdrew from the Pentecostal Assemblies of the World in order to organize a church composed entirely of white people.

At the time of the merger the Pentecostal Assemblies of Jesus Christ had about 450 churches and 17,000 members, and the Pentecostal Church, Incorporated, was about the same size. Their doctrines were identical in all essentials and did not differ materially from the tenets of the other "latter rain" churches.

The INTERNATIONAL PENTECOSTAL ASSEMBLIES represents a continuation of a body known as the National and International Pentecostal Missionary Union, founded in 1914, and the Association of Pentecostal Assemblies, formed in 1921. It departs from the "latter rain" or Pentecostal theology in no essential particular, stressing sanctification of the second-blessing type, Spirit baptism accompanied by the gift of tongues, divine healing by prayer, anointing with oil, and laying on of hands, premil-

[53] *Census of Religious Bodies,* 1936, II, 1328. The language of much of its historical statement is identical with the statement of the Pentecostal Assemblies of the World.

lenarianism, baptism by immersion, foot washing, and pacificism. It has around one hundred congregations and six thousand members.

The PENTECOSTAL CHURCH OF GOD OF AMERICA was organized at Chicago in 1919 under the name of the Pentecostal Assemblies of the U.S.A., the title becoming the Pentecostal Church of God in 1922. The headquarters were moved to Ottumwa, Iowa, in 1927, and to Kansas City, Missouri, in 1933. Finding there a local church bearing the same name, the words "in America" were added to its title. The body is a typical Pentecostal sect; it believes in immersion, Spirit baptism attended by the gift of tongues, foot washing, divine healing, and the premillennial return of Jesus Christ. There are several hundred churches and around forty thousand members.

The CALVARY PENTECOSTAL CHURCH arose in 1931, when a group of Pentecostal preachers, dissatisfied because of what they regarded as "a sad departure from the entire dependence on the power of God that had brought the pentecostal revival," formed a conference or fellowship at Olympia, Washington, which in the following year became the Calvary Pentecostal Church. It has around fifty churches with twenty thousand members, and is confined largely to the northwestern states, though it carries on missionary work in India and Brazil.

The CHURCH OF JESUS AND THE WATCH MISSION is the creature of its bishop, George A. Luetjen, who was converted and received Spirit baptism when he threw away a cigar while walking on the streets of New York in December, 1910, after a period of depression and conviction in which family troubles figured. He began preaching in his own home in Long Island City in 1922, and his mission is still located in that city. According to a published statement the group has "branches all over the U.S.A.," with ministers in eight states and Canada, but none of these have churches and there are only thirty-five members and in good standing.[54] In apparent fellowship with this group are the MIZPAH MISSION, Taft, Florida, and the ISRAEL GOSPEL CHURCH at Long Island City, New York.

The CHURCH OF GOD, INCORPORATED, was formed as Alldreds, North Carolina, in November, 1942, by persons who had withdrawn from various churches of the Tomlinson order because they believed these churches had departed from their original faith. On March 5, 1944, it was joined by a group which left the Original Church of God because they claimed the overseer had married a woman with four living husbands, and the church had received "double married" persons into its membership, and even allowed divorced and remarried men to serve as bishops. The leader of this group, W. B. Davis, was chosen as general overseer, and the

---

[54] Communication from Bishop Luetjen, July 31, 1947; *My Conversion,* a tract by the bishop; the *Prophetic Age,* a periodical.

headquarters were moved to Pulaski, Virginia. In 1947 the sect had ten churches and five hundred members but expected to bring other small groups into its body.[55]

The CHURCH OF GOD IN CHRIST (PENTECOSTAL) was founded in the early thirties and reported nine churches and two hundred members in the census of 1936. The headquarters of its bishop are at Bluefield, West Virginia.

The CHURCH OF THE FULL GOSPEL, INCORPORATED, was formed by the Rev. R. H. Askew, of the Free Will Baptist Church, at Goldsboro, North Carolina, in 1935. Two years later there was a reorganization, and churches at Dunn, Rocky Mount, Elm City, and Snow Hill were incorporated into the body. The headquarters remained at Goldsboro. There is a co-operative relation with the PENTECOSTAL FULL GOSPEL CHURCH of Baltimore, Maryland, and the two bodies jointly publish a periodical known as the *Full Gospel Herald*. In 1936 statistics reported four churches and three hundred members. Sanctification and the baptism of the Holy Spirit are the main tenets.

The PENTECOSTAL FIRE-BAPTIZED HOLINESS CHURCH grew out of the Pentecostal fire-baptized movement, which originated in Georgia in the last decade of the nineteenth century, and its adherents were known as the Fire-Baptized Holiness Church. In 1911 there was a consolidation with the Pentecostal Holiness Church, but this union was dissolved in 1918 because of a controversy over the wearing of adornments and elaborate dress. The old fire-baptized group was reorganized under the name of the Pentecostal Fire-Baptized Holiness Church. This united with the Pentecostal Freewill Baptist Church in 1920.

The sect exerts a strict discipline over its people in the matter of dress, amusements, association between the sexes, the use of tobacco, and various other practices. Its general rules forbid "filthiness of speech, foolish talking or jesting, or the use of slang," "attending fairs, swimming pools, or shows of any kind," "jewelry, gold, feathers, flowers, costly apparel, neckties, hobble skirts, split skirts, low necks, short sleeves, and indecent dress," and instructs "our young women to wear their dresses at least half-way from knee to floor, and our older women wear theirs longer, and not to have their hair bobbed or waved."

In matters of doctrine the customary Pentecostal pattern prevails. Sanctification is subsequent to justification and regeneration, and the baptism of the Holy Ghost is accompanied by speaking with tongues. Immersion, the washing of feet, anointing with oil for healing, and laying on of hands are practiced.

[55] *Declaration of Bible Order of the Church of God;* communication from the overseer, August 1, 1947.

This church reports about ninety congregations and eighteen hundred members in Georgia, Alabama, and the Carolinas.[56]

The FIRE-BAPTIZED HOLINESS CHURCH OF GOD OF THE AMERICAS is a Negro Pentecostal sect. It was at one time a part of the white body, but a separation occurred at a meeting held in 1908 at Anderson, South Carolina. Originally known as an "association," it took the name of the Fire-Baptized Holiness Church of God in 1922, and added the words "of the Americas" four years later. Its doctrines follow closely the Pentecostal pattern, and include sanctification, Spirit baptism attested by speaking with tongues, divine healing, and premillenarianism. It has headquarters at Atlanta, and reports three hundred churches and six thousand members.

The APOSTOLIC FAITH MISSION differs from other Pentecostal sects mainly in the fact that it is largely confined to cities and is of the "mission" type. It has 17 congregations, mostly urban; the same is true of most of its 2,200 members. In other respects it runs true to form; it exhibits distrust of other churches, has confidence in its own conformity to the New Testament pattern, uses revival technique, and holds to sanctification, Spirit baptism accompanied by the gift of tongues, divine healing, biblical literalism, opposition to scholarship, foot washing, puritan morality, and premillennial hopes.

The moving spirits of the Apostolic Faith Mission were Miss Minnie Hanson and Mrs. M. White. It originated as the Apostolic Faith Movement in Topeka, Kansas, in 1900, under the preaching of two evangelists named Crossley and Hunter. The ideal of the founders was, and that of the sect remains, "the restoration of the faith once delivered to the saints." The body claims to be "not a denomination" but "an evangelistic movement on a scriptural plan," carried on by persons especially called to the work by the Holy Ghost. The charismatic principle is fundamental. The gifts bestowed are in the nature of the usual emotional and motor reactions, resulting not only in personal perfection but also in selection and equipment for special work, as in the primitive church. The charism of healing is quite important and firmly grounded in Scripture: "All sickness is the work of the devil" and Jesus gave his disciples authority to exorcise demons.[57] When sick persons can be visited, they are healed by prayer and the laying on of hands; otherwise, "absent treatment" is given by sending to the afflicted handkerchiefs and other articles that have been blessed.

This sect, like others, not only feels that it is not a sect but is actually out to rid the world of sects. This phenomenon of groups splitting off

[56] Communication from A. O. Hood, general secretary, Jefferson, Georgia, July 30, 1947.

[57] *Eventide*, periodical of the sect. It carries no date, volume, or number.

from sects, perfecting definite organizations, and even securing legal incorporation, and themselves splitting and resplitting until they have spawned a multitude of well-organized bodies, all being firmly convinced that not only are they not sects but are eradicating sectarianism, is a psychological peculiarity difficult to understand.

The psychology of the Apostolic Faith Mission may be understood by studying the process through which Miss Hanson became its prophetess. She was reared a Lutheran, but early sought and experienced emotional uplifts, and joined the Methodists. Hearing about sanctification at a holiness camp meeting in 1906, she became a seeker and underwent the typical conviction depression, an experience similar to that which had preceded her conversion. After considerable struggle she was "calmly sanctified" at the altar and two weeks later received the emotional witness. The next year she heard of the baptism of the Holy Spirit, and once more was thrown into the melancholia of conviction. On two nights she remained until midnight in a holiness revival and at last "the power" came. According to her own testimony she "was under the Power of God from ten o'clock in the evening until almost four in the morning." She went back to the altar the following night to "get through," although she was already "so satisfied I could not hold any more."

In this she was mistaken, however, for at this point the gift of tongues fell upon her:

I had no more than reached the altar than the Power fell on me and I was again prostrated on the floor, where I remained until almost six o'clock the following morning. Those who tarried with me said it was about four o'clock when I received the Bible evidence and talked and sang distinctly in two different languages. I knew nothing about these languages, but they were understood by parties who were there and themselves knew the languages.

Strange to say, the good woman was not even then satisfied, for the devil gave her more trouble after the outpouring than before it.[58]

The CATHOLIC APOSTOLIC CHURCH, whose members are popularly called "Irvingites," is, in theory at least, the most thoroughgoing of all charismatic sects, in that personal experience and church government are divine gifts. To a certain degree it is an exception to the rule that such groups take their rise among the ignorant poor, the leaders of the original band being Englishmen of considerable culture and position.

The turmoil of the French Revolution and the Napoleonic Wars, as is always true of such dreadful events, gave rise to premillennial views, and devout groups in various parts of the world saw in the upheavals the fulfill-

---

[58] *Overwhelmed with the Holy Ghost: A Wonderful Experience* (pamphlet). See also *Sanctification and the Great Fundamental Truths*, provided by the sect.

ment of apocalyptic signs presaging the end of time. In 1828 a group of about fifty clergymen and laymen were invited to the country estate of Henry Drummond at Albury, West Surrey, to study the prophecies. These meetings were repeated from time to time. In 1830 reports of supernatural speaking emanated from near Glasgow, and a deputation was sent by the Albury confreres to ascertain whether the utterances were "of the spirit." An affirmative report was returned, and soon similar speaking was heard in an Anglican church in London. The exercises were suppressed by the bishop, whereupon the Presbyterian church served by Edward Irving became the headquarters of the persons giving credence to the gift.

This was the origin of the Catholic Apostolic Church, which the adherents believed, and still believe, to be the church of all true Christians. The reception of charismata constituted its fundamental features, all officials being chosen by the direct agency of the Holy Spirit. Twelve men of prominence were designated as apostles. Prophets, bishops or "angels," and others were selected according to the order mentioned by Paul in Eph. 4:11-13. These leaders did not conceive their duty as that of founding a new church, but as working within the existing bodies for the restoration of the primitive and apostolic order. The apostles visited various countries to deliver their message and presented their "testimony," in person or by documents, to the rulers of church and state in all Christian lands. Their revelations were ignored by those in authority but were accepted by considerable numbers of private individuals, both in England and upon the continent, whereupon an independent ecclesiastical body resulted. The first church in the United States was established in 1851 at Potsdam, New York, and the second was set up in New York City soon thereafter. There are now seven congregations in the United States; the total number of members is approximately three thousand.

Specific enduement of the Spirit as the qualification for official leadership and an intense millenarianism are the cardinal tenets of this body. There is a twelvefold apostleship after the primitive pattern, this constituting the supreme governing order. Local churches are ruled by "angels" or bishops. Angels and priests are assigned to the ministry as elders, prophets, evangelists, and pastors. There are no elections, save that seven deacons may be chosen by each church; all ministers of every rank, save the deacons, are selected by God but are under the control of the apostles. The last apostle died in 1901 and the angels and priests are gradually diminishing, since God has made no new designations. "The members describe themselves simply as waiting upon the Lord, for whatever it may please Him to do; and above all waiting for the promised coming of the Lord in visible power and glory." [59]

[59] *Census of Religious Bodies*, 1936, II, 350.

The NEW APOSTOLIC CHURCH is a schism from the original body. The division resulted from the selection of apostles to fill vacancies caused by death in the ranks of the twelve. Disputes arose over this question in England in 1860. The innovators claimed that there must always be twelve apostles and pointed to the selection of Matthias to take the place of Judas (Acts 1:15-26) as a precedent for election. The prophet Geyer designated the evangelists Bohm and Caird, who were recognized as coadjutor apostles. Geyer was not satisfied, and at Königsberg in 1861 he proclaimed the elevation of the evangelist Rogasatzki to the apostolate. The latter soon made his submission but a schism resulted. In 1863 Geyer himself was called. Bishop Schwarz of Hamburg was excommunicated for proposing elections, but a priest named Preuss was selected "through the spirit of prophecy" in 1863. For a time Bishop Schwarz served under Preuss and was later himself selected to be an apostle.

The New Apostolic Church began with the activities of Preuss and Schwarz. The movement spread to America, where John Erb, of Chicago, is the head of all the churches in the United States, serving under the head apostle, Herman Niehaus, who resides in Steinhagen, Germany. The sect in America has sixty-five churches and five thousand members. Its tenets and polity are similar to those of the parent body.[60]

The HOLINESS CHURCH stems from about 1880, when Hardin Wallace and James A. Singer, of the Methodist Episcopal Church, and Henry Ashcroft, a Free Methodist, set out to "recover the New Testament church." They traveled through southern California and Arizona, preaching climactic sanctification and organizing "holiness bands." There was no thought of a new denomination and the sanctified retained their connection with the various churches. The churches, however, were not sympathetic to the "bands" within the fold, and when difficulties over the holding of property arose separation was inevitable. In 1896 the bands were incorporated as the Holiness Church.

The sect has remained small. It has eighteen churches and about four hundred members, most of which are in the "happy hunting ground" of perfectionism, Kentucky. It exhibits all the familiar features of the holiness groups. The members are convinced that theirs is the true Church; in their stand against what they regard as unscriptural denominationalism it is declared that "all other bodies are neither recognized as the true church nor as branches of it." [61] The charismatic principle is dominant. All members

[60] See Oliphant, *Life of Edward Irving*; Miller, *History and Doctrines of Irvingism*; Prior, *My Experiences of the Catholic Apostolic Church*; Andrews, *God's Revelations of Himself to Men*; articles "Irving" and "Catholic Apostolic Church," in Schaff-Herzog, *Encyclopedia of Religious Knowledge*.

[61] Teel, *The New Testament Church* (pamphlet).

are filled with, and led by, the Holy Spirit, hence are "perfect." In the meetings all take part as the Spirit dictates and speak "as the Spirit gives utterance." Miraculous healing is practiced and the various "gifts of the Spirit" are received. There is an especial antipathy to "episcopal pretensions," and, as Gaddis remarks, the polity, "being governed by the charismatic principle, is of course democratic almost to the point of being anarchistic." [62] There is the usual puritan morality, opposition to a regular salaried ministry, and an earnest watchfulness for the return of the Lord in power and glory.

The INTERNATIONAL CHURCH OF THE FOURSQUARE GOSPEL is the following of "Sister" Aimee Semple McPherson, whose sensational and spectacular career at Angelus Temple in Los Angeles made her name and doctrine familiar all over the country. This fact makes unnecessary a detailed discussion of the sect.

Mrs. McPherson (she was married three times, but was known by the names of her first and second husbands) was born in Canada in 1890 and received only a secondary education. At the age of seventeen she was converted, married a Baptist evangelist, Robert Semple, and became a preacher by divine revelation. She traveled widely, preaching in England, Australia, and China, and achieved an unusual success, due to her physical attractiveness, fluency in speech, and dramatic ability. In 1918 she settled in Los Angeles. In 1921 she founded her Echo Park Evangelistic Association and built her famous temple. She attracted thousands of followers, and late in 1927 incorporated the International Church of the Foursquare Gospel. In all this she professed to be under the direct guidance of God.

More than any other group in the country, save some obscure Negro sects, the Foursquare people illustrate the tendency of certain elements to rally around and follow a leader of striking personality. "Sister" possessed all the qualities necessary to a messiah of ardent souls. Handsome in appearance and fluent in speech, she knew all the secrets of crowd psychology. Her preaching services were highly dramatic, and she used publicity, costuming, lighting effects, music, and her personal charm to secure the most striking effects. Her message was the most simple orthodoxy; she claimed and exercised the gifts of healing and tongues, and professed to be under the direct guidance of God; she abounded in good works to the poor; she turned the opposition of the regular preachers to her own advantage and to the discomfiture of her enemies.

Thus "Sister" grappled her followers to her with hoops of steel. Their devotion was not shaken by the many notorious escapades in which she was involved, family quarrels, lawsuits, alleged kidnaping and subsequent

[62] *Op. cit.*, p. 464.

criminal prosecution, marriage, separation, and so forth. Scandals which would have destroyed any decorous religious leader were used by this prophetess to strengthen her position. Following a kidnaping episode, which her enemies openly declared was an illicit amorous adventure, she published in a Los Angeles daily paper of wide circulation and sensational character a series of articles featuring both her love affairs and divine leadings. Her whole career was an interesting study in sexual charm and religious devotion. During nearly a dozen years of rumor, opposition, and publicity she held her position and following and capitalized every attack to her own advantage.

The Foursquare gospel is thoroughly fundamentalistic. Nearly every tenet of the older theology appears in the declaration of faith, expressed in plain and simple language and bolstered by pertinent quotations from the Bible. The sect is fundamentalist, adventist, perfectionist, and charismatic. Among its doctrines may be mentioned the verbal inspiration, literal interpretation, and absolute authority of the Bible; Spirit baptism subsequent to conversion; speaking in unknown tongues and interpreting the same; divine healing and the performance of other miracles; the imminent second coming of Christ, including "the rapture" and other concomitants; the final judgment of a literal nature; an actual heaven of indescribable bliss for believers; and a literal hell, including an eternal lake of fire and brimstone into which sinners shall be cast.

According to the only statistics available (1936), there are around 400 Foursquare churches in the country, with a total membership of 21,000.

Negro Charismatic Sects. It would scarcely be amiss to characterize most of the small Negro sects as charismatic, since primitive traits, attributed to the Holy Spirit, are prominent among them. Negroes are given to emotional exercises, and shouting, trances, and bodily movements of various sorts are common among them; formal worship is rather an exception and is found mainly in a relatively few large churches in the greater cities. Even there the familiar charismatic demonstrations frequently break out in their revivals.

An example, which I witnessed, may be cited from a revival in one of the largest Negro Baptist churches in St. Louis. The evangelist was named Becktin, the self-styled "Black Billy Sunday." The preliminary "warming up" was featured by a song service led by a brass band. When the rhythm was at its height the preacher entered in dramatic fashion and took charge. His prayer was to the accompaniment of the soft strains of "Sweet Hour of Prayer." The sermon was on heaven and hell. When the "call of mourners" was made only two persons responded. Then the preacher seemed to go into a sort of trance, after which he announced that God had pointed out to him five others who must either be converted that night or it would be "everlastingly too late." He said the sinners designated were two nonchurch members, two backsliders, and "one sinner." In a previous meeting, he declared, a woman had been thus "revealed" to him, but she refused to come to the altar, and on leaving the church she had stumbled on the step, fallen, and broken her collar bone. Then in a voice of thunder he "dared any sinner to try to leave the church without seeking pardon." His words created a noticeable stir in the audience and when the music again started eleven persons rushed to the altar. The evangelist then related several experiences of "grace": one girl was released from prison through prayer, a man secured some private papers from his estranged wife, another needed $5.00, and upon conversion received a gift of $2.00 and earned $3.00 from an unexpected bit of work, while still another was enabled to pay an overdue note in the sum of $110. The third call was made and the altar was crowded with penitents. An aged prophetess then sprang up, plainly possessed of "the Spirit," and delivered a weird testimony of a revelation. Pandemonium broke out among the large audience of nearly two thousand Negroes and the scene of trances, shouting, leaping, and dancing beggars description. The meeting was termed by all to have been a "divine success." Such experiences are common in nearly all Negro churches and may be observed at any time during "seasons" of revival.

No adequate census of colored denominations has ever been made. In any large city unheard-of sects can be located, frequently consisting of only one or two churches. A dissatisfied preacher finds it easy to lead off a group and start a new denomination of his own. The tendency of unlettered people to follow a talented, peculiar, or spectacular leader is responsible for many of the smaller sects. Most of the little groups have no history save a church quarrel, and few of them possess any distinctive doctrines or practices. Only a few of the holiness type need to be considered in this book.

The PENTECOSTAL ASSEMBLIES OF THE WORLD, a Latter Rain sect, follows the somewhat general practice of tracing its history direct to the day of Pentecost by way of the Los Angeles and similar revivals. It grew out of the General Council of the Assemblies of God, and was formed at Hot Springs, Arkansas, in 1914, removed to Springfield, Missouri, in 1916, and later to Indianapolis, Indiana. The cause of the division was certain additional revelations of doctrine received by the leaders of those who formed the Pentecostal Assemblies of the World. It was originally an interracial body, but in 1924 the white members withdrew and formed the Pentecostal Church, Incorporated, which was one of the constituent bodies of the United Pentecostal Church, formed by merger in 1945. It has around ninety churches and five thousand members.

The Pentecostal Assemblies of the World follow the practices and beliefs of the Pentecostal movement, including entire sanctification attested by speaking with tongues. It teaches divine healing, practices foot washing, and opposes secret societies, church festivals, collecting money on the streets, and wearing jewelry, bobbed hair, cosmetics, "attractive hosiery, short dresses, low necks, short sleeves (that is above the elbow) and bright ties." With reference to the problem of divorced persons, which has disrupted some of the Latter Rain churches, this body teaches that

there shall be no divorce and remarriage where both have or have had the baptism of the Holy Ghost, no matter what a person's matrimonial adventures might have been before they were brought to God and filled with the Holy Ghost, the Church can only judge them from the time they come within the Body. If there be any entanglement (previous marriage where no divorce was procured or marriage was illegal) in their previous married life, our duty is to help straighten them out. Where unbeliever departs and legally severs the marriage bond, the believer is free to remarry. (I. Cor. 1.) This statement must be understood to mean that the unbeliever MUST procure the DIVORCE. No one having had the baptism of the Holy Ghost shall be classed as an unbeliever. That where one unsaved departs and lives common-in-law, it shall be considered as having departed. In such cases the saved shall be permitted to divorce and remarry where positive proof that unbeliever is living in common-in-law or concubinage. No one having come into the Holy Ghost life shall be permitted to sever relation with the wife with which he lived when saved and commit an abomination by returning to any former marriage alliance.

The UNITED HOLY CHURCH OF AMERICA grew out of a revival at Method, North Carolina, a suburb of Raleigh, in 1886. The first convocation or conference was held at Durham in 1894 and the headquarters were established in that city. It was a typical holiness body and its early meetings were attended by the customary emotional manifestations. There was a division over the belief in the necessity of the Lord's Supper for salvation, and two groups emerged, but the schism was healed in 1907.

When the original revival spread to other North Carolina towns, two organizations were formed, the United Holiness Convention and the Big Kahara Holiness Association. Other groups accepted the holiness principle but retained their previous denominational connections; these were known as the "in-church people" as distinguished from the "come-outers," and their meetings were called holy convocations. Criticism gradually drove the "in-church people" out of their churches and into one of the holiness bodies.

In 1900 a meeting of all the groups was held at Durham, and a denomination was formed under the name of the Holy Church of North Carolina. As the movement spread, the words "and Virginia" were added, and at the convocation in Oxford, North Carolina, in 1916, the name was changed to the United Holy Church of America. The individual congregations are allowed to select any name they choose, and this has sometimes led to confusion because some of the names adopted are also the titles of other denominations; among these local names are Union Pentecostal, Church of God, Holy Temple, Holy Tried Stone, House of Prayer, House of God, Pentecostal Tabernacle, and many others.

There is nothing distinctive about this sect. It teaches entire sanctification subsequent to justification, the baptism of the Holy Ghost accompanied by various gifts, including the gift of tongues, divine healing, the imminent return of Christ, and a literal hell of fire for the lost. It bans membership in secret societies, as well as ornaments and superfluity in dress, and practices immersion and the washing of feet. In 1946 the body reported about 275 churches and 25,000 members.

Negro Churches of God. There are several Negro holiness sects bearing this title, with qualifying words (two prefer Church of Christ), two of which are distinctly Pentecostal in character.

THE CHURCH OF GOD IN CHRIST was founded by C. H. Mason, of Memphis, Tennessee, "chief apostle" of the sect. Mason withdrew from the Baptist Church in 1895 in order to found a church "which would emphasize the doctrine of entire sanctification through the outpourings of the Holy Spirit." His first group was organized in an old gin at Lexington, Mississippi. According to the *Census of Religious Bodies* of 1936 the sect has around 750 churches and 30,000 members, though larger claims have been made. It has no distinctive doctrines. The members wash each other's feet, and their supernatural gifts are attested by the usual emotional exercises, including speaking with tongues.

The FREE CHURCH OF GOD IN CHRIST dates from 1915. In 1921 the Church of God in Christ was joined by a group bearing the same name, but the union lasted only four years, however, and in 1925, as a result of dissensions over a state charter, the group withdrew and became again an independent sect, this time taking the name of the Free Church of God in Christ. In 1915 sixteen Baptists in Enid, Oklahoma, were baptized by the Holy Spirit and formed the new sect. Most of these persons were in the family of the Rev. J. H. Morris. His son, E. J. Morris, "felt he was selected" as the leader of the one congregation formed, and he remained in the ascendency. The group differs in no way from the Church of God in Christ save in its leadership and a greater emphasis on divine healing; the gift of tongues is the mark of the Spirit's approval. It has twenty churches and nine hundred members.

The FREE CHRISTIAN ZION CHURCH OF CHRIST, a somewhat similar sect, though less insistent on tongues, is a Methodist offshoot. This originated at Redemption, Arkansas, under the leadership of E. D. Brown in 1906. The cause of schism in the ranks of the Methodists was an "attempt to tax members of the Church." The sect has twenty congregations and eighteen hundred members.

The CHURCHES OF GOD, HOLINESS, was formed by the Rev. K. H. Burrus, in Atlanta, Georgia. He began by preaching entire sanctification to eight people, and his group is a typical holiness body with thirty-five churches and six thousand members.

The CHURCH OF CHRIST, HOLINESS U.S.A., is almost exactly similar. It has 100 churches and 7,500 members. Its organizer was C. P. Jones, a Baptist preacher at Selma, Alabama, who "was dissatisfied with his religious experience and longed for a new faith which would make him one of wisdom's true sons and, like Abraham, 'a friend of God.' " He received his inspiration after fasting and prayer, whereupon he called a holiness convention from which, in 1894, the present sect eventuated. It is simply another holiness sect and stresses the supernatural outpourings common to many of the same order.

Churches of the Living God. The CHURCH OF THE LIVING GOD, CHRISTIAN WORKERS FOR FELLOWSHIP and the CHURCH OF THE LIVING GOD, THE PILLAR AND GROUND OF TRUTH, are two sects of Negro Christians operating under this general name. The original body was formed as the result of a revelation vouchsafed to the Rev. William Christian at Wrightsville, Arkansas, in 1889. Since that date there have been several secessions and consolidations.

In 1902 a group left the original body and took the name of the Church of the Living God (Apostolic Church); in 1908 this sect was reorganized as the Church of the Living God, General Assembly. It later rejoined the parent organization. Then the Church of Christ in God seceded but soon returned. In 1915 the name was changed to Christian Workers for Fellowship. Various other groups drew away, and these, in 1925, were consolidated by the Rev. E. J. Cain under the name of the Church of the Living God, the Pillar and Ground of Truth, which grew by the accession of two or three other sects. The census identifies two distinct bodies: the Church of the Living God, Christian Workers for Fellowship, with 100 churches and 4,500 members, and the Church of the Living God, the Pillar and Ground of Truth, having 120 churches and 5,000 members.

In the constitution of the Church of the Living God, Christian Workers for Fellowship, bearing the date of 1926, it is asserted that on the death of chief Christian his successor should be elected by the general assembly. In the constitution of 1927, adopted at Decatur, Illinois, the provision providing for the election of a successor was annulled. It was declared that the chief "was neither elected nor appointed, but holds his office by virtue of a divine calling. . . . No man has been given power to judge God's anointed." Christian died in 1928 and his wife, Mrs. Ethel L. Christian, at once laid claim to his office, calling herself "chiefess." She was in turn succeeded by her son, the Rev. John W. Christian.

The "C.W.F.F." makes much of divine revelations. The chiefess declared that "in 1889 strange revelations began to unfold to me concerning the Bible and I denounced the sectarian religion and left the Baptist Church and have since preached an unadulterated doctrine." [63] It thus appears that the original revelations came jointly to her and her husband. She "learns or receives revelations and they are imparted by the leader to other members." The usual emotional manifestations are displayed in the various meetings; in the assembly at St. Louis in 1930 the "holy spirit of the Lord" was constantly felt and once "the spirit of the Lord moved in the house with such force that the reading of minutes and collection was neglected. . . . We all had a glorious time." [64]

The "C.W.F.F." publishes a catechism which provides materials of instruction in the church and Sunday school. It rehearses biblical history, and with reference to "genealogy" contains this passage:

Q. Was Jesus a member of the black race?
A. Yes. Matt. 1.

Q. How do you know?
A. Because He was in the line of Abraham and David the king.

Q. Is this assertion sufficient proof that Christ came of the black generation?
A. Yes.

Q. Why?
A. Because David said he became like a bottle in the smoke. Ps. 119:83.

Q. What color was Job?
A. He was black. Job 30:30.

Q. What color was Jeremiah?
A. He said he was black. Jer. 8:21.

Q. Who was Moses' wife?
A. An Ethiopian (or black) woman. Num. 12:1.

Q. Should we make difference in people because they are black?
A. No. Jer. 13:23.

Q. Why?
A. Because it is as natural to be black as the leopard to be spotted. Jer. 13:23.

[63] Communication to me.
[64] Minutes, p. 8.

The APOSTOLIC OVERCOMING HOLY CHURCH OF GOD was incorporated in 1916 at Mobile, Alabama, by W. T. Phillips. He was a preacher in the Methodist Episcopal Church, but having received certain supernatural revelations and enduements, and finding in the Methodist fold no opportunity to "exercise his gifts and graces," withdrew and joined a Negro arm of the Apostolic Faith Mission. Here again he found his liberty cramped, and as the result of a quarrel with his superior he led his entire flock in a schism. The outcome of all this was the establishment of an independent sect. Phillips has established more than a hundred churches in southern Alabama and gathered several thousand members.

The bishop is supreme in this group. An interesting illustration of this is seen in the financial system. Expenses of local churches are paid by "free-will offerings," but the clergy are compensated by tithes, which are obligatory. Pastors receive the tithes of the members and the bishop receives the tithes of the pastors—and Phillips is not only the bishop but also pastor of the largest church. The bishop is not immune from the law of the tithe; ten per cent of his income goes to the poor fund—which is administered by the bishop.[65]

This is a holiness body and exhibits the emotionalism that characterizes the extreme charismatic groups. "We believe," runs the Manual, "in the baptism of the Holy Ghost as it was on the day of Pentecost. We believe all those who receive the Holy Ghost will speak with other tongues." Foot washing is one of the ordinances and divine healing is insisted upon. From the Bible has been gathered a history of the Ethiopians, from which, as published in the Manual, one obtains the quite startling information that "even from the days of Enos Christianity has been existing in that country" (Abyssinia).

The HOUSE OF PRAYER, the full name of which is the "House of Prayer for All the People," is one of the most extreme charismatic sects in the country and exhibits features peculiar to itself. The creator and dictator is one Bishop Grace; he has several churches in both the South and the North, but definite statistics are not available.[66] Grace's movement seems to have been independently initiated on his own responsibility; the sect is not a schism from another church in the ordinary sense, though it has already suffered secessions from its own ranks.[67] Its devotees are unlettered, emo-

[65] Some of this information comes from the *Manual* of the sect, but most of it was obtained from Bishop Phillips himself. I spent a Sunday at the Adam Street Church in Mobile as the guest of the bishop.

[66] The group has no literature that can be trusted. My information was gathered through observation and inquiry at the church in Augusta, Georgia.

[67] Within a few rods of the House of Prayer in Augusta there is a House of Faith, which split off from the larger body and set up for itself.

tionally starved, and nervously unstable Negroes drawn from all other sects and from the general population.

The House of Prayer is theologically as chaotic as the other small Negro sects. The only element of which it seems to be certain is the charismatic principle, the direct operation of the Holy Spirit through "gifts." Perhaps its psychology and practices may best be set forth by describing a quite ordinary meeting of the group, held in midweek and in the absence of Bishop Grace.[68] The church was a large, barnlike structure of the "tabernacle" type, a flimsy wooden frame covered with tarred building paper. There was no floor, sawdust being liberally sprinkled on the ground. On the occasion mentioned it was packed with Negroes from the lower cultural level. Considerable opposition had been aroused in the city by the frenzies indulged in at the House of Prayer, and there had been agitation for suppressing the sect as a public nuisance or menace to the safety of the community. The preacher adroitly used this situation to create a "martyr psychology," quoting Scripture pertaining to the persecution and suffering of the saints, drawing an exact parallel between the despised early Christians and his hearers, and definitely comparing Bishop Grace to Jesus and Paul. On either side of the preacher several female saints, robed in white as a sign that they had "got the blessing" or "come through," stood rigidly at attention, these guardians being changed from time to time as those on duty became weary. Many saints, similarly attired, occupied the front benches.

The motor automatisms which appeared when the right atmosphere had been created and inhibitions broken down seemed to follow a definite routine. On the first appearance of the seizure the body of the victim swayed rhythmically, the eyes were closed or uplifted, and inarticulate mutterings akin to an unknown tongue were heard. In the next stage the subject fell prone on the ground, where he lay in a state of trance or coma for a considerable period. The worshipers paid no attention whatever to persons in this condition but stepped over them or even pushed them aside with the foot. The third stage was characterized by the jerks. Twitchings appeared in the prone body of the stricken individual, and increased in intensity until the jerking body bounded about on the ground like a ball. Consciousness, or a semiconsciousness, returned, and the victim struggled to his feet. The jerks continued to increase in severity; the head whipped forward or backward or from side to side, and at times the body was bent double by a sudden paroxysm. Nothing in the descriptions of the strange seizures in the Kentucky wilderness surpassed the experiences of these jerking people. Still the worshipers gave no special heed to the sufferers. The fourth or final stage was a wild dance, which gradually emerged and

---

[68] I was present as a sort of guest of honor at the meeting, was given every facility of observation, and took copious notes on the whole proceedings.

eliminated the jerks. Then for the first time the attention of the leaders was attracted. A song was "lifted" and a circle of hand-clapping, laughing, ejaculating saints surrounded the dancer. At last the dance ended in a state of near collapse; the individual had received the "power," and if the convert was a woman she was robed in white and took her place among the blessed.

FATHER DIVINE'S PEACE MISSION is unique. In Harlem, in New York, and Philadelphia an insignificant-looking little brown man reigns as God Almighty over a multitude of black "angels," with a liberal mixture of white ones, variously estimated from 1,000 to 21,000,000 in number. The movement can scarcely be called a sect. It lacks organization and has no intelligible doctrines. It is a chaotic surge of unthinking and superstitious people about a sensational leader. Father Divine has attracted wide attention and the many newspaper items about him render unnecessary a detailed description of his peculiar enterprise. He has been called an "incredible Messiah" and his movement regarded as most extraordinary. But as a matter of fact he differs little from many other self-acclaimed messiahs who have risen among colored people, several of whom have already been mentioned. Father Divine has the advantages of working in the center of the nation's largest Negro settlement and having attracted the interest of New York's great newspapers.

The visitor to Father Divine's chief "heaven" or "kingdom," in Harlem, sees on a somewhat larger scale what he might see in the centers of independent Negro cults elsewhere, with the addition of two large dining rooms. Photographs of the leader are prominently displayed. There is the customary run-down appearance and third-rate atmosphere. In the various rooms devotees are at all times found, and the greetings of "Peace" and the ejaculations "Thank you, Father," and "It's wonderful" are heard everywhere. There are a hundred tinseled signs, among which one reads: "Father Divine Is God," "Father Divine, God Almighty," "Father Divine Is the Messiah," "Father Divine Is the Only Redemption for Man," "Father Divine Is King of Kings and Lord of Lords," and similar sentiments. In this "kingdom" there are two dining rooms and an auditorium. One may secure a cheap meal or dine free in "Father's Banquet Hall."

This prophet cultivates an air of secrecy. He is openly called "God," but when pressed on his supernatural status, he will neither affirm nor deny. Large sums of money are spent on lavish banquets, his numerous "heavens" or "extensions," the great motor busses which transport his people, the "Promised Land," an estate of four farms in Ulster County, New York, and the large legal and secretarial staff maintained. The source of this wealth is something of a mystery. Divine says it comes from "the abundance of the fullness" to which he has access, his angels declare it comes from

Father Divine, who owns all things, but courts and investigators assert that it comes from the people who turn their earnings over to the leader.

Even the prophet's name and origin are in doubt. Father Divine refuses to divulge when or where he was first "combusted on the Earth plane," or any other information about his antecedents. But the most reliable information obtainable makes it fairly certain that his real name is George Baker and that he was born of Gullah slave parents on Hutchinson's Island, near Savannah, about 1878.[69] During his childhood more than one so-called messiah arose among the Negroes of South Georgia, and Baker became familiar with, and a believer in, this phenomenon. In Savannah he announced himself as the "Son of Righteousness" and opened a mission, but soon found himself in the county chain gang, doing a six-month sentence. Later he went to Charleston, but when news of his career reached that city he proceeded to Baltimore.[70] Here, about 1906, he worked as a gardener until he fell in with a colored preacher called "Father Jehovah" (his real name was Samuel Morris), who taught doctrines not dissimilar to modern New Thought. Baker then became the "Messenger," and went to Valdosta, Georgia, where he was tried for insanity because of his divine pretensions, but was freed on condition that he leave the state.

In Harlem the "Messenger" attached himself to John Hickerson, a cultist known as Bishop St. John the Divine, and a picturesque convert known as "Steamboat Bill." From Hickerson, and the various religious isms that abound in the black belt of New York, Baker learned the doctrine of "the God within," a mixture of Christian Science, New Thought, Theosophy, Spiritualism, and plain foolishness. He moved to Brooklyn, set up a communal religious house on Prince Street, and assumed the name of Major Morgan J. Devine, later changing the spelling to the more significant "Divine."

About 1919 he transferred his community to Sayville, Long Island, where he purchased a house and set up an employment agency. The combination of communal living, offers of help and employment, abundant food, and a joyous religion, attracted visitors in large numbers. By 1931 the place had become something of a nuisance to Sayville residents; legal action was taken, and Divine found himself in jail. At the trial it was elicited that many followers even then regarded the little Negro as a divinity and credited him with miracles. The court found that his real name was Baker, that he induced his disciples to transfer property to him,

[69] There are two books on Father Divine, both more or less uncritical: *God in a Rolls-Royce, the Rise of Father Divine, Madman, Menace, or Messiah*, by John Hoshor, and *The Incredible Messiah, the Deification of Father Divine*, by Robert Allerton Parker.

[70] See Parker, *op. cit.*, ch. iv.

that the woman with whom he lived was not his wife, and that he was an immoral man and a menace to society.

Divine was fined $500 and sentenced to a year in jail. "That jedge can't live long now. He's offended Almighty God," a disciple allegedly declared. Three days later the judge died suddenly of heart failure, and from his cell Divine is said to have remarked, "I hated to do it!" Whereupon he became a real God to his adherents.[71]

This strange man is actually worshiped as a divine being by multitudes of people, as I can personally testify, and he accepts this adoration as his right. He maintains several "heavens" in the metropolitan area of New York, and his movement has spread to the Pacific Coast, England, Canada, and elsewhere. He entered politics on a Righteous Government Platform, which had some strange planks; it would censor the press, abolish labor unions, establish racial equality, forbid life insurance, abolish "hello" and substitute "peace," and compel doctors to guarantee cures and be liable for the deaths of all patients. His political influence has been courted by city and national political machines, and candidates for mayor have visited his meetings and fraternized with him. He invited the president of the United States to attend his political convention and urged the pope to support his platform. "Unless the officials co-operate with me, I will move them out of office," he once declared. "I have around twenty million with me." In July, 1935, a London newspaper announced that Father Divine planned to enter the White House, to which a follower commented that "the spirit and mind of Father Divine will reach the White House." [72]

Father Divine was investigated and haled into court on several occasions, but no conviction was secured after the Sayville incident. Many cases concerned the effect of his teachings on his followers. In obedience to his "celestial life" teachings, and his taboo on sex relations, homes were broken up and children neglected or abandoned. In such cases the courts diligently tried to discover whether he actually claimed to be God, his responsibility for debts and judgments against his followers and his "heavens," and the source of his income. But he evaded all questions or obscured his meaning under a mass of words. He testified that millions called him "God," but would neither affirm nor deny on his own account. Sworn evidence was offered to show that he took the earnings of his disciples, profits from various "peace" business enterprises, and the free labor of those who had no funds. "I have money without limit," he declared, "because my money comes from God. When I spend a dime I make a dollar, when I spend a dollar I

[71] Hoshor, *op. cit.*, pp. 84-86. A follower told me that if the "God" should be placed in jail again rain would fall until he was released and New York would be washed away if his detention continued.

[72] Parker, *op. cit.*, p. 261.

make a hundred dollars, and when I spend a hundred dollars I make a thousand dollars, and when I spend a thousand I make a million." At the Sayville trial he had $7,000 in cash on his person.[73]

On the other hand he said he owned nothing. He kept no records of any kind, either of finances or membership. He paid no taxes. No property was held in his name. He had no bank account. Judgments against him could not be collected.[74] His legal difficulties became so involved, however, that he moved to Philadelphia, out of the jurisdiction of the New York courts, and returned to the metropolis only on Sundays, when writs could not be served on him. One of his recent sensational escapades was his marriage to a young white girl.

Some of the Divine followers were not so successful before the courts, however. In June, 1937, John Wuest Hunt, the "Revelator," "Mary Magdalene" Gardner, and "Peaceful Martha" Peters went on trial in the federal court at Los Angeles on charges of transporting "Delight" Jewett, seventeen-year-old schoolgirl, from Denver to California for immoral purposes. The girl testified that she was seduced on several occasions by Hunt, who persuaded her that she was a modern Virgin Mary and would become the mother of the "New Redeemer" by immaculate conception. The women defendants refused to affirm or deny that they regarded Father Divine as God, but the Gardner woman admitted that Hunt "was entitled to the name Christ." When Hunt was sentenced to prison, he was comforted by Father Divine's assurance that his term might have been longer.[75]

There have been evidences of good results ensuing from Father Divine's teachings, however. He frowns on all physical contact between the sexes and presumably insists on continence. A young woman detective, assigned to his household as a follower by a district attorney, failed to tempt him, and discovered no irregularities in his relations with his female saints.[76]

Many debased and notorious characters have been reformed and are now among the "angels." Businessmen have reported the payment of debts long considered uncollectible when the debtors came under Divine's influence. One disciple, Famaca Real, is reported to have addressed all shopkeepers of Pittsfield, Massachusetts, asking to be put in touch with "Sezar." She had once made a purchase on credit from a Pittsfield merchant whose name had been forgotten, and she was endeavoring to follow God's advice to "pay to Sezar what belongs to Sezar, and to God what belongs to God." [77]

[73] Hoshor, *op. cit.*, pp. 92, 93.

[74] Parker, *op. cit.*, ch. ix, on "Celestial Finance," reviews the facts and explains his sly business methods and the source of his wealth. See also the chapter on "Legal Conflicts."

[75] See Associated Press stories, June 24, 1937, *et seq.*

[76] Hoshor, *op. cit.*, pp. 58-64.

[77] *Time*, August 9, 1937, p. 30.

The NATIONAL DAVID SPIRITUAL TEMPLE OF CHRIST CHURCH UNION is a Negro Pentecostal body which was organized at Kansas City, Missouri, in 1932 by David William Short, its bishop and national president. It rejects the designation of "denomination" because it claims that it originated on the day of Pentecost.[78] It is thoroughly charismatic in character and claims the gifts of tongues, interpretation of tongues, healing, miracles, and prophecy. It does not claim that no one has the Spirit of Christ who does not also experience the gift of tongues and other enduements, but does insist that "a full and complete baptism of the Holy Ghost as poured out on the day of Pentecost" is always accompanied by the gift of tongues or some of the other powers.[79] This sect claimed thirty churches and fifteen thousand members in 1944.

The LATTER HOUSE OF THE LORD FOR ALL PEOPLE AND THE CHURCH ON THE MOUNTAIN, APOSTOLIC FAITH, is the double name of one sect, a Negro body, founded in 1936 by its bishop, L. W. Williams, a former Baptist pastor, at Cincinnati, following a spiritual blessing and enlightenment which he received while at prayer. It is a typical Negro Pentecostal body, but it is hardly possible to derive any logical meaning from its incoherent printed statements. The 1936 census reported only six churches, two of which had twenty-nine members, but Bishop Williams, in 1947, claimed four thousand members in several states.[80]

The SOUGHT OUT CHURCH OF GOD IN CHRIST AND SPIRITUAL HOUSE OF PRAYER, INCORPORATED, is a Negro holiness sect of the charismatic type, established early in 1947 at Brunswick, Georgia, by "Mother" Mozella Cook. The foundress was converted in a "yard service" by her mother, a holiness enthusiast who was "often absent from this world while she talked with God," and was once examined by a court on a lunacy charge. "Mother" Cook became a Baptist in Brunswick, but became a member of the Church of God in Christ at Pittsburgh, Pennsylvania, where she claims she was divinely called and sent out to organize the true church. Her chapel is a refurnished garage in her yard in Brunswick, and she has organized three other groups with a total membership of about sixty persons. The group displays the emotionalism common to its type, and has no distinctive doctrines other than the holiness and pentecostal position.[81]

TRIUMPH THE CHURCH AND KINGDOM OF GOD IN CHRIST is a Negro sect with headquarters at Birmingham, Alabama. Its status is uncertain; the census of 1936 mentioned only two churches and sixty-nine members

---

[78] Letter from Bishop Short, August 5, 1947. See also *Census of Religious Bodies*, 1936, II, 1259-60.

[79] *The Orthodox Christian Spiritual Canon Creed and Doctrines*, p. 11.

[80] Communication from the bishop, May 18, 1947. Among the published statements are *Jesus Is Coming Soon; Decree and Doctrine and Historical Record*.

[81] This sect was investigated for me by Mrs. Leland Moore.

but its own *1947 Year Book* lists an imposing array of ministers, with seven bishops in charge of that many districts, but gives no statistics of congregations or membership.

The sect resulted from a divine revelation to "Father" E. D. Smith in 1897, though it was not "speeded to the earth" until 1902, and "opened to the world" until 1904. Its founder seems to have been in charge until 1920, when "he went to Addis Abbaba Absenia, Africa, and never returned," and since that date there have been several "chiefs." It regards itself as somewhat unique among religious bodies, as the following extract from its catechism indicates:

Q. Was there another Church in the earth before Triumph?
A. Yes. Church Militant.

Q. Is there any difference between the Triumph Church and Church Militant?
A. Yes. Church Militant is a Church of warfare, and Triumph is a Church of Peace.

Q. What happened to Church Militant when Triumph was revealed?
A. God turned it upside down and emptied His Spirit into Triumph.

Q. Is Triumph just a Church only?
A. No. It has a Kingdom with it.[82]

This sect is a typical Negro holiness body of the second-blessing type. It stresses the second coming of Christ and "the baptism by fire."

Other Charismatic Bodies. Without attempting to exhaust the list of such groups, two or three other Negro sects should be mentioned.

The HOUSE OF GOD, THE HOLY CHURCH OF THE LIVING GOD, THE PILLAR AND GROUNDS OF THE TRUTH, HOUSE OF PRAYER FOR ALL PEOPLE is not to be confused with the Churches of the Living God and Bishop Grace's House of Prayer previously mentioned. It "traces its origin to Abyssinia," though it was organized by Bishop R. A. R. Johnson, in 1914, at Washington, D. C. It has only four or five churches and around two hundred members. The sect's doctrines include "twenty-four principles which were revealed to Bishop Johnson by the inspiration of God," though they are by no means unique. Among them are immersion, washing of feet, eligibility of women for the ministry, equality of the races in the church, and sanctification.

The HOUSE OF THE LORD was founded in 1925 by Bishop W. H. Johnson at Detroit, Michigan, where it has headquarters, and has several congregations with a total membership of three or four hundred. Among its articles

[82] *Junior Guide and Easy Lessons* (combined) *of Triumph the Church and Kingdom of God in Christ,* p. 15.

of faith are some unusual principles: Members cannot work at jobs involving liquor, tobacco, or "policy rackets," and neither can they be "bell hops." Women must dress in plain and modest fashion and should be subject to their husbands and to the elders of the church. Members may "eat anything that is sold in the market," but they may not become members of secret societies, participate in war, carry life insurance, unless it is required by an employer, attend theaters, ball games, dances, horse races, or similar places of amusement, nor can they "go pleasure riding or play cards." The "saints should not marry anyone who is not baptized with the Holy Ghost." This baptism is attested by the gift of tongues. "When an individual is born of God he cannot sin as he is a perfect man," but "he is not sanctified if he owns houses, lands, and goods." [83]

CHRIST'S SANCTIFIED HOLY CHURCH, COLORED, arose from the preaching of white holiness evangelists among the members of the Colored Methodist Church at West Lake, Louisiana, in 1903. The believers formed a separate sect the following year, and since that time about thirty churches have been formed and these have a total membership of around seven hundred. The only distinguishing mark of the body is its belief in sanctification and spirit baptism.

The PURGATORIAL SOCIETY is a very peculiar movement started in 1931 by Mrs. Luci Mayer Barrow of Brooklyn, New York, who declared herself a member of the Purgatorial Society of that city. In a somewhat incoherent "revelation," filled with irrevelant scriptural references, she boldly announced that she was prepared to take charge of the world's affairs as the Lord's anointed. She proposed to move the royal family of Great Britain to Canada and install the returning Jesus in Buckingham Palace. John the Baptist is to be born again, under the sponsorship of a committee which included two United States senators, who were named. The pope will be brought to the United States to occupy the capitol at Washington and summon a world-wide conclave of the churches. The Jews will at last come into their own, since Mrs. Barrow and her husband will collect all the money in the world and turn it over to them. The good woman herself will be president of the United States, her husband will be the speaker of the House of Representatives, and a certain Jewish rabbi of Kansas City will be vice-president and "king of the world." These interesting changes in the body politic are only a few of the important events which are to transpire when this revelation has been translated into actuality.[84]

Latter-day Saints or Mormons. These are the followers of Joseph Smith, who received his revelations near Palmyra, New York, during 1820-29.

---

[83] *Census of Religious Bodies*, 1936, II, 1253.

[84] This revelation is contained in a folder *Warning Information*. It is utterly incoherent, and correspondence with Mrs. Barrow failed to throw light on its real meaning.

These revelations were engraved on certain golden plates buried in a hill called Cumorah, and their location was pointed out to Smith by the angel Moroni. With these plates Smith found some spectacles called Urim and Thummim, by the use of which he was able to translate the inscriptions. This he did while sitting behind a curtain and dictating the translation to five persons. It was published as the *Book of Mormon*, which the Latter-day Saints accept as divinely inspired and possessing authority equal to that of the Bible. The plates disappeared after they had been translated, but sworn statements were produced from several persons who claimed to have seen them.

The *Book of Mormon* contains a history of early America. It declares that this continent was settled by the "Jaredites," who were dispersed by the confusion of tongues at the Tower of Babel. On one occasion Jesus Christ visited this country. The American Indians are the descendants of Hebrews who came from Jerusalem about 600 B.C.

The early Mormons established colonies in Ohio and Missouri and at Nauvoo, Illinois, but in each case they were driven out by hostile people. Smith was killed at Carthage, Illinois, on June 27, 1844, while in jail awaiting trial for treason. Much of the hostility to them was the result of their practice of polygamy. Smith realized this in 1843, but he had begun taking plural wives seven years earlier; before his death he married, or "sealed," forty-nine women, according to the most authentic list.

After Smith's death Brigham Young led the Mormons to what is now Utah and established the State of Deseret and its capital Zion—Salt Lake City. Polygamy and resistance to federal authority brought about an armed conflict and the "sealing" of plural wives was abandoned in 1890, not because the Mormons gave up the doctrine, but because it was prohibited by law. It continued in an underground way, however, and as late as 1944 a group of Mormon "fundamentalists" were convicted and sentenced for the practice.

Mormon theology simply adds the revelations of Joseph Smith and the inspiration of the *Book of Mormon* to a fundamentalist type of Protestantism. The doctrines include baptism by immersion, speaking with tongues, and the imminent second coming of Christ. There are two orders of priesthood, the Aaronic and that of Melchizedek. The leadership of the church is vested in a president and two counselors.

The Mormons have split into six sects:

THE CHURCH OF JESUS CHRIST OF LATTER-DAY SAINTS is the Utah body and the largest group. It has around 2,000 congregations and 900,000 members, mainly in Utah and Idaho.

THE REORGANIZED CHURCH OF JESUS CHRIST OF LATTER-DAY SAINTS has headquarters at Independence, Missouri, and claims approximately

600 churches and 115,000 members. It repudiates polygamy and denies that the practice was ever endorsed or indulged in by the Mormon founder. This group claims to be the true successor of the original body, and it secured a court ruling to that effect in 1894.

THE CHURCH OF CHRIST (TEMPLE LOT) represents the continuation of a group of Mormons at Bloomington, Illinois, which remained independent after Smith's death. As the result of a revelation from God, members of this group in 1867 purchased a lot at Independence, Missouri, on which to erect a temple and set up the New Jerusalem. The Reorganized Church later won possession of the lot, but this church still claims it and believes that it has the responsibility of building a temple thereon. It claims around fifty churches and two thousand adherents.

THE CHURCH OF JESUS CHRIST (BICKERTONITES) was organized at Greenock, Pennsylvania, in 1862. The founder was William Bickerton, who left the Utah church ten years earlier as a protest against Brigham Young's practice of polygamy. There are thirty churches and about fifteen hundred members of this sect.

THE CHURCH OF JESUS CHRIST (CUTLERITES) resulted from a revelation given to Alpheus Cutler, one of Smith's elders, in Fremont County, Iowa, in 1853. It has but two or three churches and two dozen members and practices community of property.

THE CHURCH OF JESUS CHRIST (STRANGITES) declares that it is the only true Mormon church, and that its founder, James J. Strang, was designated as Smith's successor by divine revelations made to both Smith and himself. Strang claimed that he, like Smith, had received certain "plates of Laban" with the miraculous spectacles which enabled him to translate them. He established his church at Burlington, Wisconsin, soon after the death of the prophet.[85]

---

[85] There is a mass of literature on the Mormons. The *Book of Mormon* and *The Doctrines and Covenants* are the original sources of its doctrines. See also Roberts, *Comprehensive History of the Church of Jesus Christ of Latter-day Saints*, Vols. I-VI; Smith, *History of the Church of Jesus Christ of Latter-day Saints*; Riley, *The Founder of Mormonism*; Brodie, *No Man Knows My History*.

CHAPTER V

COMMUNISTIC SECTS

THE PREVIOUS DISCUSSION HAS SHOWN THE DIFFICULTY OF CLOSELY CLASSI-
fying religious sects, and the large degree of overlapping that must be taken
into account in any attempt at systematic grouping. In this chapter certain
groups are discussed which might with reason be included among the perfectionists; a philosophy of perfectionism constitutes their real basis, though
none of them have clearly stated this in their theology, and some may even
not clearly recognize it. Communistic experiments historically spring from,
and logically imply, a doctrine of the perfectibility of human nature when
unhindered by adverse environmental conditions. There is thus an affinity
between perfectionist, communistic, and charismatic groups which the
sects themselves do not always recognize and may even deny.

It should be pointed out that the term "communistic," as here used, has
no reference to the political theory which the Union of Soviet Socialist Re-
publics, under the hegemony of Moscow, is attempting to apply in national
affairs. Nor does it necessarily include the abolition of private property
and the adoption of absolute community of goods, though most of the
sects to be discussed have attempted this in some form and at some time.
By the term is meant only the groups which, for whatever reason, have withdrawn more or less from the society about them into colonies, where they
have set up their peculiar principles as the rules of conduct for the group.
There have been multitudes of such colonies; they are indeed encountered in
almost every period of history.

The religious element has been the leading feature in most of these colonies, though it has not been universal among them. None have been able long
to survive, but those of a distinctly religious nature have shown by far the
greater vitality. A few American communities are still maintaining a struggling existence, but these are either at the point of death or have abandoned
their communistic principles. Taylor enumerates the reasons for their decline as follows: (1) Their failure to solve the problem of the family; (2)
the surrender of liberty involved; (3) the inability to hold the young peo-

ple; (4) the neglect of man's desire for culture; (5) the increased idleness, lack of thrift, insufficiency of capital, and inefficiency in its use.[1]

Underlying Ideas. The underlying principle of those groups which have undertaken to build up self-contained colonies of like-minded people is that of the essential perfectibility of human nature. Their ideas are, nevertheless, diametrically opposed to those of the evangelical perfectionists already discussed. The latter proceed from the assumption that human nature is inherently corrupt and totally depraved; perfection is possible only as the nature is totally changed and purged of original sin by the direct agency of God or the Holy Spirit operating through one or more emotional upheavals. Communistic sects, however, deny natural depravity and teach that man is inherently good; human ills are caused not by inbred Sin, with a capital S, but by the environment in which man lives. In a corrected environment man would attain perfection by "living naturally" or following his impulses. Hence the attempts to establish colonies in which ideal conditions will obtain.

While prevalent among the Greeks, and emerging in the Pelagian and other theological controversies from the fifth century onward, this philosophy came to fullest bloom in France before the Revolution. It was set forth by Rousseau in *Émile,* and its economic implications were elaborated in his *Contrat Social,* where he pointed out that the social system is an artificial arrangement and can be altered at any time by the plain people. Morelly, in the *Code de la Nature* (1755), dealt more specifically with those features which had been regarded as the special field of theology. Man is not naturally depraved, but virtuous, he pointed out, depravity being due to imperfect institutions. If, therefore, these institutions are improved man's virtue will immediately assert itself and all will be well. The reforms needed are mainly economic, the leading obstacles to perfection being the fear and hopelessness of poverty and the laziness and selfishness induced by the possession of riches.[2]

Two other considerations have operated in the colonizing adventures of communistic sects. Certain groups have withdrawn to await the millennium and the end of the world, which they conceived to be near at hand. The desire for a better economic order, the search for Christian perfection, and millennial hopes have always shown affinity. The communism of the Jerusalem church in the first century was undoubtedly based on the belief that the world order would soon end, hence capital stock in the form of land might safely be consumed. Elsewhere it has been noted that the early Adventists in America closed up their business affairs as "the day" approached. The Shakers, Rappists, Mormons, and others among the American commu-

[1] See "Communism," in Hastings' *Encyclopedia of Religion and Ethics.*
[2] *Ibid.*

nities were ardent millenarians, as were the various Anabaptist and Mennonite bodies in Europe.

Social pressure has also operated to force groups apart from the common run of their fellows. Along with, and frequently overshadowing, their theological and social ideas, some sects have developed vagrant theories which have proved obnoxious or ridiculous to the society about them. By a well-recognized process of social psychology these have been driven into colonies by the urge for social approval. The sexual practices of Noyes's Perfectionists, the polygamy and peculiar revelations of the Mormons, and the absurd "cellular cosmogony" of Teed's "Koreshanity," to mention examples, incurred ostracism or ridicule which, even more than economic or theological theory, caused the groups concerned to form colonies.

It is a strange anomaly that very many communistic sects which were based on the perfectibility of human nature and the essential goodness of human impulses have run into antinomianism, outraged moral conventions, indulged in sexual and orgiastic excesses, and perished through failure to control and direct the human desires. So true has this been that charges of immorality easily spring up against the colonies even when the suspicions have no foundation in fact. Mormon polygamy, Shaker abstinence, community of women among Noyes's Perfectionists, and the scandalous revelations at the House of David are examples of the violations of conventional customs on the part of the colonists.

This phenomenon is easy to understand. Even aside from notions about human nature, which tend to give free rein to the passions on the one hand, or result in attempts at abnormal suppression on the other hand, communism and other adventures in equality encounter the sexual problem at the threshold of their existence. With the shifting of individual responsibility to the society there emerges the danger that children will be brought into the world so recklessly that the population cannot be supported. Facing this possibility, communists have all been forced to deal with the family as an institution, and various modifications have been proposed: community of women, community of children, celibacy, abstinence, and various free-love ideas.

In his *Republic* Plato, the greatest of the idealizing theorists, encountered this problem and settled it frankly and consistently. There must be community of women, he held, and the family as hitherto known must be abolished. The state must supervise the begetting of children and regulate their number and parentage; the young are social property and must be brought up together in equality and in ignorance of their parentage. Plato anticipated that a surplus population would result and proposed migration and colonization as remedies. Sir Thomas More, in his *Utopia,* was not so drastic, and for that reason his system was more hazy with reference to this primary problem. He did not alter the family, but, aware that too many children would result, proposed that they be distributed more or less equally among households and that emigration take care of the surplus.[3]

Early Communistic Experiments. It is no part of the present purpose to trace in detail the history of communistic theory or practice, but as a background for a study of American colonies it seems advisable to glance at the earlier developments. The doctrine arose among the Greeks, and as early as 1300 B.C. was practiced in Crete, where the citizens were uniformly trained by the state and ate at public tables. Lycurgus established a similar regime in Sparta, where the land, though privately owned, was equally distributed; Plutarch remarked that "no man was at liberty to live as he pleased, the city being like one great camp where all had their stated allowance." Marriage was preserved, though a certain looseness in sexual relations was allowed "in the interest of race-culture." [4]

Among the Jews, members of the well-known sect of Essenes were communistic and lived in scattered wilderness groups throughout Judea; they shared all forms of property, practiced sexual continence, and refused to marry.[5] Their usages, however, were based in a profound pessimism and were intended not as a solution of social difficulties but as a mechanism of escape therefrom. The example of the Essenes may have influenced the Jerusalem Christians to adopt the celebrated communistic scheme described in Acts 4:34-35. The community of goods there adopted, however, was of a limited, temporary, and entirely voluntary nature and affords no argument that the early church inclined in any noticeable degree to communism; it was a signal failure at Jerusalem, as is evidenced by the fact that the other churches in the Empire were soon sending offerings to the Jerusalem saints who had pauperized themselves. The Buddhist monks of the Orient, the Therapeutae of Egypt, and the religious orders of the Roman Catholic Church likewise practiced communism, not, however, as a measure of reform but for purposes of individual spiritual improvement.

The same may be said of the various heretical sects of the Middle Ages

[3] Soviet Russia represents the only attempt to apply a form of communism on a large scale. It is, of course, not pure communism. Here for the first time the experiment is antireligious. Discussion is outside the province of this book, and the adventure is too young for definite conclusions. In the present period of propaganda and counterpropaganda reliable factual data are difficult to secure. On the attitude to religion and its ideas see Spinka, *The Church and the Russian Revolution;* Cooke, *Religion in Russia Under the Soviets;* McCullagh, *The Bolshevik Persecution of Christianity.* Newer works are Bolshakoff, *The Christian Church and the Soviet State;* Anderson, *People, Church, and State in Modern Russia;* Miliukov, *Outlines of Russian Culture* (Part I, "Religion and the Church"); Lauterbach, *These Are the Russians;* Johnson, *Soviet Russia Since the War.*

[4] Ryan, "Communism," in the *Catholic Encyclopedia.*

[5] An account of the practices of the Essenes was written by Philo of Alexandria, which is preserved by Eusebius in his *Apology for the Jews.*

which professed to be following the examples of primitive Christianity. Among these may be mentioned the Circumcelliones of North Africa in the fourth century, the Waldenses, Apostolic Brethren, Catharists, Brothers and Sisters of the Free Spirit, Beghards, and Lollards. More important communistic tendencies appeared among the Taborites, Bohemian radicals of the Hussite Wars. In the city of Tabor everything was held in common and private possession was proclaimed a deadly sin. Some of the Taborites, especially the Adamites, and perhaps also the Nicolaitans, taught community of women. During the stirring period of the Reformation communistic doctrines and practices were not uncommon. The Bohemian Brethren showed early leanings in that direction. The madly fanatical Thomas Münzer, Nicholas Storch, and the Zwickau prophets waged war on the existing order and were accused of practicing antinomian and sexual excesses. Many of the Anabaptists, especially those of Moravia, were outright communists, establishing large households and colonies after what they regarded as the primitive example.[6]

In France the views of Rousseau, Morelly, and others gave rise in 1796 to the conspiracy of Babeuf and the "Sect des Egaux," who preached "real equality, no matter what it costs"; their manifesto declared for the abolition of private ownership in land, which they held, in common with the Physiocrats, to be the source of all wealth, and insisted that "if it is needful, let all civilization perish provided that we obtain real equality." Meetings of the "Equals" were forbidden by Napoleon, whereupon they organized a secret society which boasted seventeen thousand armed members. The agitation ceased when the conspiracy was discovered and Babeuf killed himself.

Saint-Simon and his followers desired the abolition of every form of privilege, especially those of birth and bequests, which were the main sources of inequality. Saint-Simon himself conceded a life interest in private property, but his followers after his death insisted on the socialization of "all instruments of labor, land, and capital," the social fund to be "operated on principles of association by a hierarchy, so that each one will have his task according to his capacity, and wealth according to his work." At one time, it was said, "nearly every well-known thinker in France was a Saint-Simonist."[7]

When Saint-Simon died in 1825 his views were taken up by two of his followers, Bazard and Enfantin. The former soon seceded from the colony that had been established and it was moved by Enfantin to Menilmontant. Vagaries and excesses appeared, a priestess was enthroned, and free love was taught and practiced. In 1832 Enfantin was condemned for promulgating

---

[6] See Kautzsky, *Communism in Central Europe in Time of the Reformation.*
[7] Taylor, *art. cit.*

ideas inimical to the public morality and "Saint-Simonianism was extinguished in a burst of popular laughter."[8]

Charles Fourier (1772-1837) was a dreamer of apocalyptic dreams which bore fruit chiefly in America. Fourier believed time would have a duration of eighty thousand years. He imagined the world as divided into 2,985,984 *phalanges*, the whole ruled by an *Omniarque* from Constantinople. In the phalanges communism would be practiced, the workers would do whatever they chose, laboring, however, under something like military discipline; nationality would disappear and the marriage relation would be a sort of polyandry. As fantastic as the theory of Fourier undoubtedly was, it attracted some powerful intellects and several serious attempts were made to give it practical expression in the United States.

Some American Colonies. The United States has provided the most fertile field for communistic adventures, though it has contributed little or nothing to the theory of communism. "The willingness of a new people to make sociological ventures," and the easy availability of large areas of land have brought about the formation of approximately two hundred colonies of the type being discussed.[9] Most of these possessed no special religious significance, being only economic experiments along the usual communistic lines, and practically all of them passed away without leaving anything of permanent value. Only a few can be mentioned in the present discussion, which must be confined to the colonies of a distinctly religious nature.

One such community, very short-lived, was established quite early in Pennsylvania and known as the Woman in the Wilderness. Johann Conrad Beissel sought this group, but finding it no longer in existence this German pietist, after first joining the Dunkers, established his famous Ephrata colony on the banks of a creek at the present town of Ephrata. In 1733 buildings were erected to accommodate the considerable numbers who joined him; several of these are still standing, occupied by the remnants of the colony, affiliated now with the Seventh-Day Baptists (German). Perfection was the goal of this colony. Voluntary celibacy was the rule; married persons were received, but required to live apart. Brothers and sisters occupied separate buildings, living in tiny cells and undergoing a rigorous discipline. The doors were very narrow, to remind the inhabitants that "straight and narrow is the way that leads to eternal life," and very low, that those passing through must "bow the head in humility."

For many years the holding of private property by individuals was regarded as sinful, though this feature was eliminated about 1786. A regular monastic rule of life was adopted, the saints were called by monastic names,

[8] *Ibid.*; Booth, *St. Simon and St. Simonism.*
[9] For histories of these colonies see Hinds, *American Communities*; Noyes, *History of American Socialisms*; Nordhoff, *The Communistic Societies of the United States*; Hilquitt, *History of Socialism in the United States.*

and such observances as trine immersion, laying on of hands, washing of feet, and love feasts were celebrated. Saturday was kept as the Sabbath. The colony at its largest size numbered about three hundred persons, who refused to take oaths, bear arms, or take part in any features of the social life about them.[10]

On Zion Hill, near Ephrata, was founded an allied community known as the Zionitic Brotherhood, or Zionites, under the leadership of the Eckerling brothers. This group, with which Beissel was also connected, though not in harmony with their extreme views, indulged in mysterious and magical initiatory and perfecting rites designed to render the elect as pure in body and morals as was Adam before "the fall." [11]

About 1725 one Matthias Bauman, an immigrant from the Rhine Palatinate, established at Oley, in eastern Pennsylvania, his colony of "Newborns" or Baumanites. The leader was an ignorant individual given to visions, by means of which he had secured the gift of prophecy. Through a new birth Bauman and his followers attained sinlessness, in which state they dispensed with the Bible, sacraments, prayer, the ministry, worship, and marriage. It was a typical antinomian group and the extremes to which the devotees carried their doctrines brought upon them the stern opposition of their neighbors and the colony existed but a short time.[12]

George Rapp came from Württemberg in 1803 with a number of followers and settled on a tract of land in Butler County, Pennsylvania, calling the colony Harmony. Goods were held in common and marriage was abolished. In 1818 all records of contributions were burned, and the members renounced their claims on the property in case of withdrawal. The group moved to New Harmony, Posey County, Indiana, in 1814, but sold their holdings to the irreligious communist, Robert Owen, in 1824, and moved to Economy, Pennsylvania, where the organization was continued through various internal dissensions and vicissitudes until 1903. Salvation and perfection were the goals of the Harmonists. They taught a peculiar doctrine not unlike that of the Shakers. Adam was created androgynous and fell when God separated the female part from him. Christ was a dual being, and in the perfect and renewed world man will be restored to the original dual condition. As was true of the Ephrata, Zionist, and Newborn groups, the Harmonists believed that the return of Christ and the end of the world order were at hand.[13]

[10] See Gaddis, *Christian Perfectionism in America,* manuscript in the library of the University of Chicago, pp. 185-87; Sachse, *The German Sectarians of Pennsylvania; Critical and Legendary History of the Ephrata Cloister and the Dunkers;* Zerfass, *Souvenir Book of the Ephrata Cloister.*

[11] Gaddis, *op. cit.,* pp. 186-87.

[12] *Ibid.,* p. 187.

[13] Williams, *The Harmony Society;* Lockwood, *New Harmony Communities;* Bole, *The Harmony Society.*

Another German colony was founded by Joseph Baumler, who settled with a company of emigrants at Zoar, Tuscarawas County, Ohio, in 1817-19. They were known as Separatists and by 1832 numbered 500 persons; there were 222 in the colony when it disbanded in 1898. The Separatists of Zoar early discouraged marriage, but adopted it at a later date. They had no ceremonies and rejected all ecclesiastical connections, refused to uncover the head, bend the knee, or employ any words of courtesy in address, holding that all such honors belong to God alone. Members were of two classes, minors and those who had not signed the full covenant, and full members who gave up all property forever and covenanted to obey the trustees in all things. In the early period all children were under the care of the trustees as community wards but later were left with their parents.[14]

From 1861-96 there existed in Massachusetts, first at Athal and later at Petersham, a Millerite adventist communistic colony known as the Adonai Shomo ("the Lord is here"). The group never had more than 25 or 30 members; they lived in one house and owned 840 acres of land. It was founded by Frederick I. Howland, a Quaker who had been converted by the adventist prophet William Miller. Howland and his followers practiced communism in preparation for the imminent end of the world, observed the seventh day as their Sabbath, and believed that they and all true followers of Christ had already begun the eternal life. This peculiar sect declined as its members died and new recruits failed to materialize until in 1896, one member remaining, the charter was annulled and the property sold.[15]

The groups mentioned will serve to illustrate the general type of religious communities which have flourished in America. French theories were responsible for many colonies, though these usually were not religious. The French revolutionary Étienne Cabet drew up a scheme in 1848 to establish a colony on the Red River in Texas, but the plans were frustrated by the yellow fever epidemic. Two years later Cabet came to the United States, and with his followers occupied the Illinois town of Nauvoo, recently evacuated by the Mormons. The colony failed and Cabet himself was expelled. A group of the colonists founded Icaria, in Iowa, which existed amid dissensions, lawsuits, and splits until 1895.[16]

The doctrines of Fourier, despite their fantastic features, attracted the attention of many able minds in America, among them being Horace Greeley, Albert Brisbane, George Ripley, William Henry Channing, C. A. Dana, Nathaniel Hawthorne, and Elizabeth Peabody. The views were

[14] Randall, *The History of the Zoar Society.*
[15] Hinds, *op. cit.*, pp. 403-7.
[16] Shaw, *Icaria, A Chapter in the History of Communism.*

expounded by Brisbane in his *Social Destiny of Man* and by Greeley in the *New York Tribune*. The result was the establishment of about thirty Fourierist Phalanxes, which had an average life of only two and a half years.[17] Among these were the noted Brook Farm, North American Phalanx, Wisconsin Phalanx, Alphadelphia Phalanx, and the Altruist Community. Similar in nature were the Bethel-Aurora Communities in Shelby County, Missouri, Ruskin Commonwealths in Indiana, American Settlers' Co-operative Association at Duke Georgia, and the Woman's Commonwealth, a group of women organized at Belton, Texas, and later moved to Washington, D. C. Thomas Lake Harris, an English spiritualist, in 1851 founded his Mountain Cove Community of Spiritualists in Virginia, on what he believed to be the actual site of the Garden of Eden. This failing, he established the Brotherhood of the New Life at Salem-on-Erie; he ruled there as patriarch, the members being his guests or slaves and required to do his bidding. This collapsed in 1880, whereupon Harris founded another colony at Santa Rosa, California, which broke up in 1900.[18]

The ONEIDA PERFECTIONISTS was the most famous of all American religious communistic communities. The Perfectionists, or Oneida Community, was founded by John Humphrey Noyes, first as the Putney Corporation, at Putney, Vermont, in 1845, and removed to Oneida, New York, two years later on account of adverse public opinion. Noyes, a cousin of President Rutherford B. Hayes, was converted in the wave of revivalism which swept New England under Finney. His strange career can scarcely be understood apart from that revival.

As previously mentioned, Finney's movement was perfectionist in character, though the evangelist himself refused the term on account of the vagaries connected with the current perfectionism. Two groups were especially notable, causing wide scandal and greatly vexing Finney and other sane leaders. These groups were known as the New York and the New Haven Perfectionists; Noyes referred to the former as "wild and barbaric like Esau," and to the latter as "like Jacob, more intellectual and civilized." [19] Finney refers to both groups as "antinomian perfectionists" and refused to be classed among them.

About 1828 one James Latourette, in New York city, announced that he had attained perfection and gathered about him a group of Methodists and others. He taught an extreme doctrine of faith as opposed to "works"

---

[17] Hinds, *op. cit.*, lists all these colonies. See also Hawthorne's *The Blithedale Romance*; Codman, *Brook Farm*; Frothingham, *Life of George Ripley*. A newspaper called the *Phalanx*, later the *Harbinger*, was published at Brook Farm.

[18] McCulley, *The Brotherhood of the New Life and Thomas Lake Harris*.

[19] *Religious Experience of John Humphrey Noyes*, p. 183.

and in this lay the germ of his antinomianism. Fired with an abnormal zeal, the group sought to reproduce the condition which allegedly prevailed in the early church, cultivated "gifts" of various sorts, reported miraculous answers to prayer, and indulged in what they regarded as Pentecostal exercises. The movement spread through the territory "burnt over" by the revival. John B. Foot and the Annesley sisters organized a group at Albany, and a perfectionist colony grew up at Delphi in central New York. These groups disrupted the churches throughout the whole territory and gloried in their divisive influence.[20]

The New Haven group were saner, though they later fused with the New York party and the whole antinomian movement became one. In 1834 a monthly periodical called the *Perfectionist* was established at New Haven, with one Bayle, a former Free Church pastor expelled for embracing holiness views, as editor and Noyes as associate; the paper continued for two years and was a powerful influence in spreading the propaganda over the revival area and in consolidating the groups.

These perfectionists were strong individualists, as are all holiness people, and relied strongly upon "spirit guidance." In his *Lectures on Systematic Theology*,[21] Finney cites one of their confessions of faith as teaching that "spirit guidance" is above scripture and theology, true Christians are free from sin and the law, Christ returned at the destruction of Jerusalem in A.D. 70, and then instituted a covenant which made Christians perfect and secured their eternal salvation and "full freedom from written law and human instruction." Such theories blossomed into scandalous excesses. Prayer was abandoned in some places. At Brimfield, Massachusetts, women defied all the conventions in order to prove that "the spirit triumphs over the flesh," but even Noyes admitted that here the contrary turned out to be the case.[22] Here at Brimfield the practice of "bundling" began.[23]

"Spiritual affinity" and "gospel liberty" were talked of, and resulting unions did not reverence existing marital bonds or the principle of monogamy. The house of one Dr. Gridley at Southampton became "the scene of scandalous practices" in the name and under the protection of religion. The perfectionists at New Haven next fell prey to the contagion of "spiritual mating" and sanctified debauchery; and letters from this center to colonies of perfectionists in central New York and elsewhere spread the degradation. Revelations and visions were thought to be received confirming the practices. At Delphi, ascetic notions were strangely grafted on to the spiritual mating theory, and couples were thus joined on a Platonic basis. How-

[20] *Ibid.*, p. 187.
[21] II, 167-69.
[22] Noyes, *op. cit.*, pp. 197, 198.
[23] In the old practice of "bundling," once widespread among the poor of New England, courting couples were put in bed together. The original purpose was to save firewood and candles, but it gave rise to much sexual irregularity. There is a work on the subject, reprints of which are available, Squires, *History of Bundling*.

ever, Noyes indicates that the Platonic modification did not prove to be popular.[24]

All this was perfectionistic antinomianism running amuck; as Gaddis remarks, "Massachusetts perfectionism became little more than a religiously veiled free-lovism." Scandals, hysteria, and fanaticism became rife and opposition naturally increased; the perfectionists reported that God would destroy Brimfield with fire from heaven because of the public indignation aroused by their practices. It all became too much even for Noyes, whose own indulgences were sufficiently unconventional, and

he left the scene of these activities very early one morning in sub-zero weather and did not halt until he had covered the sixty miles to Putney, Vermont, the home of his relatives. He had for the time being given up the New Haven mess, but not the cause of perfectionism.[25]

Noyes was subject to temptations of a sexual nature, and while still a student he organized a band of "Brethren" who met to listen to each other's confessions and mutual criticism. On February 20, 1834, a date celebrated as a spiritual New Year's day by the Perfectionists, Noyes publicly avowed himself as morally perfect, an act which led to the cancellation of his license as a Congregational minister. In his development Noyes became thoroughly antinomian and the doings of himself and his followers scandalized the orthodox. Noyes himself indulged in sexual lapses as well as in tippling, explaining the same as necessary to free him from "the law." He remarked, for example, that during his career in "legal religion" he had practiced temperance, but in his new experience he felt impelled "to assert practically my liberty from the rules of my old bondage." Therefore, "I drank ardent spirits, that I might reprove the spirit of legality which still hovered about me, and that I might practically transfer the keeping of my soul from the temperance pledge to the Spirit of God." [26] Concerning sexual relations Noyes said:

The turn which my mind took in regard to sexual morality had much influence on my subsequent course. . . . I did nothing of which I had occasion to be ashamed, but I lost reputation with those who saw only externals. . . . I was loosed from the moorings of ordinary prudence, and set adrift once more with no pilot but God.[27]

In the Oneida Community this antinomianism was reduced to a system. Community of all things (women included), free love or "complex marriage," and the expectation of the approaching end were outstanding features. There was an attempt "to live as angels" and to create in the colony a small section of the kingdom of heaven on earth. Hence there

[24] Gaddis, op. cit., p. 357 n.; for details see Noyes, op. cit., pp. 195-202.
[25] Gaddis, op. cit., p. 357.
[26] Noyes, op. cit., p. 123.
[27] Ibid., pp. 225, 226.

was "no marrying or giving in marriage"; those who had wives were "to be as though they had none." "Love without lust" was the ideal, and no man could have exclusive right to any one woman, and vice versa. "If a man cannot love a woman and be happy in seeing her loved by others, he is a selfish man, and his place is with the potherds of the earth." [28] In order to guard against exclusive attachments on the part of the Perfectionists, old and unattractive persons imparted "first impressions" to the young before the more desirable saints were admitted. Over this "ascending fellowship" or method of imparting sexual "impressions" Noyes was supreme, a fact which his biographer cites as "proof of the strength of a spirit that could afford to 'stoop to conquer.' " [29]

Each man was the husband of every woman and each woman the wife of every man. It was polyandry rather than polygamy, however, since the woman controlled her own love affairs, summoned her wooers and dismissed them at will; "the man must love on in silence until unmistakably summoned." [30] The plan of mutual criticism inaugurated by Noyes in his student days was the instrument of government and discipline.

Public criticism and threatened legal measures forced the Perfectionists to give up the system of "complex marriage" in 1880. On January 1, 1881, the community was dissolved and a joint stock company, with the members as stockholders, took over control of the properties and industries. The business had been well managed and flourishes today in Kenwood, New York, and Niagara Falls, where traps, chains, silk, and the famous Community silverware are manufactured.[31]

The SHAKERS are now nearly extinct. The United Society of Believers, popularly known as the Shakers, one of the two bodies listed as communistic societies by the United States *Census of Religious Bodies*, was sexuocentric in character and made sexual indifference the leading mark of perfection. Mother Ann Lee was an illiterate, neurotic, emotionally unstable, and sexually unbalanced English woman. Joining the "Shaking Quakers" at the age of twenty-two, she entered a nine-year period of mental struggle in which sexual features were prominent. Her friends induced her to marry one Abraham Standley, a blacksmith, and she gave birth to four children, all of whom died in infancy. She roamed the streets carrying on "a war on lust" and reports of irregularities were current; she was finally imprisoned and while in jail passed a crisis and experienced

[28] Eastlake, *The Oneida Community*, p. 35.
[29] *Ibid.*, p. 55; Gaddis, *op. cit.*, p. 366.
[30] Gaddis, *op. cit.*, pp. 366, 367.
[31] There is a voluminous literature on the Oneida experiment. In addition to the works previously cited, see Noyes, *History of American Socialism*; Dixon, *New America* (a hostile criticism); Noyes, *Handbook of the Oneida Community*; and the Oneida periodical, the *Perfectionist* (1843-46), the *Berean* (1847), and the *Circular* (1854-73).

her anointing and revelations. She saw sexual lust as the cause of human depravity and a life of celibacy as the method of redemption and perfection. Furthermore, God's nature is that of sexual duality, and as he had already appeared on the male side of Jesus Christ, he now manifested himself on the female side in Ann Lee. Thus the second coming of Christ occurred in her own illumination, hence the name of the "Millennial Church." [32]

To this day the Shakers accept Mother Ann Lee as a sort of female deity, an effusion or incarnation of the Father-Mother God. While holding many of the tenets of evangelical Christianity, they reject the Atonement, Virgin Birth, and resurrection of the body; they affirm that there are seven heavens, each with its corresponding hell, a probation after death, a hierarchy of gods, Holy Spirits, and angels as well as of heavens, and they set great store by cycles and subcycles of seven in the historical process.

Mother Ann with her husband and seven other followers came to America, directed by divine revelation, in 1774, and two years later a colony was established in the woods of Niskeyuna, now Watervliet, New York. They were persecuted and imprisoned, but threw themselves heartily into all the revival movements of the period and gained considerable numbers. In 1780 Joseph Meacham, a Baptist pastor of New Lebanon, New York, was converted to Shaker principles and was instrumental in establishing the colony at New Lebanon, which now remains as the leading settlement of the sect. Other groups sprang up in the surrounding country and, as a result of the Kentucky revival at the beginning of the nineteenth century, a large Shaker community developed near Hopkinsville; here the group acquired over four thousand acres of fine land on which they erected a hundred buildings of various kinds. This colony endured for more than a hundred years and new buildings were erected as late as 1917. At one time there were 18 such colonies in the country, with probably 5,000 members and property worth $5,000,000. Decline began about 1860 and has continued steadily; there remain today the colony at New Lebanon, three or four other scattered groups, and a membership of less than two hundred.

Community of goods and celibacy were, and are, the outstanding features of Shaker practice. Persons were admitted to the novitiate or outer order and allowed to live in their own families, but in all cases sexual continence was the method of attaining perfection. "We believe," declares

---

[32] Gaddis, *op. cit.*, pp. 219-27; Evans, *Autobiography of a Quaker;* White and Taylor, *Shakerism, Its Meaning and Message;* Schaff-Herog, *op. cit.*, "Communism," and literature there cited. The literature is voluminous; consult McLean, *A Bibliography of Shaker Literature.* On the Freudian and sexual features of the sect see Schroeder, "Shaker Celibacy and Salacity, Psychologically Interpreted," *New York Medical Journal,* June 1, 1921.

one of the latest statements of doctrine, "in a continent, virgin life, in deed, word, and thought. For in no other way can we keep a clean conscience and self-respect, or preserve our hearts pure from adultery and fornication." [33] That the logical consequence must be the destruction of the race gave no concern to the Shakers. The doctrine states:

We believe that the children of God, those who are led by the Spirit of God and are "the children of the resurrection, neither marry nor are given in marriage," and that all who make that compact previous to hearing the call of Christ must forsake it and all the relationships growing out of it.

Further:

We regard it as perfectly normal, legitimate, and righteous, that the natural family on which the world relies for social order and continuance, and which, however good in its place, provides home comforts for only a small circle, and is extremely limited in its benefactions toward that large class whom death, disease, poverty, incapacity, or untoward circumstances have deprived of home, should be dissolved and pass away before the family of Christ, which is the basis of social order in the everlasting kingdom of God.[34]

The AMANA SOCIETY, whose real title is "the Community of True Inspiration," like many other similar groups, is a foreign importation to American soil. Its origins lie in a movement among "the inspired" of Germany. Dissatisfied with contemporary church life, J. F. Rock and J. A. Gruber received the gift of revelation and inspiration about 1714. They attracted followers and established congregations in various parts of Germany, but on account of opposition and persecution the inspirationists emigrated to America in 1842, settling on a tract of land near Buffalo, where the leaders, Christian Metz, Barbara Heinemann, and G. A. Weber, were joined by eight hundred followers between 1843-46. The settlement in New York was known as the Ebenezer Society and consisted of four villages. In 1854 the group removed to Iowa, where the town of Amana was laid out; within about eight years six other villages, West, South, High, East, and Middle Amana and Homestead, were founded and here the society has continued to the present day.

[33] Hollister, *Synopsis of Doctrine Taught by Believers in Christ's Second Appearing*, art. 9.

[34] *Ibid.*, art. 10 and note. This group is not alone in thus seeking the elimination of the race. E. H. Roberts, M.D., of Corsicana, Texas, president of the Church of Jesus of Nazareth, Inc., thus expressed himself in a letter to me under date of April 27, 1928: "By sending and carrying the gospel to every part of the globe, we hasten the return of Christ and thereby cut off hatred, selfishness, divorce, murder, theft, all manner of disease, prevent the birth of untold generations who would be born, reared, be hellhounds, die, and be in torment. Look at all the damnable things I could prevent and the souls I could keep out of hell by their not being born, not because I have done anything to carnally prevent conception, but by fulfilling Christ's mission, he returns and then no more souls born for hell and all the wretchedness that is becoming more rampant."

The society is communistic and wholly religious. Its fundamental principle is that "God can now as well as of old inspire men to declare his word and will, and thus act as messengers of divine teaching to the world." But since the death of Barbara Heinemann (1884) no member has been inspired with the gift of prophecy. Unlike many recipients of special outpourings of the Holy Spirit or inspiration these persons seem never to have engaged in unusual orgiastic or emotional exercises. They have no ministry and their religious services consist mainly of prayer, testimony, and reading from the writings of the inspired. They do not practice baptism, but wash each other's feet and observe the Lord's supper solemnly on biennial occasions. Young people are confirmed at about fifteen years of age. Marriage is permitted, but those who marry suffer a temporary loss of standing. Members will not take oaths or bear arms; they eschew all amusements, and commonly dress in the clothing of the ordinary German peasantry.

The Amana saints are divided into three classes: young people and probationers, those further advanced in the faith, and full members who have proved their loyalty to inspirationist principles through many years of faithfulness. There are seven congregations or churches in the seven villages of the Amana group, and the membership, which is slowly declining, is about thirteen hundred. Adherents may depart at will or be expelled, in which cases they receive back what they placed in the community fund. Orphans are wards of the society.[35]

The CHURCH TRIUMPHANT is a communistic society with a peculiar philosophic and religious basis. The original group was formed at Chicago in 1886 by Cyrus R. Teed. In 1903 the founder moved his followers to Lee County, Florida, where the town of Estero was established and where the group still exists. The sect claims five thousand adherents.

Teed claimed to have undergone a special spiritual illumination in 1870, receiving by revelation the set of tenets which he denominated "Koreshanity," from Koresh, the Hebrew form of the founder's name, Cyrus. Teed thereafter called himself Koresh. He apparently had acquired a smattering of the Americanized Hinduism taught in Chicago by the Bahais, Vedantists, and similar groups following the World's Parliament of Religions at the Chicago World's Fair. On the religious side his system embraced the principle of reincarnation; men attain eternal life or the final resurrection through a series of re-embodiments under various forms of life.

In true sectarian style, the other churches and contemporary religion

[35] *A Brief History of the Amana Society or Community of True Inspiration;* Shaw, *Life in the Amana Society,* in the *Chautauquan,* VIII (1888), pp. 300 ff.; Ely, *Amana, A Study of Religious Communism,* in *Harper's Magazine,* CV (1902), pp. 659 ff.

are depicted as degenerate; both church and state are to be destroyed preparatory to the emerging of a new *religiare,* or "new heaven and new earth." The second coming of Christ is near at hand, this being pronounced by Koresh "from the authority vested in us and under the light of divine illumination." Koresh claimed to have discovered the "philosophers' stone," and alchemy is a part of Koreshan doctrine. Astrology is also taught.

Koreshanity utterly repudiates the Copernican astronomy and other features of modern science and has its own scientific system. Its central idea is "the cellular cosmogony," allegedly revealed to Koresh in 1870. The convex shape of the earth's surface, the movement of the earth around the sun, the existence of other planets beyond our universe, and other commonly accepted facts are all denied. Koreshanity insists that the earth's surface is concave; this world is not a solid sphere with humanity living on the outside, but a hollow ball, eight thousand miles in diameter, with men living on the inside. Instead of *bending down* at the horizon the surface really *bends up.* What we know as sun, moon, and stars are not beyond or outside the earth, but are inside it. The direct route to China is not down through the earth but straight up through the air. What we know as the earth's surface, its oceans and continents, is spread over the inside wall of the hollow ball, which is really the earth. Moving about within the ball are seven mercury discs, the planets of our solar system, and the reflections from these discs make what we call the stars. "The planets seen in the sky are not solid bodies like the earth, but are reflections from the seven mercurial discs moving between the metallic layers of the concave shell of the earth." [36]

This, according to Koresh, is not "a matter of controversy," but a fact which he was prepared to demonstrate to all comers; indeed "the truth carries conviction to every open receptacle of its fluxion."

Says Koresh:

We are prepared not only to show the contradictions, absurdities, and impossibilities of the Copernican theory of astronomy, but to meet every argument that may be deduced against our own, and to conclusively demonstrate the correctness of the Koreshan system. [37]

At Estero was erected an elaborate instrument by means of which the "Koreshan Geodetic Staff" claimed to disprove the apparent depression of a line horizontal to the earth's surface, and to prove that such a line really

[36] *The Flaming Sword,* May, 1932, pp. 11-12.

[37] Koresh, *Fundamentals of the Cellular Cosmogony* (leaflet). The whole theory is set forth in Koresh, *The Cellular Cosmogony.*

"curvilineates upward eight inches to the mile." The customary opinion to the contrary is due to "geolinear foreshortening!" [38]

The cellular cosmogony is to this group not merely an interesting discovery in the realm of physical science, but a truth on which all issues of life and death hinge. "This discovery is the key to the solution of all the problems of life and creation." [39] The earth is a cell and the cellular theory applies to all being; the adoption of the Koreshan cosmogony is the necessary prerequisite to any understanding of God, humanity, immortality, and social relations.

The Church Triumphant is communistic, following the example of the early church; but communism did not continue there because the church "in its declension went, body and soul, over to paganism." [40] Now that the church has completed its mission and "has nothing left to recommend it to the favor of the world," men are called to "come out of her." Great things are predicted of the new faith:

Koreshanity will build up the Capital city of the world; it will be located at the point where the vitellus of the alchemico-organic cosmos specifically determines. The position of the sign marks the head of the coming dispensation will define the location of this greatest of cities. The world will be governed from this Capital. [41]

In the new order the saints are divided into three classes: the investigative court the marital order, and the highest or celibate order. It is held that thousands now living "will pass out without the ordinary corruptible dissolution of the body, for the time is at hand when there shall be no more death." [42]

The customary reports of immorality have floated about the Estero colony and its celibate practices. Koresh was something of a social figure in Fort Myers and neighboring towns, where "the tourists and town top set made a show out of him." A minister who resided in Fort Myers during the period knew Koresh but "counted him a scandal to polite and Christian intercourse." He drove a costly equipage and was accompanied by three handsome women, the youngest of whom adverse rumor called his queen. It was whispered that he had "disposed of his legal wife" and was "living in sin with all three women." He was called "a braggart, fanatic, and utterly corrupt" man who "ended as a rank imposter." Koresh taught that he would rise from the dead and his followers kept a strict watch over

---

[38] Koresh, *Geolinear Foreshortening Proves that Scientists Are Deceived* (leaflet).

[39] Letter from the Guiding Star Publishing House.

[40] *What Is Koreshanity?* (leaflet).

[41] *The Flaming Sword*, May, 1932, p. 3.

[42] *What is Koreshanity?* (leaflet).

his grave. The body was swept out of the grave by the waves of the sea in a hurricane, but was recovered and reburied. The present colony is reported to be in poverty and the property is in a rundown condition.[43]

The LLANO COLONIES, a communistic colony of the conventional type, was founded in California by Job Harriman, in 1914, but proved a failure. In 1917 the group moved to Vernon Parish, Louisiana, where, on property vacated by a sawmill, was established the village of Newllano and the Llano Co-operative Colony. This colony never flourished but was able to maintain itself for nearly a quarter of a century before it went out of existence.

The Llano Pledge, assumed by all, provided that members would accept any work assigned to them, would not disparage the colony, would call or attend no meeting to which all members were not invited, would expect no compensation other than food, clothing, shelter, and services such as the colony would be able to provide, would expect nothing which all others might not have on the same terms, and would settle all differences by colony action. Marriage was not interferred with, but all children were to be placed "under the general control and discipline as it is in use at the colony now or may be hereafter adopted." [44]

The Llano Co-operative Colony was an economic venture without any religious basis. There was no church, but any group might worship in any of the public buildings. The goal was the attainment of universal brotherhood "by working and living together in peace and harmony with one another, with all vanity and superior complexes eliminated." [45] Its career was somewhat checkered. Once the whole enterprise was abandoned by the leaders, but "a small group of stalwarts" remained and secured twenty thousand acres of cheap land.[46] Deserters criticized the experiment and spoke disparagingly of the colony, its lack of proper streets, roads, houses, sewer and lavatory provisions, and other facilities.[47] Appeals for financial help were made, with but little success. In reply to a request for an accounting of funds the general manager replied that only $16 had been received recently and not more than $3,000 had been donated in twelve years. "I am interested," he wrote, "in making a report upon that question some day when we have time to stop and look the matter up. Right now we are too busy." [48]

[43] From a letter to me from the minister above mentioned. The colony publishes many books and leaflets on Koreshanity. Also a monthly periodical called the *Flaming Sword*. See Teed, *Koresh;* Borden, *The Logos or Word Book;* Morrow, *The Cellular Cosmogony;* and the works cited.

[44] *The Llano Pledge* (leaflet).

[45] Carl Henry Gleeser, "The Llano Movement," in *Religion and Philosophies in the United States,* edited by Julius A. Weber, pp. 305-11.

[46] The *Llano Colonists,* June 11, 1932.

[47] A bitter attack is made on one such critic in the *Llano Colonist,* June 11, 1932.

[48] *Ibid.,* June 4, 1932.

The Llano group developed a plan for the organization of "units" or similar enterprises elsewhere, and published directions whereby two or three farmers might pool their interests and form a colony. Only one such unit materialized. This was a religious colony established three miles from the Llano site under the name of the Christian Commonwealth. The superintendent was the Rev. Samuel W. Irvin, formerly a Methodist missionary and president of Collegio Monte Maria at Rome. The venture was "not sectarian, but rather interdenominational and altogether undogmatic"; the creed was a vague statement about brotherhood. Membership was based on terms similar to those of the Llano Colony; $1,800 was required, one-third for a house and the balance for tools, equipment, social privileges, and old-age benefits. In case of withdrawal the $600 paid for the home was to be refunded, but all other fees were forfeited. The rules of this colony were similar to those of the parent groups.[49]

The CHURCH OF GOD AND SAINTS OF CHRIST ("Black Jews") is one of the most interesting communistic colonies in the United States. It is located in the village of Belleville, in Nansemond County, Virginia, near Portsmouth. Here a company of several hundred Negroes own and cultivate a thousand acres of land and operate several small industries, a commissary, school, and homes for orphans and the aged.

The Church of God and Saints of Christ owes its origin to a series of revelations vouchsafed to "Prophet" William S. Crowdy, a cook on the Santa Fe Railroad. These revelations consisted of the "Stone of Truth" or the "Seven Keys," and certain ancestral data concerning the Negro race. It is somewhat difficult to say just what the "Stone of Truth" is.[50] The "Seven Keys" are set down as follows:

(1) The Church of God and Saints of Christ; (2) Wine forbidden to be drank in the Church of God and Saints of Christ forever; (3) Unleavened bread and water for Christ's Body and Blood; (4) Foot washing is a commandment; (5) The Disciples' prayer; (6) You must be breathed upon and saluted into the Church of God and Saints of Christ with a Holy Kiss; (7) The Ten Commandments.

Accompanying each key are numerous scripture references (over a hundred in one case) which may or may not bear upon the subject or key in point.

[49] *The Dawn* (leaflet). A minister of a near-by city, in a communication to me, said reports of immorality had been current, but added that "these may be attributed to common prejudice against anything named socialist in a conservative community." He says the associate superintendent was a man of radical socialist ideas who had experienced a divine leading but lost the vision; he had tried in vain to secure ministerial work in the Methodist Church. Another correspondent writes that the Llano groups "are held in favor as a business institution, but are referred to as 100 per cent fanatics, bolsheviks, communists, and radicals."

[50] I must make this confession, even though it lies before me as I write and has not only been studied but also been carefully explained by a prominent elder of the sect.

These seven statements and the attached biblical quotations are the most important symbols of the sect; they are prominently displayed in its literature and constitute practically the whole subject matter studied in the Sunday schools and congregations of the sect. The "Seven Keys" and the Ten Commandments are recited at each service and are regarded as the essentials of Christian doctrine.

The prophet's other revelation was to the effect that the Negro people are in reality Jews and descendants of the "lost tribes of Israel"; the Jews were originally black, but changed color as a result of mixing with whites. Accordingly all the rites of the Old Testament are added to New Testament requirements as binding upon the saints. Foot washing, the holy kiss, circumcision, baptism, sacrifices, and many other ceremonies are observed. Special attention is given to a literal observance of the Passover; this annual feast is continued for a week, and on the appropriate night houses are liberally smeared with blood and the saints, appropriately, and, in the case of high officials elaborately, robed, march out in commemoration of the historic event of antiquity.[51] The Jewish calendar, with Jewish names for the months, is used by the group. The faithful quite commonly bear the names of saints, as St. Benjamin Watkins, St. Ethel Mai Tutwiler, St. Joshua Hurt, St. Zebedee Daniels, St. Isaiah Williams, and the like.[52]

Crowdy is recognized as the founder and only prophet of the sect and is held in an esteem akin to worship. His mantle, by appointment of the prophet himself, fell on Bishop William H. Plummer, who styled himself "Grand Father Abraham" and became virtual dictator of the church. Due recognition is given to the prophet and the incumbent bishop in all services; the columns of the *Weekly Prophet*, official periodical, are usually filled with the edicts and pronouncements of the bishop, and reports of service in the various churches. These reports uniformly begin:

All Hail! To the Weekly Prophet. We, the Church of God and Saints of Christ, met on another blessed Sabbath Day. We rejoice for Prophet William S. Crowdy, the founder of the Church of God and Saints of Christ, also for our present grand and noble leader, Grand Father Abraham.

Only the Belleville group is communistic. Here resides the bishop and the faithful lay their possessions at the feet of the Grand Father Abraham, receiving nothing save what he chooses to give them. An elder superintends each industry in which the members are assigned to work. Weekly or semi-

[51] The *Weekly Prophet*, July 31, 1931, published the names of eighty-two bishops, evangelists, and elders who attended the Passover Feast of Abib (April 14-21), nearly all coming from a distance.

[52] These are names of real members of the sect and are not fictitious.

weekly rations and clothing are doled out to the saints through the commissary. In line with Old Testament precedent a Sabbatic year is observed for the land, during which no crops are planted.[53]

The HOUSE OF DAVID, the peculiar and notorious religious colony, was established at Benton Harbor, Michigan, by "King Benjamin" Purnell in 1903. The leader's previous career is obscure. It seems that he was born in Jasper County, Kentucky, in 1861, and there married a woman whom he later deserted for the "Queen Mary" who ruled with him in their colony. It was written of Purnell by one of his followers:

> Benjamin was born in 1861,
> Which was the year the Civil War begun;
> Perhaps he felt at home
> 'Mid the environment of war,
> For he had been a warrior
> In the war in heaven, before.[54]

It appears that Purnell, after a career as a roving preacher, joined a religious colony in Detroit headed by one Michael Mills, who died in jail. In 1895 Purnell received a revelation that he was the "seventh messenger" of Rev. 8:6; 11:15. The six "angels" preceding him were Joanna Southcott, Richard Brothers, George Turner, William Shaw, John Wroe, and James Zereel, all of England. Purnell culminated the series. His mission was to prepare for the imminent end of time by the "ingathering of Israel"— hence his movement was called the "ingathering" and his followers were "Israelites." The Benton Harbor colony was on a communistic basis; believers surrendered all their possessions to Benjamin, who reaped the rewards of their labors in various industries and pursuits and provided for their support from a "commonwealth fund." The colony at the height of its prosperity included a large farm, some small industries, several buildings, each with a biblical name, and about nine hundred residents.

The theology of the House of David is typical adventism with the addition of several unique touches and unusually fantastic interpretations of Scripture. As the divinely appointed seventh messenger, King Benjamin was supreme in all temporal and spiritual affairs. It was generally believed among his followers that he had conquered death and would either live

[53] When I visited the colony in 1931 it was a Sabbatic year, but the saints did not scruple to buy and reap the crops of their "Gentile" neighbors. I was informed that the schoolteachers in the colony were salaried and nonmembers; only college graduates are allowed in the school and the bishop declared none of his "children" could then qualify. There is no literature on this sect save the *Weekly Prophet*, and a pamphlet of conglomerate Bible studies, largely nonunderstandable, by Prophet Crowdy, called *The Bible Story Revealed*.

[54] *The What? Where? When? and How? of the House of David*, p. 13.

forever or enjoy a speedy resurrection after death. The customary signs of the end were drawn from Scripture and the current environment.

In bolstering his tenets with biblical authority, Benjamin allowed nothing to stand in his way; hence one finds in the literature of the House of David a very peculiar exegesis. For example, the men of the colony wear long hair because, according to Scripture, man is the head of the woman and, also according to Scripture, it is a shame for *the head of the woman* to be uncovered! [55] Airships, automobiles, phonographs, telephones, radios, and motion pictures are all prophesied in the Bible as sure signs of the approaching end of the world.[56] In a booklet entitled *Where Did Cain Get His Wife?* it is explained that the serpent of the Genesis story was not a snake but a *black man* and a *preacher,* a special creation of God, who committed adultery with Eve. Cain was born of this sin and sought his wife among the black and evil people who were multiplying from the original creation. Adam's sin consisted in his sexual relations with Eve after she had transgressed with the colored preacher! [57]

In 1923 certain members of the colony, disillusioned by unconventional practices on the part of Benjamin, brought suit for the restitution of their property and wages for the time they had worked without pay. Counter-charges were made, and the ensuing investigation released the most sensational scandal in the history of American sects. It was alleged that ordinary members of the group lived in dormitories and were given poor food and clothing for their labor, while King Benjamin lived in great luxury at Shiloh "palace" surrounded by the young girls of the colony, whom he clothed in the finest of silks. There were sordid tales of sexual "initiations" and the seduction of these girls by the sixty-two-year-old "angel." To avoid exposure the girls were at intervals married in groups to the young men of the community; at one time twenty-four couples were thus united at the command of the leader.

These and similar allegations were proved to the satisfaction of the court. Mr. and Mrs. John W. Hansel, of Nashville, Tennessee, were awarded $26,188.18 as damages or recompense for property worth $5,000 turned over to Purnell and nine years' labor on the part of the parents and children. Criminal proceedings were instituted against the leader, who succeeded in eluding officers for a considerable period by hiding in the secret rooms of Shiloh. After being apprehended he died while the scandal was at is worst.

The CHRISTIAN CATHOLIC CHURCH, at Zion City, Illinois, forty-two miles north of Chicago, exists as a theocracy. The colony has attracted

[55] *Shiloh's Messenger of Wisdom,* XXVII, No. 4, 8.
[56] *Ibid.,* p. 1.
[57] *Where Did Cain Get His Wife?* pp. 3-5.

wide attention because of the supernatural pretensions of its founder and the conviction of its leaders, unshaken even by a trip around the world, that the earth is flat.

John Alexander Dowie, founder of the sect and colony, was born in Edinburgh in 1847. He went to Australia in young manhood, returned to Scotland for two years to study, was ordained as a Congregational minister, and returned to Australia in 1870. After preaching in the Congregational Church for eight years, Dowie became convinced that he had the gift of healing, whereupon he abandoned his ministry, established the International Divine Healing Association, and built a tabernacle at Melbourne.

Dowie came to the Pacific Coast about 1888 and worked there as a divine healer. He removed first to Evanston, Illinois, and later to Chicago, where he erected a tabernacle and healing room and attracted a large following. He established his Christian Catholic Church in 1896.

About this time Dowie announced himself as Elijah III, John the Baptist being Elijah II, and assumed the title of "Elijah the Restorer." Arousing opposition among the churches in Chicago, he built Zion City in 1901, established his theocracy there with himself as "first apostle," attracted a considerable population, enacted and enforced a strict set of "blue laws," and established a number of business enterprises and industries for the people.

"Elijah's" missionary operations were almost uniformly unsuccessful. He failed in New York and London in 1903 and 1904. The following year he went to Mexico. In his absence severe criticisms were directed at the financial operations of Zion City, and it was charged that his teachings conduced to immorality. He was deposed from office during his absence and a receiver was appointed. It was said that the indebtedness at Zion City totaled more than $6,000,000 with assets estimated at only $2,500,000. Returning from Mexico, Dowie fought the receivership and his deposition and secured a partial vindication in the courts, which made provision for his support. He died in 1907.

Dowie's successor as general overseer of the Christian Catholic Church in Zion was Wilbur Glenn Voliva. Born in Indiana in 1870, he became a minister of the Disciples of Christ in 1889 and held various pastorates until he joined Dowie and became an elder in charge of the North Side Zion Tabernacle in Chicago in 1899. Two years later he went as overseer of the work in Australia, returning at the time of Dowie's legal difficulties in 1906. He was an assistant to Dowie until the latter's death.

There is nothing distinctive in the doctrines of the Christian Catholic Church. It is a group of an extreme fundamentalist character. To the customary reactionary type of orthodoxy and literalism it adds divine healing, opposition to the findings of modern science, insistence on the flatness of the earth, and a rather tense expectancy of the immediate second coming of Christ. Its monthly periodical is called the *Final Warning*. The communistic character of the sect is seen in the withdrawal of the community from the world into a self-contained colony and not in an actual community of goods. Its government is supposed to be in the hands of God. There is a general overseer, and under him are other overseers and elders charged with various duties.

On account of its peculiarities and the enthusiasm of its meetings, the sect has encountered the ridicule and opposition of its neighbors. On April 2, 1937, its great Shiloh Tabernacle was destroyed by fire of alleged incendiary origin. This misfortune was attributed to the agency of the devil, who was angered because preparations were under way for the presentation of the *Passion Play* in the tabernacle.[58]

[58] The *Final Warning*, May, 1937, p. 4.

CHAPTER VI

LEGALISTIC OR OBJECTIVIST SECTS—PART ONE

THE SECTS DISCUSSED IN THE PREVIOUS CHAPTERS MIGHT BE CLASSED AS "personalistic" or "subjective" to indicate the emphasis placed by them on individual experience. While they all have their rules, rites, and ideas of authority, these are regarded as aids to the supreme end of an immediate and mystical touch of the soul with God. The reality of this relation is never attested by objective "works," but always by an inner witness. Immediacy is a fundamental principle.

There are other groups which may be classed as "objectivist." They set up an objective act or "thing" as a mediating requirement between the divine influence and the human spirit. I shall call them legalistic bodies, for want of a better name. The mediating element may reside in the peculiar power possessed by a priest or in the quasi-magical efficacy of material objects like the sacramental bread, holy water, or sacred medals. More frequently it is found in the performance of some concrete act, like baptism or foot washing, in obedience to Scripture. In some cases the legalistic principle is seen in opposition to something, usually instrumental music, missions, or Sunday schools, not mentioned in Scripture and therefore allegedly forbidden. Some of the sects under discussion make these objective "things" necessary to eternal salvation, actually if not in theory.[1]

Sacramentarian bodies like the Roman Catholic and Orthodox groups, and in lesser degree the High-Church wing of the Anglicans and Episcopalians, mediate divine power to the individual through an infallible church or pope, a divinely instituted and hence peculiarly endowed priesthood succeeding in unbroken line from Christ or the apostles, and the potency of the sacraments and other objects administered by such priests. The Roman Catholic Church carries this principle to the point of actual magic.[2] In

[1] A word of caution must be uttered in justice to these groups. In many phases of belief and practice they do not depart from the general religious position. They are as "spiritual" as the perfectionists, for example, in most cases. The mediating or objectivist element is their only point of difference from the groups already considered.

[2] For a Catholic defense against the charge of magic see Martindale, *The Faith of the Roman Church*, pp. 94-95.

the mass, it is claimed, the priest causes wine to change into blood and bread into flesh. The miracle occurs at the exact moment when the priest speaks the words, "This is my body. This is my blood." If any other words are spoken, or if the same words are spoken out of the exactly prescribed setting, nothing occurs. The flesh thus created is not ordinary flesh, but the actual flesh of Jesus Christ, as the wine becomes his actual blood. When this flesh is eaten (the wine is denied to the laity) Christ physically enters the believer's body, and divine grace is bestowed in exactly the same manner that muscle is built by eating food. Even the leavings of the sacrament are divine and to be adored, hence the practice of exhibiting and adoring the host.

To the Catholic it matters nothing that a chemical analysis of the consecrated elements proves with scientific conclusiveness that there is no flesh and blood, but only bread and wine. The answer is that while the "accidents" of taste, color, and weight remain the same, the "substance" is changed, and only the "accidents" can be reached by science. Not the faith of the believer or the psychological influence is important, but the correct doing of the act itself by an ordained priest. "A sacrament is not fulfilled by the fact that one believes in it, but by the fact that it is performed," runs the ancient doctrine.[3] The absolute necessity and miraculous efficacy of certain exact words uttered in a prescribed way at a definite moment on a specific occasion is very like magic. The Roman Church denies the validity of Anglican orders, though admitting that they were originally conferred by authorized bishops, because the form of words used in the ordination of Englishmen (based on the Ordinal of 1662) differed by the addition of a clause which did not appear in the Ordinal of 1552! On this basis all Anglican orders were declared invalid in 1896.[4]

In Catholic theology a kind of divinity and miraculous power attach to many material things that have been propery handled by authorized persons. This is particularly true of bones and relics of saints, holy water, and medals blessed or dedicated to saints. Routine prayers and "telling of beads" and burning of candles may shorten the years of souls suffering in purgatory. Among Catholics, and also among many Protestants, baptism, to be valid, must be performed in the *name* of the Father, the Son, and the Holy Ghost. It has been contended that the insistence upon the *name,* and the prominence given to the *name* of Jesus generally, is a survival from pagan magical rites. Certainly baptism was a feature prominent in the mystery religions.[5] Catholics hold that baptism performs a miracle in washing away sin and that there can be no salvation apart therefrom. They also

[3] Adam, *The Spirit of Catholicism,* p. 185.
[4] See "Anglican," in the *Catholic Encyclopedia.*
[5] Angus, *The Mystery Religions and Christianity,* pp. 81-82.

insist that the validity of baptism depends upon the correct pronunciation of a certain formula; the word "baptize" must be used and the phrase "in the name of the Father, the Son, and the Holy Ghost" are likewise indispensable.[6] When the performance of a miracle can eventuate through an ordinary material act, coupled with the speaking of certain carefully prescribed words, it seems plain that we have something closely akin to magic.

Some Protestant groups attribute spiritual efficacy to baptism and insist that the rite must be performed in a certain manner and in the Triune name, but none make the divine influence depend upon an exact form of words. Outside the Anglican and allied bodies, Protestants commonly deny apostolic succession and hold that it would convey no power even if proved. They reject the Catholic position that a line of succession in the purely physical act of laying on of hands to the accompaniment of certain uttered formulae confers divine authority even on criminal priests, holding against Rome that moral purity is more likely to constitute a channel of grace than any such act. They look upon orders as offices of administration and service rather than special enduements of the Holy Spirit. As an aid to worship many find value in the sacraments, but no representative Protestant would admit that "the act's the thing."

Protestants generally locate the seat of authority in the Bible, at least in the New Testament or the teachings of Jesus, as "containing all things necessary to salvation." "Whatever is not contained therein or may be proved thereby is not to be required of any man" is the common Protestant assertion. This does not necessarily imply a literal interpretation of the Scriptures, certainly not among the great denominations, though this is assumed by most of the small sects, as has already been shown. An intense devotion to the very word of Holy Writ characterizes the little groups classed as legalistic. "The Bible not only *contains* the word of God, it *is* the word of God," is a well-known attitude. From this position the bodies in question draw the principles which mark them as legalistic. The sects ordinarily hate the Roman Catholic Church and would angrily deny any kinship with it. But they are alike in their devotion to "tangibles" as a medium of grace and in requiring something concrete and material as an avenue of access to God. There is a common principle of mediacy or objectivity.

The Craving for Objectivity. The craving for something tangible to which they can cling is deeply implanted in the psychological make-up of many people. Pure "spirituality" is beyond them. They are unable to approach God by prayer, communion, or any mental process alone; the

[6] See "Baptism," in the *Catholic Encyclopedia.*

concrete object is essential. Of course the value of rites, music, pictures, and similar aids to worship is recognized by all Protestants, but those being discussed go beyond that position. The aid is elevated into a necessity and becomes a requirement—a fundamental part of the worship itself.

Among Christians the "objectivist" type of mind demands something tangible as a medium through which to approach God, and this is found in acts which have a scriptural basis. God is the object of worship, but the medium is necessary and sometimes is invested with great power. Usually the mind is satisfied with one or a very few such media. It is an interesting commentary on the type that while it supposedly insists on literally observing scriptural precepts and injunctions, it usually selects one or two models for adherence and disregards scores of others. One group observes foot washing, another covers the heads of women, some reject organ music, others anoint with oil, still others immerse three times forward, and so on and on. But no group practices all the rites mentioned in the Bible, and none, of course, opposes all things not mentioned. No person ever did, or indeed could, literally live up to the "whole Bible," though many profess to do so. Persons select something congenial and are satisfied, though a hundred other things are just as plainly in the Bible.

Judaism. According to the *Census of Religious Bodies* of 1936 (the latest available) there are around 3,800 Jewish congregations and 5,000,000 members, the latter figure including all the Jews residing in places where congregations have been organized; the Jews themselves, however, are quick to point out that these figures provide no true picture of the actual situation. Nevertheless, the vitality of Judaism, in the face of the vicissitudes of the people through the whole of the Christian era, is one of the most amazing phenomena of religious history.

As everybody knows, the Jewish religion is based upon the Old Testament, with special emphasis upon the Pentateuch or the so-called books of Moses. This is the Torah, the teaching of the fathers and the revelation of God. Around the actual words of the sacred record, explaining and adjusting it to the actual needs of life, there has grown up a mass of tradition and authoritative interpretation, the Talmud, with guidance covering nearly every detail of life from the cradle to the grave. The regulations best known to non-Jews are the dietary laws which prescribe in some detail the foods which may or may not be eaten, and the ritual for the killing of animals to be eaten. In their present situation it seems probable that comparatively few Jews attempt a meticulous observance of the Talmudic rules, though they constitute a pattern of conduct by which the life of the faithful should be ordered.

A scholar has explained:

Judaism is a detailed system of ethical *practices* by which its adherents conse-crated their daily lives to the *service* of God. The cornerstone of Judaism was the *deed*, not the *dogma*. . . . Salvation for professing Christians is not a consequence of duty *done* in the conscious service of God; it is something mystically *received* as a gift of divine grace. . . . Christianity and Judaism appealed to different sides of human nature; the former to the passive side, the latter to the active side. Chris-tianity stressed *faith*, Judaism *right action*.[7]

The high points of Jewish worship are the Sabbath ritual and the ob-servance of certain festivals and holy days related to the historical ex-periences of the people interpreted into messages pertinent for the life of the Jew in this and every age. The chief festivals are Pesach or the Passover in April, commemorating the liberation of the Israelites from the Egyptian bondage (Exod. 2); Shabuoth or the Feast of Weeks or Pentecost in June, celebrating the reception of the Ten Commandments by Moses (Exod. 19; 20); and Succoth or the Feast of Tabernacle or Booths in October, commemorating the wilderness period of Hebrew history (Lev. 23:42; Deut. 16:13-15). The Holy Days are Rosh Hoshanah or the New Year, and Yom Kippur or the Day of Atonement in October (Lev. 16:29-34). Other festivals are Hanukah or the Feast of Lights in December, in cele-bration of the purification of the Temple after its defilement by Antiochus Epiphanes (I Macc. 1-4), and Purim or the Feast of Lots in March, honoring the work of Esther. The Fast of Tebeth in January recalls the siege of Je-rusalem, that of Tammuz in July is related to the breach in the walls, and the Fast of Ab in the same month commemorates the fall of the city and the destruction of the Temple.[8]

As in the case of all religious movements, Judaism has not remained static and uninfluenced by the currents of modern thought. There are well-defined cleavages within the body, and the word "denomination" has been applied to some of them, but the ethnic consciousness and mutual devotion to certain great principles and causes have prevented outright schisms and the development of separate Jewish sects. Some of the differences are of a minor nature and trace back to European divergencies in language or liturgy. More important are those that have resulted from the application of modern scientific methods of study.

There are four great schools of thought in present-day Judaism, and at least three of them are sufficiently marked to be characterized as "denomi-nations" within the Jewish whole. These are Orthodoxy, Reform, Conser-vatism, and Reconstructionism.

ORTHODOX JUDAISM is what its name implies; it represents the orthodox

---

[7] Herford, *The Truth About the Pharisees*, pp. 36, 37.

[8] For a brief description of Jewish religious rites see Idelsohn, *The Ceremonies of Judaism*. See also the various articles in the *Universal Jewish Encyclopedia*.

or traditional position and might be called the "extreme right" of Jewish theology. It accepts the inspiration of the Old Testament and the Talmud and lives up to the precepts of the Torah in so far as modern conditions permit. "Orthodox Judaism holds to one principal doctrine, the doctrine of revelation, which means that the Torah contains absolute truth, that it is not the work of Moses, but of God."

Orthodox Jews practice the various rites and ceremonies, observe the dietary regulations, use Hebrew in their services and largely English in their sermons, and expect the coming of a Messiah and the establishment of the Messianic age. The voice of Orthodoxy in the United States is the Union of Orthodox Jewish Congregations and the Union of Orthodox Rabbis of the United States and Canada, and its central institution is the New York Yeshiva University, which consists of a Talmudic Academy and a College of Liberal Arts.

REFORM JUDAISM represents the complete adjustment of Jewish religion to modern life and culture. It is in general the liberal arm of the faith and is the result of critical methods of study; its theory of biblical inspiration is not unlike that of liberal Protestantism. It teaches that revelation is progressive in character, rejects the dietary laws and many of the older rites and ceremonies, and accepts as binding only the moral laws and "such ceremonies as elevate and sanctify our lives." "We consider ourselves no longer a nation," runs one of its earliest declarations of principles, "but a religious community, and therefore expect neither a return to Palestine, nor a sacrificial worship under the sons of Aaron, nor the restoration of any of the laws concerning the Jewish state." It does not expect a personal Messiah but recognizes "in the modern era of universal culture of heart and intellect the approaching of the realization of Israel's great Messianic hope." A later declaration supported the rehabilitation of Palestine as a Jewish homeland and a haven of refuge for the oppressed, and the preservation of the Sabbath, festivals, and Holy Days, and such customs and ceremonies as possess inspirational value. The mouthpieces of Reform Judaism in the United States are the Central Conference of American Rabbis and the Union of American Hebrew Congregations, and its leading institutions are the Hebrew Union College at Cincinnati and the Jewish Institute of Religion in New York.

CONSERVATIVE JUDAISM may be said to occupy a position between Orthodoxy and Reform, and it seeks to conserve the values of both. It regards itself as "a positive embodiment of Traditional Judaism, a movement which, on the one hand, recognizes the necessity of change, and on the other avoids the excesses of radicalism." It upholds the Torah, the Sabbath, the dietary laws, the use of Hebrew, and other basic ideas of Judaism, but it adopts the scientific attitude and the modern method in education, utilizes the English language in sermons and in some of its prayers, and permits the use of family pews in the synagogues. The leading Conservative institution is the Jewish Theological Seminary in New York, and its main organization is the Rabbinical Assembly of America.

RECONSTRUCTIONISM is a new movement which has not yet created an organization, though it is sponsored by the Jewish Reconstructionist Foundation, Inc., founded in 1940. It rests on the work and teachings of Mordecai M. Kaplan, and its emphasis is not so much upon differences in theology as upon a reorganization of Jewish life. Its program centers around six points: the establishment of a homeland for Jews and their culture in Palestine; the reorganization of Jewish community life in America; the broadening of education beyond mere training in ritual or catechism; the reinterpretation of Jewish concepts in terms of modern thought; the development of Jewish esthetic life; and the establishment of a co-operative society throughout the world.[9] Reconstructionism may be regarded as the "extreme left" of American Judaism.

There are no available statistics which reflect the relative numerical strength of these four groups or movements among American Jews, although Reconstructionism is by far the smallest.

The COMMANDMENT KEEPERS OR BLACK JEWS is a Negro sect which adheres to Judaism and has a synagogue in the Harlem section of New York City. Its members regard themselves as Jews in every sense, and their services follow the rites of Orthodox Judaism. They refuse to be known as Negroes and declare that all so-called Negroes are of Hebrew stock and trace their ancestry back to biblical times through Ethiopia, whose first king, Menelik I, is said to have been the son of King Solomon and the Queen of Sheba; it is claimed that this son was confirmed in Solomon's faith at the age of thirteen and was later sent by his father to colonize Ethiopia.

The Commandment Keepers was established in a Harlem basement in 1919 by its chief rabbi, Wentworth David Matthew. Rabbi Matthew is a native of Nigeria and his father was a Fallash or Ethiopian Jew. He received a rabbinical education in Cincinnati and Berlin. Around 1927 a rival group of Black Jews sprang up in Harlem under the leadership of a West Indian Negro known as Rabbi Josiah Ford, but Matthew succeeded in consolidating the two groups when Ford departed for Ethiopia in 1932.

Rabbi Matthew declares that there are 150,000 Fallash Black Jews in the United States and 100,000 in the near-by West Indies. He claims 3,300 members of the Commandment Keepers in Harlem and an equal number in congregations in Brooklyn, Jersey City, Philadelphia, St. Louis, Salt Lake City, Youngstown and Warren, Ohio, and other places. There is a subsidiary

[9] See Jung, Philipson, Goldstein, and Eisenstein in the *Universal Jewish Encyclopedia*, VI, 239-46.

fraternal society known as the Royal Order of Ethiopian Hebrews. The sect has a home for the aged, operates several cigar and stationery stores, a laundry, and some other business enterprises in co-operation with white Jewish merchants in Harlem, and has announced plans to establish a co-operative agricultural project on Long Island.

Two other Negro groups centering in and around the Harlem area are known as the HOUSE OF ISRAEL and the MOORISH SCIENCE TEMPLE. The members of both of these sects wear full beards. In January, 1943, several adherents of the House of Israel were arrested by federal agents for violation of the Selective Service Act. These bodies teach that the Negroes are the real Hebrews, that Adam was a Negro, and that the black race was once supreme on earth. They operate schools in which the Abyssinian language is taught and claim that they are enslaved by the white race because that language is excluded from the public schools.

The EASTERN ORTHODOX CHURCH represents the ancient faith of the Byzantine Empire and is the dominant religion of eastern Europe and the Slavic peoples. It was the first great break in papal Christianity and historically it found its center in Constantinople. One of its main departures from Roman Catholic doctrine, the principle around which the early controversies raged, is its rejection of the so-called "filioque" phrase in the Nicene Creed; Eastern Christianity holds against Rome that the Holy Ghost proceeds from the Father alone, and not from the Father and the Son. It rejects the dogma of the Immaculate Conception of the Virgin Mary, works of supererogation, indulgences, and purgatory. It also rejects the use of carved images, but reverences icons or holy pictures and relics of the saints.

On the other hand Eastern Orthodoxy accepts the teachings of the seven ecumenical councils of the early church and honors Mary as the mother of God; it also accepts the Virgin Birth of Christ, the seven sacraments, holy unction, and transubstantiation. Baptism is by trine immersion, although the forms of other communions are recognized. Marriage is permissible to clerical candidates, but is forbidden after ordination.

Orthodoxy does not exist in a solid bloc as does Roman Catholicism. It has no acknowledged head or center, but flourishes as numerous autonomous national bodies. In recent years, however, there have been signs of an attempt to consolidate Orthodoxy under the hegemony of the Russian church and the patriarch of Moscow. The Soviet authorities have relaxed their efforts to stamp out religion in Russia and are said to be supporting the movement to organize Orthodoxy and use it as a buffer against the Vatican and the Roman Catholic Church.

This is reflected in current movements within the Russian Orthodox Church in this country, which has been torn by internal conflicts and rivalries. It came to these shores by way of Alaska, where it was a missionary offshoot of the church in Russia when Alaska was Russian territory. It became autonomous in the United States after the Bolshevik revolution. While recognizing its spiritual relationship to Moscow, and mentioning the Russian patriarch in its prayers, it broke all official connections because its leaders would not recognize any allegiance to the Soviet regime. The leader of the autonomous body was Metropolitan Theophilus. Strong efforts were made after World War II to bring the American church back under the control of the Moscow patriarch Alexei, who named Archbishop Makarius as his representative and exarch of the church in this country. Much strife ensued and at one time Theophilus demanded police protection. Early in 1948 the Moscow patriarch summoned five American leaders to stand trial for "their stubborn attempts to split the church." The indictments were ignored by the men against whom they were directed. A few days later Alexei announced in Moscow that the Russian Church supported the Soviet power and its philosophy.

There are eight Eastern Orthodox bodies in this country which recognize their foreign attachments in their names: the Albanian, Bulgarian, Greek, Roumanian, Russian, Serbian, Syrian Antiochan, and Ukranian Orthodox Churches. There are no official or administrative connections between them. There are three others which have sought to Americanize themselves: the American Holy Orthodox Catholic Apostolic Eastern Church, organized in New York in 1932; the Apostolic Episcopal Church, otherwise known as the Holy Eastern Catholic and Apostolic Orthodox Church, which adheres to the Chaldean rite, and was formed by the ordination of a bishop in 1925; the Holy Orthodox Church in America, which began as a mystical movement in 1924 and became a full-fledged denomination in 1927 by the consecration of a bishop.

The numeral strength of the Eastern Orthodox Churches is in general comparable to the number of immigrants from the various countries from which they stem. The three American groups have only a handful of adherents. The official census figures (1936) indicated that there were around 700 congregations and 350,000 members of all the groups. However, the Russian Orthodox Church reports 250 parishes and 1,000,000 members, and large claims are made by the Greek Orthodox Church; such claims are probably based on the number of Russians and Greeks in the areas where congregations have been organized rather than the baptized communicants. The Orthodox bodies have a dual system of membership; communicant members are baptized persons who have received the confirmatory chrismation or anointing with holy oil, and parish members include the families whose heads are in the congregations.

The ASSYRIAN JACOBITE APOSTOLIC CHURCH is one of the so-called "separated Churches." It originated in the controversies of the fifth century concerning the person of Christ and the doctrine of the procession of the Holy Ghost.

The Jacobites take their name from Jacobus Baradaeus, a wandering bishop of the sixth century. They are Monophysites, or Eutychians, holding that the divine and human in the person of Christ are so blended as to constitute one nature. Many Assyrians are Nestorians, and accept the doctrine of Nestorius, the ancient patriarch of Constantinople, that there are two persons or natures in Christ.

Jacobus, a monk of Constantinople, was consecrated a bishop in 541 or 543. In danger of his life because of his Monophysite views, he clad himself in rags and wandered about for nearly forty years, preaching his doctrines and organizing groups. It is said that he consecrated 2 patriarchs and 27 bishops, and ordained 100,000 priests and deacons. From his activities came the Assyrian Jacobite Church. It endured bitter persecution at the hands of Roman Catholics, Persians, Mohammedans, and even the fellow Assyrians, the Nestorians. In fact antagonism between the Jacobites and Nestorians has practically destroyed the unity of the Assyrian people.

The Jacobites agree with Eastern Christianity on the doctrine of the procession of the Holy Ghost, rejecting the Roman Catholic "filioque" and teaching that the Holy Ghost proceeds from the Father only and not from the Father and the Son. It was the controversy over the "filioque" which, more than any other one point of doctrine, rent the church into its Eastern and Western branches, and the difference persists to this day. The Jacobite phrase runs: "The Holy Ghost proceeded from the Father *and is with the Son.*"

In other respects the Jacobite Church approaches the doctrinal position of the Roman Catholic Church. It regards the ecclesiastical traditions and ordinances as of equal importance with the Bible as the source of authoritative truth. The Virgin and the saints are venerated and prayers are offered for the dead. Auricular confession is accepted. In the Communion the real presence of Christ is regarded as present in the elements under the appearance of bread and wine; the sacrament is offered to the laity in one kind only, the wine being denied. All baptized persons are regarded as members of the church. Baptism takes place a few days after birth and is usually, but not always, by immersion; the priest breathes on the water and the child, and the baptismal ceremony includes the laying on of hands and anointing the body with sacred oil or chrism in the form of a cross. The sign of the cross is made with one finger.

The Assyrian Jacobite Church is not numerically strong throughout the world and appears to be dwindling; estimates of its membership vary from twenty to eight thousand. But it claims an impressive hierarchal organization. Its lineage is traced directly back to the apostles, particularly to Peter, who is regarded as the first patriarch of Antioch, and from whom the apostolic orders were derived. The head of the church is the Patriarch of Antioch; he takes his title from the ancient see of Antioch, although he has never been permitted to live there because the Greeks regard his group as heretics. His seat is not fixed and the present patriarch lives in Syria. Under the patriarch is the metropolitan (called mifrain) of Mosul, who ordains the bishops (koorie). Other officials are iskiffs, rhahibs, priests, and deacons. The clergy can be married or celibate, but the higher orders are not open to the former.

The church was established among the Assyrian immigrants in the United States about 1907. A considerable group had organized a Jacobite congregation at Paterson, New Jersey, and in 1907 they sent their leader, Hanna Koorie, to Jerusalem, where he was ordained a priest and a bishop. On his return to the United States he gathered the Assyrians, formally organized a church, and the group began worshiping in St. Luke's Episcopal Church at Paterson. In the course of time other congregations were formed in near-by states. Headquarters are at West New York, New Jersey, where the official periodical *Beth Nahrin* (Mesopotamia) is published. Several thousand Assyrian Jacobites have been gathered into the various congregations but no institutional work has been undertaken.

CHRIST'S MISSION, INC., located in the heart of New York city, is staffed exclusively by ex-priests and former Catholic laymen. Its purposes are to rehabilitate priests and nuns who leave the Roman Church, and to controvert Catholic doctrine. It was founded in 1887 by James O'Connor, an Irish priest who renounced his orders in 1878. The present director is Leo H. Lehmann, who was ordained to the priesthood in the basilica of St. John Lateran, the cathedral of the popes, in Rome, after completing his studies in the College of Propaganda. After serving in Capetown, South Africa, and in the United States, he left the priesthood in 1929. Several other ex-priests are associated with him in Christ's Mission and in the publication of its monthly periodical the *Converted Catholic*.

Christ's Mission claims that priests are leaving the Catholic Church in this country at the rate of from seventy-five to one hundred annually, and that the exodus in other countries is even greater. Around three hundred such converts have been served by the mission, although they were not all converted there. Its work consists mainly in advising and finding jobs for these men, trying to re-educate them, and shielding them from persecution. Regular services are held in the mission headquarters and staff members are sent about the country on lecture tours. One of its workers, who is now a Baptist minister, went to Italy soon after the close of World War II to form an evangelical organization among the two thousand priests who were said to have deserted the Catholic Church in that country.[10]

The REFORMED EPISCOPAL CHURCH split from the Protestant Episcopal Church. The Episcopal Church holds to apostolic succession. Many in this communion acknowledge little or no debt to the Reformation and do not regard themselves as Protestants. The Tractarian Movement espoused the Roman Catholic view of the sacraments, holding, however, that the Real Presence in the elements was mystical rather than material, though its efficacy did not reside in the faith of the believer but in the actual presence of Christ. The Anglo-Catholics in England and the High-Church wing of the church in the United States approach very near to Catholic doctrine in several particulars. Episcopalians generally insist that the historic episcopate or apostolic succession is preserved through the ordinations of their church, against the almost unanimous opinion of other Protestants. The Episcopal Church is quite active in the interest of church unity, but on the basis of a principle which is denied by all those to whom approach is made.

The growing tendency to ritualism and exaggerated sacramentarianism was the occasion of the only schism experienced by this church in America. In 1873, at the conference of the Evangelical Alliance of the World in New York city, the dean of Canterbury, Dr. Payne Smith, and Bishop George David Cummins, assistant bishop of Kentucky, participated in a union Communion service in the Fifth Avenue Presbyterian Church. Their action in joining a sacramental service with ministers outside the apostolic succession aroused widespread dissatisfaction among Episcopalians and the two participants were more or less severely criticized. Dean Smith paid no attention to these objections, but Bishop Cummins, who had long been disturbed by ritualistic trends which he considered to be destructive of true catholicity, felt them most keenly. He addressed a letter to his diocesan, Bishop Benjamin B. Smith, of Kentucky, who was also presiding bishop of the church, in which he declared his "purpose of transferring his work and office to another sphere." He was expostulated with in vain, and was finally arraigned for trial and deposed from his office and ministry.[11]

In the meantime, a month after his letter to the presiding bishop and nearly seven months before his trial and deposition, Bishop Cummins met a company of seven clergymen and twenty laymen in New York and formally organized the Reformed Episcopal Church. Cummins became presiding bishop and Charles Edward Cheney of Chicago was elected a bishop

[10] See Lehmann, *The Soul of a Priest* and *Out of the Labyrinth;* the publications of the Agora Publishing Company, New York; the *Converted Catholic* magazine; "The Trek from Rome," by Jeanne Kellar, pamphlet reprinted from *World Outlook,* October, 1947.

[11] Tiffany, *History of the Protestant Episcopal Church,* p. 535.

and consecrated subsequently in Chicago by Bishop Cummins. Thus the new body possessed the historic episcopate, a fact which could not well be denied by the parent body.

The Reformed Episcopal Church has survived as an evangelical body, preserving, as it believes, the true spirit of the church before it was influenced by ritualism and High-Church developments. It uses the Book of Common Prayer and accepts substantially the Thirty-Nine Articles. Though the apostolic succession has been preserved, the body regards episcopacy "as an ancient and desirable form of church government rather than as of divine right." The idea that the church consists of only one order of ecclesiastical polity is denied, as is also the theory that the ministry constitutes a priesthood separate from other believers. This group also rejects baptismal regeneration, the real presence in the sacramental elements, and the theory that on the altar Christ's body and blood are offered anew as an oblation to the Father. Save in the matter of origin and the theory of apostolic succession the Reformed Episcopal Church is not essentially legalistic. It is in full communion with all other Protestant groups and receives members therefrom on letters dismissory and accepts their clergy without reordination. The body now has around 65 churches and approximately 7,500 members.

Old Catholic Churches. There are in the United States a large number of Catholic churches which have broken away from the Roman hierarchy and are classed as Old Catholic bodies. This classification is accurate only in the matter of doctrine, for none of the groups are connected with, or recognized by, the Old Catholics of Europe. The continental bodies organized in protest against the dogma of papal infallibility promulgated in 1870, and received their orders indirectly from the Roman Catholic Church through the Jansenist Church of Holland. The leaders of the various bodies in America were at one time or another connected directly or indirectly with authentic European Old Catholic Churches and in many, but not all, cases derived orders therefrom, though such connection has now ceased to exist.

There is, however, general agreement with original Old Catholic doctrine, which is practically the same in all the American churches. This doctrine is essentially Catholic, though approaching nearer that of the Eastern than the Western or Roman branch. The authority of the pope is rejected, as is clerical celibacy. Communion is offered to the laity in both kinds and the liturgy is mainly in the vernacular. The great creeds are accepted, but the "filioque" clause of the Nicene Creed is rejected. Apostolic succession, as constituting the only valid ministry, is insisted upon, but the typical Roman Catholic intolerance of other religious bodies is largely absent. In most other points of doctrine and practice there is agreement with the Roman position.

Old Catholic history in this country is a sad record of schisms, personal rivalries and jealousies, depositions and counter depositions, and other events that constitute a scandal to Christian charity and unity. Many of the groups are so small that they can hardly be located, and in some cases apparently consist of a lone bishop without followers but claiming valid apostolic orders.

The most interesting part of this history revolves about the name of Father Joseph Rene Vilatte. He was a Parisian who, after serving in the Franco-Prussian War, went to Canada as a teacher and lay assistant to a French mission priest. He studied later in preparation for the priesthood in Belgium and Canada. Becoming unsettled by the anti-Catholic lectures of the ex-priest Father Chiniquy, he entered the Presbyterian College at Montreal, where he became convinced of errors in both Protestantism and Catholicism. After six months in a monastery at Bourbonnais, Illinois, he undertook mission work among the French and Belgians of Wisconsin, who had imbibed Old Catholic doctrines in Europe but were drifting, without a ministry. Here he was markedly successful and organized several congregations.

The need for a bishop soon became apparent. Some Protestant Episcopal authorities had lauded Vilatte and his work and desired to incorporate his converts, but when the missionary declined, they turned against him and gave him unending trouble.[12] He went to Switzerland and was ordained to the Old Catholic priesthood by Bishop Herzog of Berne in 1885. He later arranged for consecration as bishop at the hands of Archbishop Heykamp of Utrecht. Protests from Bishop Grafton, Episcopal bishop of Fond du Lac, caused the consecration to be deferred, and Vilatte wrote declining the orders previously offered. The Russian Orthodox Bishop Vladimir of New York then took the young priest under his protection, referring to the holy synod the matter of his consecration in the Russian Church.

In the meantime Vilatte had correspondence with Archbishop Alvarez of Ceylon, who had received orders from the Syro-Jacobite Church of Malabar. He went to Ceylon and on May 29, 1892, by order of the patriarch of Antioch, he was consecrated archbishop of the archdiocese of America, under the title of Mar Timotheus. Bishop Grafton had written and cabled Alvarez to refuse the orders, but received the reply, "We shall consecrate Mgr. Vilatte if he is the only Old Catholic in America." Bishop Grafton deposed Vilatte "from the Protestant Episcopal ministry," and the Episcopal house of bishops pronounced his consecration null and void for the reasons "that it was derived from a church separated from the rest of Christendom since the Council of Chalcedon, and that he had been de-

[12] *American Old Catholic*, May, 1915.

posed by Bishop Grafton shortly beforehand." To this the partisans of the new prelate replied that "as the Archbishop had never been an Episcopal minister the deposition actually affected our leader as would the deposition by the Grand Lama of Tibet." [13] There could really be no doubt as to the validity of Vilatte's orders, derived as they were from the ancient see of Antioch. Bishop Coxe of the Episcopal Church wrote that "whatever the House of Bishops may say to the contrary, no Roman Catholic prelate in the United States has an Episcopate as valid as yours," and the Episcopal *Catholic Champion* editorially declared that "Vilatte is as true a bishop as ever wore a miter." [14] The Holy Office at Rome later solemnly recognized Vilatte's episcopal character.

On his return to America from Ceylon the new archbishop organized the American Old Catholic Church, which had a considerable growth under his leadership. In 1898 he went to Rome and made his submission to the pope. His orders were recognized, but after vainly waiting in a monastery in Ireland for a determination of his status in the Roman Catholic Church, he withdrew his submission and returned to America to continue his independent work. He consecrated various persons, later to be mentioned, to the episcopate, but since these acts were not authorized by the patriarch of Antioch the bishops thus created were not recognized, and with their work all connection with the Syrian Church ceased. Archbishop Vilatte continued for approximately twenty years as the head of the American Old Catholic Church, when he again made submission to the pope and retired to a monastery in France, where he died. He was allowed a pension and his orders were recognized as valid though "irregular"; he did not "fit in" to the Catholic hierarchy and was never assigned to a diocese.

The AMERICAN CATHOLIC CHURCH was established by Vilatte at Chicago. In 1915 he received F. E. J. Lloyd, a prominent Episcopal priest who had been bishop-elect of Oregon, and conferred on him episcopal orders. On the retirement of Vilatte, Lloyd assumed his office and incorporated his group under the name of the American Catholic Church. Many of the former leader's congregations fell away, but Lloyd remained in charge of those that adhered, bearing the title of metropolitan and archbishop. The organization includes about a dozen congregations and fifteen hundred members, possessing, however, only two small church edifices. It boasts a rather imposing organization, with an archbishop, two auxiliary bishops, a titular bishop, and several priests.

Polish Old Catholics. According to sources friendly to Archbishop Vilatte, this leader suffered bitter calumny and persecution at the hands of

[13] *Ibid.*
[14] *Ibid.*

Episcopalians and Roman Catholics in this country and Canada.[15] Dissension in the ranks first broke out among the Poles of Chicago. Various Polish Roman Catholic priests in Detroit, Cleveland, Chicago, and other cities placed themselves under Vilatte's jurisdiction, and hopes were entertained for a Polish Old Catholic Church. In 1897 Father Kaminski of Buffalo was elected bishop and sought consecration at Vilatte's hands. Father Kozlowski of Chicago, the disappointed candidate, refused to abide by the selection and called a second convention which elected him as rival bishop. After failing to bring the factions together, Vilatte, in 1898, consecrated Kaminski. Kozlowski went to Europe and was consecrated by Bishop Herzog of Berne, who was unfriendly to Vilatte. Strife between the adherents of the two rivals reached the riot stage in Buffalo, Scranton, Cleveland, Chicago, and elsewhere. In the end a considerable number of congregations adhered to Kozlowski and others were loyal to Kaminski. The latter remained in the Vilatte jurisdiction and Kozlowski organized his followers into an independent body called the Polish Independent Catholic Church.

The POLISH NATIONAL CATHOLIC CHURCH was organized at Scranton, Pennsylvania, in 1904. Father Francis Hodur was elected bishop and was consecrated by the National Catholic bishops of the Netherlands. On the death of Bishop Kozlowski his congregations joined the Hodur group, and the combined body is known as the Polish National Catholic Church of America. It has more than 100 congregations and has reported 250,000 members, though the census listed only 63,000.

The LITHUANIAN NATIONAL CATHOLIC CHURCH was formed by Bishop Hodur in 1914. It remained under Hodur's care until 1924, when he consecrated the Rev. John Gritenas as its bishop. The body has declined, now having only half a dozen churches and around three thousand members.

The AFRICAN ORTHODOX CHURCH was founded in 1921, when Vilatte consecrated the Rev. George Alexander McGuire, a Negro physician and erstwhile Episcopalian and Anglican priest, as bishop, metropolitan, and primate of the African Orthodox Church, a body which McGuire had formed in New York three weeks previous to his elevation. He had been a missionary field agent of the Episcopal Church, and near the outbreak of World War I he went to the West Indies, the place of his birth, where he became an Anglican priest. Returning to the United States after the war, he organized the Independent Episcopal Church among Negroes, after laboring in vain to secure independence for the colored members of the Episcopal Church. Attacked by the Episcopal Church press, he was offered consecration by the Russian Orthodox authorities, but refused to become subordinate.

[15] *Ibid.*, see also June, 1915.

Formation of the present body and McGuire's consecration by Vilatte followed.

The archbishop established his "cathedral" and a theological school, called the Endich Theological Seminary, after the alleged name of the Ethiopian eunuch mentioned in the New Testament, in the basement of his home in Harlem. His church has thirty congregations and five thousand adherents.

The AFRICAN ORTHODOX CHURCH OF NEW YORK is an offshoot of McGuire's sect. McGuire consecrated a Bishop Barrow as head of a congregation in Brooklyn, and the latter proceeded to charter the group as an independent body known as the African Orthodox Church of New York. Barrow in turn conferred episcopal orders on George S. A. Brooks, who proceeded to secede from Barrow and established the Afro-American Catholic Church. He later obtained control of the African Orthodox Church of New York. The body has three congregations and seven hundred members, all in Brooklyn.[16]

The AMERICAN EPISCOPAL CHURCH is a peculiar offshoot of the Vilatte movement. It is sometimes known also as the American Episcopal Church (Lutheran). Its archbishop is Denver Scott Swain of McNabb, Illinois, where he operates in what has been described as a "dilapidated, tumbledown building." Archbishop Carfora of the North American Old Roman Catholic Church ordained Swain to the priesthood in 1942, but in less than a year Swain was suspended "because he obtained his ordination through misrepresentation, and also because he attempted to seek consecration as a bishop in some other organization." About the same time Swain obtained archepiscopal ordination from Francis Victor Krauski of Chicago, who had secured orders from F. E. J. Lloyd of the Vilatte group.

This sect has reported numerous churches and a membership running up to 100,000, but investigators have not been able to find any constituency. In fact Archbishop Swain seems to be an ecclesiastical stormy petrel. A writer in the *American Lutheran* (November, 1947) refers to him as a "several times married ex-convict" with an alias of Denver Swari, and points out that he was twice confined in Joliet prison for a confidence game to which he pleaded guilty.

At one time Swain was listed in *Who's Who in America*. It stated that he received the degree of Doctor of Laws from an unlocated college at the age of nineteen, and that in 1936 he received the degree of Bachelor of Divinity from the unknown St. Paul Theological Seminary, entered the ministry and was ordained bishop of the American Episcopal Church, all in the same year. The *American Lutheran* writer, however, points out that he

[16] Details from Archbishop McGuire.

was in the penitentiary until June of that year, and had been there since 1934, and was returned to prison in September, 1938. Swain was dropped from *Who's Who in America* after one insertion.

Swain claims apostolic succession "through seven or eight other lines" in addition to the Vilatte ordination.

The OLD CATHOLIC CHURCH IN AMERICA was organized by W. H. Francis Brothers. In 1908 the Old Catholics of Holland placed Bishop Arnold Harris Mathew in charge of Old Catholic work in England and Ireland. He later made submission to the Roman church, but before doing so perpetuated the succession by conferring episcopal orders on certain Old Catholic priests. Among these was the Prince and Duke de Landas Berghes et de Rache, who was consecrated bishop in 1912 and sent in 1914 to the United States to reunite the scattered Old Catholic groups. He seems to have been coached by the archbishop of Canterbury, and on his arrival in this country to have become a priest in the Episcopal Church.[17] He was, however, elected archbishop by the National Catholic Church in America. He consecrated on successive days in 1916 two bishops, Carmel Henry Carfora, an ex-priest of the Roman Catholic Church, and W. H. Francis Brothers. Quarrels between the two followed. Carfora deposed Brothers, who organized the Old Catholic Church in America, of which he became archbishop and metropolitan. It claims 6,000 members.

Carfora organized the NORTH AMERICAN OLD ROMAN CATHOLIC CHURCH in 1917, with headquarters in Chicago. It now has around fifty churches and fifteen hundred members. Carfora was primate and archbishop, and as such was recognized by the few remaining Old Catholics in England as the true leader of all American Old Catholics.

All was not smooth sailing in the seas of the Carfora faction. After the trouble with Brothers, Carfora consecrated Bishop Samuel D. Benedict, who seceded, went to New York, and claimed to be the true head of all the Old Catholic bodies in America under the title of archbishop and primate of the Evangelical Catholic Church. Bishop Benedict was deposed by Archbishop Carfora, but the former nevertheless proceeded to consecrate another bishop named Newmark. He seceded and became independent, consecrated W. H. Hammond to the episcopacy, who in turn seceded from Newmark. Benedict, Newmark, and Hammond were all independent, and claimed to be true Old Catholic bishops, though the census was unable to locate any congregations or members adhering to any of them.

The Vilatte group regarded all these as impostors. In the *American Old Catholic*, May, 1915, appeared warnings against Carfora, "an Italian ex-Roman priest who is masquerading as one of our bishops. His alleged conse-

[17] *American Old Catholic*, May, 1915.

crator denies having ever consecrated this man Carfora bishop." From an Episcopal paper the Vilatte periodical quotes this warning:

Caution is suggested in dealing with a man styling himself as "Bishop Gregorious," otherwise "Dom Francis" or "Rev. Willy Brothers," who claims to be a bishop consecrated by Archbishop Vilatte and the Armenian Archbishop Seropian. Archbishop Vilatte states that he ordained Brothers a priest and afterwards deposed him for cause. . . . There is likewise a man in our country just now styling himself "Prince de Landas Berghes et de Rache, Old Catholic Bishop." As this man says he "comes to this country at the suggestion of the (Protestant) Archbishop of Canterbury, and was licensed to serve in a Protestant Episcopal Diocese after his arrival," it seems rather indecent of him, while acting as Protestant Episcopal minister, still to style himself "Old Catholic Bishop." It is to be distinctly understood that no man is to be received as an Old-Roman Catholic priest unless he can show faculties from the Archbishop dated 1915.

The LIBERAL CATHOLIC CHURCH is one of the most interesting sects in the world, an amazing blend of Roman Catholic sacramentarianism, Theosophy, and esoteric vagaries derived from Hinduism. It is

one of the most curious bodies of modern Christendom, a church which opens apparently its sacred portals to the sinners and publicans, and more scandalous still, to freethinkers and creedal mugwumps, a Church with a perfectly valid spiritual chain joining it to the twelve apostles, yet free from the punctilios of usage which have accumulated in the name of the Church since the time of Nicea.[18]

In its published statements the group professes to hold that all religions are divinely inspired and that no converts should be sought from one to another; it imposes no beliefs upon the laity and insists upon its congeniality with all forms of science. But when one pierces beneath the veil it is found to be a compound of spiritualistic notions incomprehensible to the ordinary intelligence, and the total output is an astral jumble as strange as any of the philosophies transplanted from India. It is sacramentarian to the core, carefully guards its apostolic succession, heals and anoints with oil, practices absolution and holy unction, baptizes with the trinitarian formula, and persuades its devotees to see visions and indulge in pious imaginings and spirit-mongering.

The Liberal Catholic Church sprang from Old Catholic sources. Before his defection to Rome, Bishop Arnold Harris Mathew consecrated in England a Bishop Frederick Samuel Willoughby. He also went over to Rome, but not until he had similarly consecrated Bishop James Ingall Wedgebody. This prelate visited the noted Theosophist Charles W. Leadbeater, fell under the influence of Theosophy, and consecrated Leadbeater as bishop of Aus-

[18] Ferguson, *The Confusion of Tongues*, pp. 281-82.

tralia. In 1916 these colleagues began the creation of a liturgy which combined occult mysteries with Roman sacramental notions. The completed form is "filled with the ghosts of Theosophy, so that not so much as an article remains without a spooky and cryptic reference of one sort or another." [19]

In 1917 Bishop Wedgebody made an evangelistic tour to the United States and consecrated Irving Steiger Cooper as regionary bishop. He founded a procathedral at Los Angeles, the paradise of cults with an occult flavor. The body has about thirty congregations with fifteen hundred members and has secured four church edifices. [20]

Presbyterian Bodies. The greater Presbyterian Churches in the United States are far removed from legalism in every form. There are, however, some small sects which are mildly legalistic because of their insistence on singing only the psalms, refusal to participate in politics, orthodoxy in scriptural interpretation, and certain details of worship. These are the Associate Synod or Associate Presbyterian Church, its kindred body, the Associate Reformed Presbyterian Church, the Synod of the Reformed Presbyterian Church or Old Light Covenanters, its sister sect, the General Synod of the Reformed Presbyterian Church or New Light Covenanters, and the United Presbyterian Church. These bodies are the descendants of the Secessionists and Covenanters of Scotland.

Scotch Presbyterianism experienced many tribulations and divisions in its native land. One of the earliest disruptions occurred in 1733 under the leadership of Ebenezer Erskine, who, with three others, was deposed as the result of a sermon preached in connection with the "lay patronage controversy," in which the dissenters opposed the practice of installing ministers selected by a group of laymen but not elected by the congregations. The four men formed the Associate Synod or Secession Church; the group was divided in 1747 into Burghers and Antiburghers, the former upholding and the latter opposing the religious clauses in oaths administered to burgesses of Scottish cities. Both the Burghers and Antiburghers later threw off "New Light" groups as the original "Old Light" parties "developed more modern views as to the limitations of the duties of the civil magistrate in the ecclesiastical sphere."

Another controversy resulted in the formation of the Relief Church in 1761. Thomas Gillespie was deposed by the general assembly for refusing to take part in the installation of a minister not chosen by the congregation. He was joined by three local churches and a presbytery was formed "for the relief of Christians deprived of their church privileges." In 1847 the Se-

[19] *Ibid.*, p. 282.
[20] See Piggott, *The Liberal Catholic Church*; Sheehan, *Teaching and Worship of the Liberal Catholic Church*; Leadbeater, *The Christian Creed*; Ferguson, *op. cit.*, ch. xiii.

cession and Relief Churches merged to form the United Presbyterian Church of Scotland.

The well-known Scottish Covenanters have had a long and turbulent history. Their first covenant to maintain the Reformed faith was entered into as early as 1581. In 1643 the Solemn League and Covenant was sworn to by both the Lords and the Commons and was accepted by Charles II in 1650, when he was seeking to recover the English throne. On the exile of the king and the rise of Cromwell there was a division, the Revolutionists accepting Cromwell and the Protestors or Covenant Men rejecting him under the terms of the covenant as never having been chosen by the nation. Bitter war and persecution broke out on the return of Charles, the Covenanters standing firm against him. William III in 1688 perfected a settlement which was accepted for the sake of peace by the majority of the Presbyterians, but the minority of Covenant Men refused the settlement as not in full accord with the Solemn League and Covenant. The practice of covenant-making had become habitual with them and remains one of their principles.

The SYNOD OF THE REFORMED PRESBYTERIAN CHURCH and the RE-FORMED PRESBYTERIAN CHURCH, GENERAL SYNOD, date from the eighteenth century, when many members of the Reformed Presbyterian Church, or Covenanters, came to America to escape persecution in Scotland. Ministers followed, and in 1774 at Paxtang, Pennsylvania, a presbytery was formed. In 1782 a union was formed with the Associate Presbyterian Church. Scattered societies held aloof, however, and on their appeal other ministers were sent from Scotland, and in 1798 the second Reformed presbytery was organized at Philadelphia. In 1809 the Synod of the Reformed Presbyterian Church was perfected. In 1832 dissension broken out in the body; the "Old Lights" held that the constitution of the United States was an infidel document in that it did not recognize the kingship of Jesus Christ, and therefore Christians should not vote, hold office, or participate in government thereunder, while the "New Lights" took the moderate position that the constitution was defective but not infidel or immoral, and that no oath or covenant was violated in exercising the franchise. The result was a disruption. The extremists or "Old Light" party became the Synod of the Reformed Presbyterian Church and the "New Lights" became the Reformed Presbyterian Church, General Synod.

The ASSOCIATE PRESBYTERIAN CHURCH, or the Associate Synod of North America, is an outgrowth of the Secession Movement led by Ebenezer Erskine. In 1753 the Secession Church of Scotland sent two ministers to America to meet the needs of emigrants, and the following year the Associate Synod was formed. When the union of the Associate Synod and the Reformed Presbyterian (Covenanter) Church was perfected in 1782, forming the Associate Reformed Presbyterian Church, two ministers and three ruling elders refused to enter the union. They formed an associate presbytery which was recognized by the Secession Church of Scotland, and in 1801 the Associate Synod of North America was organized.

The UNITED PRESBYTERIAN CHURCH dates from 1858, when the Associate Synod of North America and the Associate Reformed Presbyterian Church united under the name of the United Presbyterian Church. Eleven ministers of the synod dissented and continued the Associate Presbyterian Church.

The ASSOCIATE REFORMED PRESBYTERIAN CHURCH dates from 1858. The Associate Reformed Synod of the Carolinas had withdrawn from the General Synod of the Associate Reformed body in 1822, being in doubt as to the regularity of the larger group in matters of doctrine, and was known as the Associate Reformed Synod of the South. When the union of 1858 was perfected this synod became the Associate Reformed Presbyterian Church and has continued its independent existence.

The approximate statistics of these bodies are as follows:

Sect	Churches	Members
United Presbyterian Church	900	170,000
Associate Presbyterian Church	10	300
Associate Reformed Presbyterian Church	150	22,000
Synod of the Reformed Presbyterian Church (Old Light Covenanters)	90	7,000
Reformed Presbyterian Church, General Synod (New Light Covenanters)	15	2,000

These bodies are all of the conservative order and insist on the plenary inspiration and literal interpretation of the Scriptures. All are strongly Calvinistic except the United body, and all, with the same exception, prescribe the exclusive use of the metrical version of the psalms in singing. The latter feature is the distinguishing mark of the general group, the only point wherein these sects differ from certain others; they are called "Psalm Singers" by many outsiders. Superlative importance is attached to the psalms. "Next in importance to the translation of the whole Bible into the vulgar tongue, and declaring every man's right to read it and judge for himself," runs a quotation in the preface of one version, "were the rhyming versions of the psalms," and the editors declare that "the present version has been prepared under the consciousness that the gathered hosts of four centuries are looking upon us and charging us to guard the songs that made the nations free." [21]

[21] The Book of Psalms, Rendered in Metre and Set to Music, authorized by the Synod of the Reformed Presbyterian Church, 1930, p. 111.

The attachment of these groups to the stately psalms of the Old Testament rendered into what is frequently mediocre verse is an interesting example of legalistic biblicism.[22]

The Associate Synod and the Synod of the Reformed Presbyterian Church oppose secret societies.[23] The latter prohibits the use of musical instruments in worship, on the theory that what is not expressly commanded in the New Testament is forbidden.[24] The Reformed Synod and the General Synod practice closed Communion. The former stands on the old position of refusing to vote or hold public office until the constitution of the United States is amended to include the recognition of Jesus Christ, and it carries on an active propaganda to secure such an amendment.[25] The General Synod admits that it "is so small as to be of little importance. . . . And worse than that, too many are looking back to past glories of the Church rather than looking forward for opportunities of service and sacrifice." [26]

The ORTHODOX PRESBYTERIAN CHURCH was formed in 1936 as the Presbyterian Church in America, but in 1939 the present name was assumed as the result of court action. The body grew out of a protracted controversy in the Presbyterian Church, U. S. A., over alleged departures from Presbyterian doctrines and standards in the larger church. The conservative group was led by J. Gresham Machen, Clarence E. Macartney, Robert Dick Wilson, and others, and the Orthodox Presbyterian Church represents the foundamentalist viewpoint.

The literature of the body traces the beginning of the controversy to what it regards as doctrinal defections in the Presbyterian Church as far back as 1801, when the General Assembly adopted a plan of union or cooperation with Congregationalists, who rejected universal depravity and predestination. The plan was abrogated in 1837, however, and over five hundred "new school" congregations and 100,000 members withdrew. Other steps in the process were the establishment of the liberal or "new

[22] "If therefore the verses are not always so smooth and elegant as some may desire or expect," says the *Bay Psalm Book* of 1640, the first book printed in America, "let them consider that God's Altar needs not our pollishings."

[23] See *Free Masonry as a Religion* (pamphlet), Witness Committee, Synod of the Reformed Presbyterian Church, Pittsburgh, Pennsylvania.

[24] See *Voice of the Ages Against Instrumental Music in the Worship of God* (pamphlet), Committee on Testimony Bearing, Synod of the Reformed Presbyterian Church, Allegheny Pennsylvania.

[25] See *Is the Constitution of the United States Christian? Why Covenanters Do not Vote, Reasons for not Voting Under the Present Constitution of the United States* (pamphlet), Witness Committee and Committee on Testimony Bearing, Synod of the Reformed Presbyterian Church.

[26] The Rev. L. A. Benson, stated clerk, Clay, Kansas, in a letter to me. On these small sects see Glasgow, *History of the Reformed Presbyterian Church in America*; Latham, *History of the Associate Reformed Synod of the South*; Scouller, *History of the United Presbyterian Church in North America*; Hancock, *Church Error, or Instrumental Music Condemned; Reformation Principles Exhibited, Being the Declaration and Testimony of the Reformed Presbyterian Church.*

school" Auburn Theological Seminary; the readmission in 1869 of the liberals who went out in 1837; the addition of a "declaratory statement" to the Westminster Confession in 1903, making concessions to Arminianism preparatory to reunion with the Cumberland Presbyterian Church; the adoption by numerous presbyteries in 1918-20 of a proposal to unite with other Protestant bodies on the basis of the generally accepted doctrines of Christendom; the presentation in 1924 of the "Auburn Affirmation," signed by 1,300 ministers, protesting the action of the 1923 General Assembly in reaffirming the necessity of accepting five fundamental doctrines, and declaring that these doctrines were "men's theories" and "there is no assertion in the Scriptures that their writers were kept from error"; the reorganization of the board and faculty of Princeton Theological Seminary in 1929 by the inclusion of men who represented the liberal viewpoint, some of whom had signed the "Auburn Affirmation"; the refusal of the General Assembly in 1933 to adopt a resolution proposed by Machen, to the effect that members and missionaries of the Board of Foreign Missions must reject the viewpoint of the book *Rethinking Missions*, and affirm the exclusive nature of Christianity and the five essentials held up by the general assembly of 1923.

As the "fundamentalist-modernist" controversy developed, the conservatives themselves were not idle. Not only did they control the General Assembly of 1923 and bring about the adoption of the resolution regarding the five basic doctrinal tenets, but in 1924 they elected Macartney as moderator, and induced the 1925 General Assembly to overrule the action of the New York Presbytery in licensing two ministers who would not declare their belief in the Virgin Birth. In 1929 the conservative Westminster Theological Seminary was established at Philadelphia, independent of church control, following the liberalization of Princeton, and in 1934 the Independent Board for Presbyterian Foreign Missions was organized.

Nevertheless the conservatives felt that the church was completely dominated by modernists. "Auburn Affirmationists" sat on the missionary and educational boards; Princeton was in the hands of the liberals and Machen; Wilson, and Macartney had been eliminated; and all the moderators after 1924 were liberals.

The immediate occasion of the secession came at the General Assembly of 1936. Machen and another minister were unfrocked for supporting the independent board and refusing to obey the injunction of the 1934 Assembly to support the official board, and Arthur F. Perkins was suspended because he had organized a Bible conference independent of church control. The conservatives took the position that the church in the past had allowed modernism and false doctrines to come to a controlling position within its body, and had actually condemned men for their adherence to historic Presbyterian doctrine. The schism followed.

The Orthodox Presbyterian Church takes an uncompromising stand on Calvinism, the inspiration and literal interpretation of the Bible, and the sovereignty of God as interpreted in the older type of Reformed theology. Specifically it adopts and construes according to the traditional pattern the "five points of Calvinism": total depravity, unconditional election or predestination, the definite or limited Atonement, efficacious grace or the doctrine that men believe and are saved only because God selected them and made them able and willing to believe, and eternal security or "final perseverance of the saints." The denomination had about 75 congregations and 7,500 members in 1947.[27]

The PLYMOUTH BRETHREN, a body of believers known to most people by this title, but by themselves referred to simply as "The Brethren," are strong literal biblicists. The movement of which they are a part developed first in Ireland and England, near the close of the first quarter of the nineteenth century, under the leadership of John Nelson Darby, George Muller, and others. Becoming dissatisfied with the contemporary state of the church, small groups began meeting for spiritual communion, prayer, and "breaking of bread." One of the first gatherings was at Dublin in 1827 and the first permanent group was organized in 1829. The largest and most important was at Plymouth, hence the name of Plymouth Brethren.

These people were ambitious to develop a brotherhood conforming to the ancient pattern as laid down in the Scriptures. They were convinced that the existing churches had departed from primitive standards, and accordingly refrained from fellowship with the various denominations. No ecclesiastical organization was developed nor does one exist at the present time. The Brethren simply gathered in small groups, "broke bread" together, listened to the discourses of any persons who felt called to preach, and "searched the Scriptures" to discover where they might be led.

The doctrines developed by the Brethren are similar to those of other sects which seek to "recover the primitive church" by obeying the literal words of the Bible. Prominence is given to adventism, with the usual concomitants, and the second coming of the Lord is momentarily expected. The pessimism of adventist groups is reflected in the absence of programs and ideals for social betterment. Runs one of their modern pronouncements:

We believe, that the proper hope of God's people is not the improvement of the world but the coming of Christ for his own, to raise the dead in Christ and change

[27] See John Patton Galbraith, *Why the Orthodox Presbyterian Church*. The figures come from Paul Wooley, registrar and secretary of the Westminster Theological Seminary.

the living and then take them all out of the world, which he will then purge and cleanse by judgment preparatory to the millennium, when Israel and the nations of the earth will inhabit it under his rule, but his Church will always be in heaven.[28]

In the matter of polity, all denominational names and "systems of human devising for Church order" are rejected as unscriptural, and the same is true of ministerial ordination.

We believe that when a company of Christians is gathered for worship there should be no human leader in charge, but that all should be left to the spirit of God to use whom He may choose. We refuse all sorts of salaries or stipulated remunerations for the preaching of the Word. We take no collections at public meetings and refuse all help from the world.[29]

In their scriptural interpretations the Brethren indulge in various speculations concerning the person and sufferings of Christ, and have developed theological details which appear meticulous to the ordinary Christian.

Though forsaking the regular churches in order to set up the "true church," the Brethren have been given to contention, excommunication, and schism. The splits, for the most part, have revolved about the principle of exclusiveness and banning of individuals or groups whose doctrines or practices displease others. In 1848, for example, a teacher at Plymouth was suspected of heresy, and some of the groups put under a ban not only the teacher himself but all the members of the Plymouth body and any group that had received anyone who had been connected with Plymouth. The Bethesda assembly at Bristol objected to such severity and received into fellowship persons from Plymouth who had not themselves been infected with the heresy, even though they might have heard the heretical teacher. Thereupon other groups placed the whole Bethesda assembly under the same excommunication which had been pronounced against Plymouth, and even went to the extreme of excommunicating all the members of any assembly that did not repudiate both Plymouth and Bethesda. Thus was occasioned the most important, though by no means the only, split in the ranks of the Brethren.

While there are today several distinct groups, all may be classified as "Open" or "Exclusive," depending on their sympathy with, or opposition to, the Plymouth and Bristol position. The Exclusives recognize no persons save those within the fellowship of their own little group and in agreement at all points of doctrine and practice, which of course excludes nearly all the Christians in the world. The Open Brethren adopt a more friendly attitude, asking the question, "What does the person himself hold?"

[28] *What Do You Believe?* (leaflet), Bible Truth Depot. New York, New York.
[29] *Ibid.*

They are "Open" to receive Christians that are personally sound in the faith, unless there is clear evidence of intentional association with known evil. They reject the theory that ecclesiastical position is in itself disqualifying, but intercommunication with the assemblies tolerating heresy has never been contemplated nor allowed." [30]

About the middle of the nineteenth century a number of Brethren came to the United States, where they preached with some degree of success. Darby and other leaders made trips to this country on evangelistic tours, and small groups sprang up here and there over the country. Close contact was kept with the English sources of the movement, and each European squabble and split immediately resulted in similar divisions on this side of the Atlantic.

The Plymouth Brethren in the United States constitute a typical fundamentalist group, narrow and intolerant of the great body of Christians, and even among themselves, viewing the Bible as the inerrant and infallible revelation of God and hence the final authority in all things, and believing that they alone have discovered the divine pattern of what the church should be. In spite of the confidence in their own conformity to the apostolic ideal, they are divided into ten different sects. Since they have no organization and refuse to accept any name, they are designated simply as Plymouth Brethren I, II, III, etc. There are no discoverable variations in doctrinal position between the various bodies. As previously mentioned, the main point of difference concerns the "Exclusive" or "Open" attitude toward others. Though regarding themselves as the true church, they are in point of fact little more than a tract society. They engage in no missionary, benevolent, or evangelistic work, and their members are drawn mainly from the conservative and dissatisfied elements of other churches.

It is difficult to define the differences between the various sects of these Brethren. Only one body—the Plymouth Brethren II—may really be considered "Open" in the sense that persons outside the group are "fellowshiped." The other bodies vary in the degree of intolerance, but all confidently maintain their own superiority, frown upon others, and are quite free with "the ban." Brethren I occupies a middle position, but admits that the term "Exclusive" is applicable to it. Brethren III insists that Christ has given absolute judicial power to the assembly and "accordingly they advocate the absolute disfellowshiping of any person whose life or doctrinal views are not in accord with the principles of the Christian faith as laid down in the Scriptures," by which of course they mean their own interpretation of the Scriptures. Brethren IV disclaims any designation

[30] *Census of Religious Bodies*, 1926, II, 268.

whatever save those that the Scriptures apply to all believers, as Christians, Brethren, etc.; to accept any specific title would imply that they are a sect, which they deny, sects or divisions being condemned in I Cor. 1:10-15. Brethren V stands upon the same ground and insists that "they are strictly orthodox in their views and look with suspicion upon cults which depart from the simple interpretation of scripture."

It is almost impossible to keep track of the history and statistics of the Plymouth Brethren in this country. They have no organization and no officials who can make authoritative statements. It seems that any person who cares to do so may open an assembly anywhere at any time. There are no formalities of joining the membership, but rather a tendency to claim any person who displays interest and adopts the fundamentalist theology. The Brethren are loath to recognize any divisions in their ranks or to give out information. According to the census reports, there are approximately 600 Plymouth Brethren churches in the United States with 25,000 members. Only 156 church edifices are reported. The groups are quite small and meetings are usually held in homes or rented halls.[31]

The COONEYITES OR GO-PREACHERS are roving evangelists who preach a doctrine known as "the way of Jesus." It was first promulgated in Ireland around 1894 by William Irvine, or Erwin, an agent for a faith mission. The movement has gained few followers in the United States. One of its favorite slogans is "Go into all the world and preach," hence the name "Go-Preachers." These evangelists are often called "tramp preachers" because they give up their secular occupations and live from the receipts of the collections taken in their services. This practice seems to have been initiated by Edward Cooney, one of Irvine's most zealous converts, who impressed his name upon the group. The sect regards itself as the only true pattern of the church and is intolerant of other religious bodies.

The Mennonites. In proportion to their numerical strength the Mennonites are the most divided group of Christians in America; their 900 churches and 115,000 members belong to 16 separate sects, in addition to

[31] I have visited and interviewed Plymouth Brethren from Florida to New York, including the Bible Truth Depot and the Gospel Book and Tract Depot, both in New York city, and which are as nearly official publishing houses of the sects as their loose organization permits. In every case I encountered a reluctance, bordering on suspicion, to furnish information. The standard history of the Plymouth Brethren is Neatby, *History of the Plymouth Brethren;* the latest is a series of thirteen articles in *Serving and Waiting* (January, 1925—February, 1926); Ironside, *History of the Brethren Movement;* see also Groves, *Darbyism, Its Rise and Development;* Dennett, *The Plymouth Brethren;* Grant, *The Plymouth Brethren, Their History and Heresies;* Whately, *Plymouth Brethrenism: A Refutation of Its Principles and Doctrines;* Carson, *Heresies of the Plymouth Brethren;* Reid, *Plymouth Brethrenism Unveiled and Refuted;* Teulon, *History and Teaching of the Plymouth Brethren; Life Among the Closed Brethren;* Gregory, *Gospel of Separation;* Miller, *Plymouthism and the Modern Churches;* see also the *Writings* of John Nelson Darby.

which there are several not affiliated with any other body.[32] They trace their ancestry back to the antipedobaptists, or Anabaptists, of the fifteenth and sixteenth centuries. The particular branch of this movement from which the Mennonites took their rise was led by Menno Simons (1492-1559), whence the name of Mennonites. He was a Roman Catholic priest who experienced an evangelical conversion and struck out in opposition to the current tendencies of both the Reformation and Catholicism. He differed not so much in theology from Luther and the other Reformers, but opposed their ideas of the church, particularly its relation to, and reliance upon, the state, and advocated a more complete separation from the world. This last principle has marked his followers down to the present day. Simons can hardly be called the founder of the Mennonites, since groups espousing their distinctive tenets were in existence several years before his conversion, but he has always been recognized as the outstanding leader.

In spite of bitter persecutions many converts were made and groups sprang up all over Switzerland, Holland, Germany, and in parts of Russia, where they are still found. There was a great variety of beliefs among them. Some were Unitarians. Those who followed Melchior Hofmann and Thomas Muenzer were ardent millenarians and looked for an early establishment of Christ's kingdom at Strassburg; Hofmann named the year 1553 as the date of the end and announced himself as one of the "two witnesses" of Rev. 11:3. Jacob Hutter and the Swiss Brethren organized a communistic body, and communism remains a principle of the Hutterian Brethren, one of the many Mennonite groups. A body of Anabaptists in 1535 seized Münster, which became the scene of uncontrolled fanaticism until the movement was subdued after a siege of several months. Such vagrant doctrines and excesses were excrescences of the general movement. The main body of Mennonites held to the absolute separation of church and state, even to the point of taking no part in government, plainness of life and separateness from the world, the necessity of regeneration, and consequently the baptism of adults only. They were called "Rebaptizers" because of their insistence that persons baptized in infancy must again undergo the rite as a sign of conversion or regeneration after reaching years of accountability.

The first internal dissension among the Mennonites occurred in Europe in the closing years of the seventeenth century. Jacob Ammon declared the groups were becoming lax in discipline and insisted on the literal observance of the teachings of Menno Simons and the Canons of Dort.

[32] The case is not as bad, however, as it is made out by Ferguson, who, in *The Confusion of Tongues* (p. 422), says there are "one hundred and twenty-odd different groups among the Mennonites of America."

His especial point of insistence was on the ban, or excommunication of disobedient members, in conformity with I Cor. 5:9-11, II Thess. 3:14, Tit. 3:10, and the Dort Confessions. Ammon's party, known as the Amish, applied the ban "to daily life and the daily table," shunning proscribed persons in all details of social intercourse, even in the family circle, while the main party excluded them only from the Communion table.

In 1690 two bishops, Ammon and Blank, investigated conditions among the Mennonites of Switzerland and southern Germany, and ordered leaders accused of laxity to appear before them and answer the charges. When the persons summoned failed to appear, the Amish leaders expelled and excommunicated them, and they in turn expelled the Amish group. The separation became complete in 1698. Later efforts at reconciliation failed and the division between the Amish and regular Mennonite factions persists to this day.

The Mennonites in America. The first group of Mennonites came from Crefeld to America in 1683 and settled at Germantown, now a part of Philadelphia. At Germantown was organized not only the first Mennonite church in this country but also the first German Quaker, Dunker, German Reformed, Lutheran, Moravian, and German Methodist congregations. Other Mennonite groups followed, a second colony was established on Skippack Creek, thirty miles above Germantown, in 1702, and soon similar companies were found all over Pennsylvania, where they are still more numerous than elsewhere.

The immigrants came mainly from Germany and Switzerland and were honest, law-abiding, and thrifty farmers; most of them have remained on the soil to the present day. In theology they were evangelical and extremely conservative. To the common evangelical tenets they added the ceremony of foot washing, commonly required their women to wear a hair covering in public meetings, frowned upon marriage with unbelievers, forbade oaths, and insisted upon extreme plainness in dress and household equipment. For the most part they baptized by pouring, made much of the semiannual observance of the Lord's Supper, and held pronounced millenarian views. Their experiences of persecution caused them to refrain from participation in politics and especially office holding; at one time the Germantown government lapsed because none could be found to occupy the offices. In polity they represented congregationalism gone to seed. The local church was a supreme unit. Its ministers were selected by lot and the person chosen was obliged to serve regardless of qualifications, for was he not called of God? Each church had its bishop, and since he carried his office with him it sometimes happened that a tiny group had several prelates. Discipline was preserved by a rather free exercise of the ban. The Mennonites have preserved most of these features in spite of the influence of modern ideas.

Their pronounced congregationalism made schism easy in the Mennonite ranks; at the same time it made organization difficult. The first conference was held in 1727, attended by fifteen representatives from five churches. After this similar conferences were held at frequent but irregular intervals. The body most closely identified with the original history is the Mennonite Church, from which most of the other sects diverged. The approximate statistics are as follows:

Sect	Churches	Members
Mennonite Church	350	50,000
Hutterian Brethren, Mennonites	6	500
Conservative Amish Mennonite Church	20	3,500
Old Order Amish Mennonite Church	100	13,000
Church of God in Christ (Mennonite)	20	3,000
Old Order Mennonite Church (Wisler)	20	3,000
Reformed Mennonite Church	25	1,000
General Conference of the Mennonite Church of North America	150	40,000
Evangelical Mennonite Brethren	10	1,000
Mennonite Brethren in Christ	30	10,000
United Missionary Church	85	5,000
Mennonite Brethren Church of North America	60	15,000
Krimmer Brueder Gemeinde	10	1,200
Mennonite Kleine Gemeinde	4	300
Central Conference of Mennonites	30	3,500
Conference of the Defenseless Mennonites of North America	10	1,500
Stauffer Mennonite Church	4	200
Unaffiliated Mennonite Congregations	5	500
Totals	939	152,200

The first split among the Pennsylvania Mennonites occurred in connection with the Revolutionary War. The members refused to take any part in the war and paid a small fine for exemption. The fine was paid with little murmuring, but some objected to paying the war tax of three pounds and ten shillings. Christian Funk stoutly maintained that the tax should be paid and was excommunicated in 1778. He thereupon organized an independent group known as the "Funkites" which persisted until 1850.

The REFORMED MENNONITE CHURCH dates from 1812, when Francis Herr was expelled because of irregularities in a horse trade. He and his friends held meetings in his house, and on his death his son John Herr was converted, took up his father's cause, was elected a bishop, and organized the Reformed Mennonite Church. The members of this group hold no conferences, publish no manuals, operate no Sunday schools, are very strict in discipline, especially in the use of the ban, refuse to fellowship with other religious bodies, are severely plain in dress, and regard as sinful all adornment of the person or the home.[33]

The STAUFFER MENNONITE CHURCH, commonly called "Staufferites," resembles the Reformed Mennonites in strictness of discipline and rejection of Sunday schools. The members use the German language in worship and have no evening services or evangelistic meetings. They separated from the Groffdale congregation in Lancaster County, Pennsylvania, in a dispute over the exercise of the ban during the decade of 1840-50, the rigid element withdrawing and taking the name of their leader Jacob Stauffer. Locally they are known as "Pikers," from the location of their church on the Hinkletown and Blue Ball Pike. Once separated from the main body, the schismatics found it impossible to agree among themselves, and there have been two splits among the four churches which compose the sect. One party, known as the "Risslerites" from their leading bishop, numbers fewer than a dozen members. Each of the three groups calls itself the "right and true Stauffer Mennonite Church."

Another division occurred in 1847 over the cut of a minister's coat, which was collarless and of a prescribed plain style. John H. Oberholtzer, a young and educated minister, objected to the coat on the ground that the Mennonite creed did not prescribe any definite form of garment. He also asked for a written constitution. As a result of the controversy the liberal Oberholtzer faction withdrew and at the same time were expelled by the conference. Sixteen ministers and several congregations, with sections of other churches, formed an independent body. They practiced open communion, intermarried with members of other churches, restricted the use of the ban, and adopted a salaried ministry. These were all departures from the accepted Mennonite traditions. The churches later became charter members of the General Conference of Mennonites, though a small number withdrew in 1853 and formed the Evangelical Mennonite Church, which was later absorbed.

The CHURCH OF GOD IN CHRIST dates from 1858, when John Holdeman, a layman in the Old Mennonite Church, in Wayne County, Ohio, had visions and dreams through which he felt called to preach, though not selected by the customary procedure of the lot. He and about twenty followers declared that the old church had departed from the faith and that his own company was the true Church of God which had maintained an unbroken continuity since the days of Christ and the apostles. The group took the name of the Church of God in Christ. It had no appreciable

[33] Muser, *Reformed Mennonite Church.*

growth until after the Civil War, when it received accessions from the Russian immigrants in Kansas and other states. In doctrine it departs from Mennonite tradition only in refusing to take interest on money loaned and the laying on of hands after baptism.

The GENERAL CONFERENCE OF THE MENNONITE CHURCH was organized in 1860. In 1859, soon after the expulsion or withdrawal of the Holdeman faction in Ohio, two small Mennonite congregations in Lee County, Iowa, met to discuss the union of all the Mennonite sects into one body. The resolutions there adopted attracted wide attention among the believers and secured the support of Holdeman, who advocated the union movement in the columns of a paper he was then publishing. Under the auspices of the Iowa churches a general convention of Mennonites was held at West Point, Iowa, in 1860, and here the General Conference of the Mennonite Church was organized. This was the first and most ambitious attempt to unite the various sects and it has made more rapid progress than any of the groups remaining detached. The principle action was, and is, to unite Mennonite groups in support of mission work. In doctrine the General Conference is in agreement with other Mennonites. Its practices are much more liberal. The head covering is not obligatory upon women, foot washing is not enforced as an ordinance, and in the matter of conformity to the world in dress and life a more modern attitude is adopted.

The OLD ORDER MENNONITE CHURCH was founded in Ohio. Just as the first Mennonites deemed themselves, in true sectarian fashion, to have recovered original Christianity, so the Old Order Mennonites or "Wislerites" have recovered the original principles of Menno Simons. The Old Order church is an amalgamation of four groups of reactionaries who opposed the introduction of "innovations." Bishop Jacob Wisler of Ohio opposed English preaching, protracted meetings, evening services, "four part singing," Sunday schools, higher education, missions, and other progressive enterprises. His constant threats of excommunication against all who advocated modern methods made him a general nuisance and he was expelled in 1870. At once he organized a congregation of his own.

As the leaven of modernism worked among the Mennonites, protests against "innovations" broke out in other sections. In 1886 a band of "Woolwichers," so named from the Ontario township in which they resided, withdrew from their church in opposition to "falling top" buggies and other evidences of defection from the faith. In 1893 Bishop Jonas Martin led out one third of the Weaverland congregation in Lancaster County, Pennsylvania, because a new pulpit had been installed. The "Martinites" were joined by a conservative group in Rockingham County, Virginia, and then "Woolwichers" and "Martinites" together adhered to the "Wislerites." There was subsequently another split when certain members in

Ohio persisted in the use of a telephone. Ultraconservative in dress, form of worship, and social customs, the Old Order people are the fundamentalists among Mennonites.

The MENNONITE BRETHREN IN CHRIST and the UNITED MISSIONARY CHURCH are Methodistically inclined. The sect was formed by the union of several small groups which had, one by one, separated from the parent body because they held prayer meetings and revivals and gave rein to emotionalism which offended against the decorum prevalent among the main group. Undoubtedly they were influenced by the Methodist camp meetings of the period.

About 1853 William Gehman, pastor of an Oberholtzer church in Lehigh County, Pennsylvania, began holding prayer meetings for the cultivation of an emotional religious life and a definite experience of conversion. For this he was expelled, and in 1858 he organized a body known as the Evangelical Mennonites. In 1871 Solomon Eby of Ontario was expelled for the same offense, and about the same time Daniel Brenneman of Elkhart County, Indiana, suffered expulsion for a like cause. In 1874 the Eby and Brenneman groups united under the name of Reformed Mennonites, not to be confused with the conservative body of the same name already mentioned. Another company called the Brethren in Christ had seceded in 1838 from the River Brethren in order more freely to exercise their emotional and evangelistic tendencies. A similar body was known as the New Mennonites. In 1875 the New and Reformed bodies came together to form the United Mennonites; they were joined four years later by the Evangelical Mennonites, and the name became the United Evangelical Mennonites. In 1883, near Jamton, Ohio, a union of this body and the Brethren in Christ was perfected and the Mennonite Brethren in Christ resulted. In 1947 the general conference, meeting at Potsdam, Ohio, voted to change the name to United Missionary Church. The Pennsylvania conference voted against the change and continued to use the name of Mennonite Brethren in Christ.

In doctrine these sects do not differ radically from the regular Mennonites, but certain distinctive elements of practice have been added. They baptize by immersion, observe open Communion and foot washing, insist on second blessing sanctification, forbid tobacco and strong drink, and look for the immediate end of the world and the second coming of Christ. Healing and anointing with oil are practiced. In their camp meetings joy is unrestrained, and the typical conversion, preceded by an agony of conviction for sin and followed by emotional exhilaration, is highly valued. Government is modeled after the Methodist pattern, and revival efforts are directed to reaching sinners outside the Mennonite tradition. These are the most evangelical of all the Mennonites.

The Immigrants from Russia. In the last half of the eighteenth century Catherine of Russia invited German emigrants to settle the territory she had acquired from the Turks and Tartars, and her offer of free transportation, loans, and religious tolerance attracted colonies of persecuted Mennonites. By 1800 over four hundred families moved thither, settling in the Chortitz and Moltschna regions, where they developed communities and established churches. These German Mennonites in Russia had an interesting and romantic history.[34] They indulged in characteristic quarrels and splits and imbibed strange millenarian ideas. Among their experiences was the trek of Claas Epp and his followers across the steppes from Saratov and Moltschna eastward into the Mohammedan country of Khiva. Epp announced that Christ would appear in 1889 somewhere in middle Asia to the "Church in Philadelphia," which was his own little flock. He was one of the "two witnesses," and a minister with whom he quarreled was "the red dragon." Untold hardships were endured, but Epp was sustained by dreams which assured him that Elijah would meet him and carry him bodily into heaven. At the proper time he stood behind a table attired in ascension robes and attended by his people who gathered to bid him farewell. When nothing transpired the prophet discovered that he had been deceived by an old wall clock which stood in a leaning position with the hands pointing to the figures eight and nine; when straightened, the hands indicated nine and one, so the parousia was postponed two years. Epp finally claimed to be the son of Christ, and adopted the baptismal formula of "Father, *Sons*, and Holy Ghost." He was finally deserted and excommunicated, but lived until 1913 with a faithful band of twenty families.

The MENNONITE KLEINE GEMEINDE originated in Russia and was transplanted to America. It is sometimes called the "Little Congregation." The leader was Klass Reimer, who objected to office holding, the use of force, and advocated a more rigid discipline in religious matters. He organized the Kleine Gemeinde, practiced severe simplicity in dress and household, opposed education, smoking, hilarity at weddings, the social features of funerals, and other evidences of a "worldly" spirit. His followers favored a spontaneous and emotional religious experience and underwent strange hardships and mortifications, fasting, praying for hours at a time, and weeping. These excesses led them into serious immorality. About 1874 the Santa Fe and Burlington Railroads transported to Kansas and other sections of the West large numbers of Mennonites from Russia, among them several groups of the Kleine Gemeinde. The sect is still found in Kansas and Manitoba; they adhere to their distinctive practices but are one with other Mennonites in most matters of doctrine.

[34] See Smith, *The Mennonites*, ch. vii.

The BRUDER GEMEINDE and the KRIMMER BRUDER GEMEINDE are other Russian sects which resulted from an evangelistic revolt against the coldness and formality of the regular congregations. A controversy broke out and the enthusiasts seceded. Similar to the Bruder Gemeinde was the Krimmer Bruder Gemeinde, or Crimean Brethren, though this sect sprang from a Kleine Gemeinde congregation. In the emigration to America in the seventies were members of both these sects. They settled in Kansas, the Dakotas, and other states, where they are still found. The Krimmer Bruder Gemeinde are strict disciplinarians and are in opposition to modern dress, large land holdings, amusements, and general worldliness. Both sects adopted immersion, the Bruder Gemeinde baptizing backward and the Krimmer Bruder dipping forward.

The DEFENSELESS MENNONITE BRETHREN IN CHRIST OF NORTH AMERICA sprang up in the Middle West. In 1873 Isaac Peters was exiled from Russia on account of emigration agitation. He went to Nebraska, where he organized some churches. About 1889 Aaron Wall drew off some conservative Mennonites in Minnesota who opposed missions, Sunday schools, and other innovations. The Peters and Wall congregations in 1910 formed a conference under the name of Defenseless Mennonite Brethren in Christ of North America. This sect has since tempered its views and now maintains both missions and Sunday schools.[35] It has in recent years called itself the Evangelical Mennonite Brethren.

The HUTTERIAN BRETHREN are a sect of communists which have a common origin with, and are classed among, the Mennonites. These people sprang from the activities of Hans Hut, a chiliastic Anabaptist prophet of Germany in the first quarter of the sixteenth century. Sympathizing with the radical Munzer, he was active in the peasant uprising, though claiming to oppose carnal force. He outlined a detailed millenarian scheme and announced that Christ would appear in two years to destroy the godless. He finally died in the flames of his prison in 1527; it was alleged that he set fire to his cot in anticipation of execution. Hut outlined the plan of communism which his followers now carry out.

The Hutterian Brethren came from Russia, whither they had fled from Germany, and settled in South Dakota in 1874. They live in large households or "bruderhops," eat at a common table, use the German language, and observe a simple form of worship. Their doctrines are in accord with other Mennonites except in the matters of communism and millenarianism. The children are reared in nurseries, but spend the nights with their parents. The men wear quaint old-fashioned clothes fastened with hooks and eyes. In their services they sing sixteenth-century hymns, in one part

[35] For fuller discussions of all these Mennonite bodies see Smith, *The Mennonites.*

only. They are strictly nonresistant and encountered trouble with the government and their neighbors during World War I; on one occasion their sheep and cattle were forcibly seized and sold by the authorities for $20,000, which was used to buy Liberty Bonds. As a result of this persecution many of the Hutterites went to Canada, but the dominion finally forbade their settlement there.

The most picturesque of the Mennonites are the Amish, who took their rise from the activity of Jacob Ammon, already mentioned. These people began coming to America about 1727, and by 1742 there was a settlement in what is now Berks County, Pennsylvania, strong enough to secure from the Provincial Assembly exemption from the oath of naturalization. There are now large numbers of the Amish in Lancaster County, and they are found elsewhere in Pennsylvania, Ohio, Indiana, Kansas, and other states. There are four separate sects still maintaining an independent existence. They are known as the "hook-and-eye" Mennonites, from the refusal of many of them to wear buttons on their coats.[36] Strictness in abstaining from worldly practices, and the application of the ban upon disobedient members are distinguishing marks of the typical Amish. In addition to the head covering of the women, and the other practices common to Mennonites, the Amish generally forbid telephones, radios, furnaces, curtains, suspenders, musical instruments, carpets, pictures, sewing machines, windmills, and top buggies, though strangely enough many of them use automobiles as necessities. They are familiar figures on the roads and city streets in Pennsylvania, where they present a striking appearance in the quaint coats, low and broad hats, long hair and beards, long and full skirts, and black bonnets. They are honest and respected folk, kindly and hospitable, loyal to kith and kin, and are commonly regarded as among the best farmers in Pennsylvania.

The strongest body is the OLD ORDER AMISH MENNONITE CHURCH. About 1850 a dispute arose over the method of baptism, whether it should be in the house or outside in running water. Other points at issue during the same period included the use of organs in the home, hymnbooks, and separation of the sexes in religious services. A conference was held in a large barn in Wayne County, Ohio, in 1862, where an unsuccessful attempt was made to reconcile the differences. The conservatives have since been known as the Old Order Amish.

[36] Ferguson, *op. cit.*, says this is due to their aversion to killing animals, since buttons are made of bone. This is an error. It is a part of their idea of separateness from the world and the maintenance of the old European custom. I have been told that they feared concession at this point would eventually mean a lapse from their traditional ideas of separateness into other and more serious worldliness.

This group preserves the practices and prohibitions mentioned above. They have few church houses, usually holding their meetings in barns or homes. The host provides a meal, which is followed by the communion service. They use the German language in preaching, have no evening services or Sunday schools, and oppose higher education. The ministers are unsalaried and chosen by lot. Their strictness in the use of the ban is a marked feature of discipline; the excommunicated must be shunned even in the household, a practice which has caused many domestic tragedies and resulted in one instance in the murder of an entire family. Until recently at least, they retained the old colonial custom of "bundling," in which courting couples are placed in bed together.

The CONSERVATIVE AMISH MENNONITE CHURCH is slightly more modern. Hooks and eyes are generally worn on coats and vests, but otherwise there is more freedom in attire. The members are somewhat fraternal in their attitude toward other churches, while the Old Order brethren fraternize not at all. The Conservative congregations have houses of worship and the sect has made a beginning in missionary and benevolent work. The only noticeable difference between the Conservative and the Old Order groups lies in the fact that the former have yielded slightly to the modern spirit.

The DEFENSELESS MENNONITES originated in 1866 under the leadership of Henry Egli, who withdrew because the Amish of Illinois and Ohio were not rigid enough in their dress regulations and did not insist on a vital religious experience. As time went on, however, the former contention was forgotten and the sect has now discarded dress restrictions. They are optional immersionists, but in all other respects are similar to the more conservative Mennonites.

The CENTRAL CONFERENCE OF MENNONITES had its beginning in a poem written in 1870 by Joseph Yoder of Illinois, in which he is alleged to have denied eternal punishment. The minister's conference ordered Bishop Joseph Stuckey to expel Yoder, but the former refused. A committee of ultraconservative Amish from Pennsylvania sat on the case, affirmed the judgment of the minister's conference, and declared that unless Stuckey expelled Yoder he and his congregation would no longer be regarded as members of the conference. For more than twenty years this church remained detached, but in 1899 other liberal congregations joined the Stuckey faction and the Illinois Conference of Mennonites was formed. The name was later changed to Central Conference of Mennonites. The sect removed dress restrictions, but otherwise differs little from other Mennonites in faith and practice. It engages in both home and foreign missionary work and supports educational and benevolent institutions jointly with other bodies.[37] In 1948 a merger of the Central Conference of Mennonites and the General Conference of the Mennonite Church of North America was reported.

[37] There is a voluminous literature on the various Mennonite bodies. I have visited extensively among them in Pennsylvania, examined their literature in the Mennonite Publishing House at Scottdale, and secured data by questionnaires from most of the groups. In the foregoing account strong reliance has been placed on Smith, *The Mennonites;* Musser, *Reformed Mennonite Church;* Weaver, *History of the Central Conference Mennonite Church;* Funk, *The Mennonite Church and Her Accusers;* Kaufman, *The Mennonite Church and Current Issues;* and *The Mennonite Year Book.* See also Grubb, *The Mennonite Church of Germantown;* Hartzler and Kaufman, *Mennonite Church History;* Hartzler, *Mennonites and the World War;* Holdeman, *History of the Church of God;* Wick, *The Amish Mennonites;* Smith, *The Mennonites of America;* Krehbiel, *History of the General Conference of the Mennonites of North America;* Vos, *Menno Simons;* Menno Simons, *Complete Works;* Cramer, *Menno Simons;* Kautsky, *Communism in Central Europe in the Time of the Reformation.*

CHAPTER VII

LEGALISTIC OR OBJECTIVIST SECTS—PART TWO

THE MAJORITY OF AMERICAN BAPTISTS WOULD JUSTLY PROTEST AGAINST being regarded as legalistic in any sense, even approximate, to that in which the sacramentarian bodies are legalistic, hence a disclaimer of so regarding them must at once be entered. Indeed few groups are farther removed from sacerdotalism than are the Baptists. They are mentioned in the category only because many of the smaller sects cling to certain objective practices, such as immersion, foot washing, and anointing with oil, as necessary, if not to salvation, at least to membership in the true Christian church. The larger and more influential Baptist bodies may be excluded from the category altogether.

It is not uncommon for Baptists to regard themselves as constituting the true apostolic church.

It is a distinct principle with Baptists that they acknowledge no human founder, recognize no human authority, and subscribe to no human creed. For all these things, Baptists of every name and order go back to the New Testament. And while no competent Baptist historian assumes to be able to trace a succession of Baptist churches throughout the ages, most of them are of one accord in believing that, if we could secure the records, there would be found heroic groups of believers in every age who upheld with their testimonies and, in many cases, with their lives, the great and outstanding principles of the Baptist churches of today.

So runs the opening paragraph of the authorized statement concerning the Baptists in the *United States Census of Religious Bodies*.[1]

That statement could doubtless be made of nearly every Protestant group in the world. They all profess to rely exclusively upon the New Testament, and if they have creeds (as do the Baptists, in point of fact) they would be quick to deny that such creeds are "human," but would insist that their formulated statements simply reduce to systematized modern terms only what the New Testament teaches. Hence they likewise would claim that in every age were found groups loyal to these principles. Other Christians,

[1] 1926, II, 77.

therefore, dismiss the Baptist claim to represent in any distinctive way original apostolic Christianity.

Baptists, however, quite generally believe and assert that they have a distinctive message, and this belief leads many of them, even the largest of all bodies, the Southern Baptist Convention, to hold more or less aloof from interdenominational co-operation. The Baptist principles which are regarded as "distinctive" are as follows: (1) The absolute supremacy of the Scriptures as the norm of faith and practice. This is applied positively and negatively. Not only must a doctrine or practice be not contradictory of Scripture, it must actually be required by the same. (2) Rejection of infant baptism, as being contrascriptural, opposed to the requirement of a converted or regenerated church membership. (3) Regeneration as a condition of membership in the church. (4) Absolute freedom of conscience. (5) Complete immersion as the only valid form of baptism and its necessity to church membership.[2]

Other Protestants deny that there is anything distinctive in these principles; many other bodies hold all of them and nearly all bodies accept some of them. In the matter of infant baptism and its compatibility with the theory of regenerate membership, it is pointed out that baptized infants *are not admitted to membership* by other Protestants; nearly all bodies hold, in theory at least, to the idea of a regenerate membership, and persons baptized in babyhood are required to accept the conventional vows after reaching years of accountability, and presumably after having become converted, before they become members of the church. No Protestant body accepts baptismal regeneration, nor are admittedly unregenerate individuals admitted to membership.

In general, Baptists are mildly Calvinistic in theology and adhere more or less closely to the New Hampshire Baptist Confession of 1833; some of the smaller sects are strictly Calvinistic and others are Arminian in belief. In evangelical temper and attitude toward modern social movements there is little difference between the larger Baptist bodies and the other outstanding Protestant churches. Only the small Baptist sects fall within the purview of the present discussion.

Antimission Baptists. The great Baptist bodies are among the most fervent and effective missionary agencies of the world. This is not true of several small sects. Opposition to missions, missionary organizations, Sunday schools, temperance societies, and an educated ministry has been vehement in Baptist ranks and controversy over these matters disrupted churches and associations, just. as the controversy over holiness led to Methodist schisms.

[2] Newman, *A History of the Baptist Churches in the United States*, pp. 1-4.

The antimission movement broke out among the Baptists in Tennessee, Kentucky, the Carolinas, and other frontier states near the beginning of the nineteenth century. It swept through the Baptist communion and disrupted its work everywhere along the frontier. The American Board of Commissioners for Foreign Missions sent out to India in 1812 two missionaries, Judson and Rice, and on the voyage, though sailing on different ships, both embraced Baptist views. The news electrified American Baptists. The event was regarded as a providential challenge to missionary activity. Rice at once returned and became "the field marshal of Baptist missions." He was largely instrumental in organizing the Baptist Mission Board.

Rice at first met little or no opposition, even along the frontier. In Kentucky and Tennessee he received larger contributions than in other states.[3] In 1818 the Illinois Association received John M. Peck, a western missionary, and declared in its *Minutes:* "Brother Peck presented the plan of a society to employ missionaries, and promote common schools amongst the whites and Indians, which we desire to see carried into effect, and which we recommend to the churches:"

One year later, however, the Wood River Church of the same association went on record as follows:

The Church is not willing for any of her members to have anything to do with the Board of Western Missions. . . . Whereas Br. Jones was appointed by the Board as a missionary for one month the Church is willing he may receive the wages appointed him for the same and then be cautious to receive no more from the Board for like service.[4]

The antimission movement soon spread through the western churches, capturing Tennessee completely and virtually sweeping Kentucky and other states.

Not a man ventured to open his mouth in favor of any benevolent enterprise or action. The missionary societies were dissolved and the associations rescinded all their resolutions by which they were in any way connected with these measures, and in this respect, the spirit of death rested upon the whole people.[5]

This antimission movement was characterized sometimes by turbulence and nearly always by bitterness. The salaried missionaries in the west were scorned. Jacob Bower related that in Missouri a company gathered near the house where he was preaching and chopped down trees to disturb his meeting.[6] The salaries were a bogey, contributions were referred to as

[3] Sweet, *Religion on the American Frontier—The Baptists*, p. 61.
[4] *Ibid.*, pp. 61, 62.
[5] *Ibid.*, p. 63.
[6] *Ibid.*, p. 64.

"taxation," presaging a state church, and collectors were compared to Tetzel and the peddlers of indulgences against whom the Reformers waged war. The Apple Creek Antimission Association of Illinois in 1830 refused to hear a missionary preacher, and declared "an unfellowship with foreign and domestic missionary and Bible societies, Sunday schools and tract societies, and all other missionary institutions." The Sugar Creek Association of Indiana in 1832 adopted a constitution which declared:

Any church suffering their members to unite with any of the Mission Conventions, Colleges, Tracts, Bible, Temperance, &c., Societies, and failing to deal with their members, shall be considered guilty of violation of the principles of the union, that the association, when put in possession of a knowledge of such facts, shall punish such Churches as being not of us.

Similiar actions could be cited in large numbers from the records and circular letters of associations and churches in all the frontier states during the period. In 1846 there were 68,068 antimission Baptists in the country; 11,603 were in Georgia, 10,186 in Tennessee, and between 4,000 and 6,000 in each of the states of Virginia, North Carolina, Alabama, Kentucky, Ohio, Indiana, Illinois, and Missouri. It is clear that antimissionism was a frontier phenomenon.[7]

The leaders in this reactionary movement were John Taylor, Daniel Parker, and Alexander Campbell. Taylor was a Kentucky preacher whose ire was aroused by the sad picture of the religious state of the frontier painted by the missionary authorities. He thought their statements reflected on the work of the wilderness preachers. In 1819 he published a pamphlet under the title *Thoughts on Missions,* in which he compared the missionaries to Judas and leeches. Though Taylor later changed his views, his writing and preaching did incalculable harm to the missionary cause.[8]

Daniel Parker, of Two-Seed-in-the-Spirit fame, was the archenemy of missions, Sunday schools, and all such "innovations." He worked in Tennessee, Kentucky, and Illinois, where the fruits of his activity still linger. In 1820 he opposed the missionary board in a vigorous pamphlet entitled *A Public Address to the Baptist Society,* and in 1829 he began publishing the *Church Advocate,* in the columns of which for two years he poured vituperation upon missions and the other movements to which he was opposed. He pointed out that in calling men, assigning them to fields, and insisting upon education the board usurped the prerogatives of God. It was an unscriptural body, having

neither precept nor example to justify it within the two lids of the Bible, [it] re-

[7] *Ibid.,* pp. 64-66.
[8] *Ibid.,* pp. 67, 68.

belled against the king of Zion, violated the government of the gospel church, and forfeited the right to the union and brought distress on the Church of Christ.[9]

Alexander Campbell, founder of the Disciples of Christ, was a Baptist from 1813 to 1830. In 1823 he began a periodical called the *Christian Baptist,* which was succeeded in 1829 by the *Millennial Harbinger.* In these papers he advocated antimission and allied principles. In 1844, after he had separated from the Baptists and organized the Disciples, he changed front and adopted the principles he had formerly condemned. He had already done much harm, however, and after his defection the conservative Baptists strengthened their position by turning his previous diatribes against him.

The antimission agitators urged four main objections to the "innovations." In the first place, boards and societies, with their centralization of authority, were subversive of the fundamental Baptist principle of democarcy and congregational polity. John Taylor spoke of "the great Board of Missions in America, and Rice their chief cook," and "their mighty convention" as being comparable to the operations of Tetzel when

the Pope of Rome and the Mother of Harlots were at their zenith. . . . Money and power are the two principal members of the old beast. That both of these limbs are found in this young beast is obvious and exemplified in the great solicitude of correspondence with all Baptist associations. . . . I consider these great men as verging close on an aristocracy, with an object to sap the foundation of Baptist republican government.[10]

Further, the "money basis" of the missionary enterprise was a ground of objection. The collections were heartily despised. Over and over the changes were rung on the ancient practice of selling indulgences. Rice was "a modern Tetzel. . . . The Pope's old orator of that name was equally innocent with Luther Rice and his motive about the same." [11] To Daniel Parker the missionaries resembled the money changers whom Christ drove from the temple, and they were to experience a similar fate.[12] Alexander Campbell delighted in exhibiting the expense of missionary operations, a practice still indulged in, and he accused the societies of greed, dishonesty, embezzlement, and stealing. Referring to Mrs. Judson's clothing, he declared, "The visiting dress of this self-denying female missionary could not be valued at less than Twelve Hundred Dollars!!" [13]

[9] *Ibid.,* pp. 68-70.
[10] *Thoughts on Missions,* pp. 21, 22.
[11] *Ibid.,* p. 9.
[12] Sweet, *op. cit.,* p. 73.
[13] Quoted from the *Christian Baptist* by Sweet, *op. cit.,* p. 71.

In the third place, jealousy of the educated and salaried preachers sent out by the missionary society was a powerful factor in arousing the ire of the frontier clergy. Sweet cites the retort of one of the latter when pressed on his objections to the missionaries:

Well, if you must know, Brother Moderator, you know the big trees in the woods overshadow the little ones; and these missionaries will all be great men, and the people will all go to hear them preach, and we shall all be put down. That's the objection.[14]

Most effective, however, was the argument from scripture. It was insisted that missionary societies were not mentioned in the Bible; the apostles were not sent out by such organizations; God never intended that the heathen should be converted by such methods; it was impious and presumptuous to educate a man to do what God had called him to do. Such contentions had much force among strict literalists and ultra-Calvinists. In his characteristic vein of ridicule Campbell pictured Paul and Barnabas before a missionary society:

On Wednesday, the 11th of June, A.D. 44, the Rev. Saulus Paulus and the Rev. Joses Barnabas were set apart as missionaries to the Gentiles dispersed throughout the world. . . . Mr. Paulus is a young man and a native of the city of Tarsus; he received his classical and theological education in the theological seminary at Jerusalem. He appeared before the committee a man of good sense, of ardent piety, and understandingly led by the Spirit of God to the work in which he is now engaged.[15]

Parker declared that Jonah was not sent as a missionary by a society, nor was he educated in a seminary for his task, nor did he look to a society for his salary.[16]

The argument against missionaries was thus stated in a circular letter of October, 1810, to the Primitive Baptist churches of Mississippi:

We are obliged to believe that inasmuch as God sent his Son into the world to save his people from their sins, that he has a people whom he designs to save. Now, if any of those whom God designs to save should finally be lost, he must either change his mind, or else he has not the power to accomplish his designs—the supposition of which we consider blasphemy.[17]

The great commission was given to the apostles only and not to elders or churches. It had already been fulfilled. At the time this charge was given

---

[14] Sweet, op. cit., p. 74, quoted from Babcock, *Memoirs of John Mason Peck*, p. 111.
[15] Quoted by Sweet, op. cit., p. 71n.
[16] Parker, *A Public Address to the Baptist Society*, quoted by Sweet, op. cit., p. 74.
[17] Benjamin Green, *A History of the Primitive Baptists of Mississippi*, p. 90.

there was no organized church, and the construction placed on it by the modern societies would imply that all Christians should go as missionaries to the heathen world.

We would now ask every intelligent Christian whether the gospel was sent to the heathen land of America by a Missionary Society, or the providence of God? The truth is, that the Holy Ghost, it seems, has never adopted any other mode than persecution in some shape for sending the gospel from one country to another. This was commenced at Jerusalem and has been continued ever since.[18]

In a circular of the Rocky Spring Primitive Baptist church, Holmes County, Mississippi, under date of April, 1839, the argument is thus stated:

It is certain that everything which God has not commanded, he has forbidden—and those who go beyond the commandments of God are saying, by their acts, that God has forgotten to command some things actually necessary in carrying on his work. Reflections of this kind are the cause wherefore we protest against Missionary, Tract, Sunday School, and Temperance Societies. . . . About Sunday Schools and Temperance Societies we shall say nothing more than that we consider them a part of the trumpery of Mystery Babylon the Great. We cannot fellowship your theological schools. . . . We challenge the learned world to show any divine authority for sending a man to school after God has called him to the ministry; nor is there any need of it, for all power in heaven and on earth is in the hands of God.[19]

In opposing collections for missions it was asserted that Rom. 15:25-27 taught the exact opposite. Paul's collections were for the saints; missionary offerings are for the heathen. Paul ministered in carnal things; the missionaries in spiritual things.[20]

In disparagement the missionary supporters were called "Means Baptists."

Means refers to those who rely upon human means of whatever character to execute the purposes of God: religiously speaking we see this in Sunday Schools, Mission Systems, Theological Schools, &c.; but all this belongs to the open and avowed enemies of gospel grace.

Against a man who insisted on taking children to religious services the following attack was directed:

I do not object to seeing young people to meeting providing they behave themselves; and of course it is especially encouraging if they seem to have an interest in

[18] Ibid., p. 34.
[19] Ibid., pp. 176, 177.
[20] Ibid., p. 63.

gospel truth; but Mr. Gold goes farther than this, seeming to hold it as a sacred duty for Old School Baptists to take their children; even *their babies* to their meetings; and see that they "give *what attention they can* to the preaching." This . . . unquestionably is the Means system. If this idea is correct, why not organize an Old School Baptist Sunday School? A move of this character has been made by some elements of this class of Baptists as well as introducing organs in their meeting houses.[21]

"Hard-Shell" Baptist Sects. The conservative "anti" Baptists of the rural frontier were in derision called "hard shells" or "landmarkers" by their more progressive brethren, and the former term is frequently applied to them at the present day. In due time the principles against which they contended were accepted by the large majority of Baptists, but in the rural districts many persisted in unbending opposition to the "innovations." These gradually drifted together and formed independent sects, the main characteristics of which may be gathered from the above discussion of the antimission movement. They are for the most part strongly Calvinistic, adhere strictly to the verbal inspiration and literal interpretation of the Bible, insist on closed Communion, generally practice foot washing, and usually condemn organs, along with Sunday schools and ecclesiastical organizations.

The PRIMITIVE BAPTISTS constitute the largest of these conservative groups, though their numbers are declining. They have about 1,700 churches and 65,000 members, nearly all in rural areas. They deny that they are a denomination and have no state conventions or general organizations of any kind. While not avowedly opposed to education, they deny that it is necessary to successful preaching of the gospel and their ministers are usually ignorant and unsalaried men. Less than half of their congregations possess houses of worship, and such churches as exist have an average value of less than $1,700. The Primitives are the most orthodox and exclusive of all Baptists.

The COLORED PRIMITIVE BAPTISTS are identical in belief and practice with the white brothers. They have around 1,000 churches and 44,000 members, nearly all in the rural South. The progressive movement has made some inroads on them, as has also been true of the white Primitives; about two dozen churches have organized Sunday schools and societies, but these are regarded with high disfavor.

The TWO-SEED-IN-THE-SPIRIT PREDESTINARIAN BAPTISTS are the survivors of Elder Daniel Parker's followers. They have about a dozen churches and 200 members, all but a handful being in the rural areas of Tennessee and Kentucky.

[21] William Middleton Smoat, *The Contest of 1886-89*, pp. 73, 77. This work was published at Occoquan, Virginia, in 1923 and has a second preface dated as late as 1929.

The Two-Seed-in-the-Spirit doctrine preserves the extreme antimission Calvinistic theology. As expounded by Parker and accepted today, it is a modified Manicheanism. Adam and Eve at creation were infused with the good seed, which is an emanation from God. The bad seed, or spirit of the serpent or devil, entered Eve when she fell, and by her was transmitted down the stream of life. Some children, to this day, are born of the good seed and hence are predestined to eternal life; others are so unfortunate as to spring from the bad seed and are children of the devil, predestined to eternal damnation. Nothing can be done about it in either case. To send the gospel to the former is useless; to preach to the latter futile. Hence it follows as the night the day that missionary activity is not to be engaged in by sensible Christians.[22]

Arminian Baptists. Five Baptist sects are distinguished by Arminian or freewill doctrines in opposition to the Calvinism or predestinarianism of other Baptists. Most of them are declining in numbers. In their conservative principles, literalistic views, and adherence to such practices as immersion, foot washing, and anointing with oil, they are at one with the other small groups.

The FREEWILL BAPTIST CHURCH, the largest such body, is found mainly in the Southern states and numbers over 200,000 members in 1,100 local churches. The Freewill Baptists are among the oldest religionists in the country. A church emigrated from Wales in 1701 and settled on the "Welsh Tract" in Pennsylvania. The American leader was Elder Paul Palmer, and his activity resulted in the organization of several churches in North Carolina and other states before the middle of the eighteenth century. The rapid growth of Calvinistic Baptists made severe inroads on the body until only a few scattered congregations remained steadfast. These rallied in due time and experienced a gradual growth. They had no distinctive name, but because of their belief in the universality of the Atonement they became known as Original Freewill Baptists. They have since dropped the word "Original." Since the Civil War they have held their own conferences and have been recognized as an independent denomination. A group in the North, known as the Free Baptists, left the others and affiliated with the Northern Baptist Convention.

Freewill Baptists hold with Methodists and other Arminians that "Christ tasted death for every man." They further differ from other Baptists in the practice of "open Communion." They observe foot washing in obedience to the precept of Christ, and anoint the sick with oil in healing. Their denominational headquarters are at Ayden, North Carolina,

---

[22] A brief statement of this Two-Seed doctrine in theological terms is found in the authorized statement of Elder E. R. Little in the *Census of Religious Bodies*, 1926, II, 219. For a fuller statement see Spencer, *A History of Kentucky Baptists*.

where they maintain a publishing house and a theological seminary known as Eureka College.

The UNITED AMERICAN FREEWILL BAPTIST CHURCH is a Negro branch of the Freewill Baptists. Originally a part of the Freewill Baptist group and tracing its history to the same sources, this body became an independent denomination after the Civil War. In doctrine, polity, and religious practice it is identical with the white Freewill body. It has 350 churches and 75,000 members, and operates Kinston College at Kinston, North Carolina. These colored Baptists are confined to the states of North Carolina, Georgia, Alabama, Mississippi, and Louisiana.

The GENERAL BAPTISTS are another Freewill group. They have 500 churches and 40,000 members, mainly in the rural districts of the South. They differ in no important respects from the Freewill Baptists; they accept a "general" Atonement and practice open Communion and foot washing. They claim to spring directly from the Arminian Baptists of Holland and England and to have received their first minister, Robert Nordin, from London in 1714. Their early history in America, however, seems to be identical with that of the Freewill Baptists. In 1823 Benoni Stinson organized an association in Indiana and drew up a confession of faith consisting of eleven articles; this statement, with slight changes, is still accepted by the General Baptists, and Stinson may be regarded as the real founder of the sect. There is a college and theological seminary, Oakland City College, in Indiana and a publishing house at Owensville in the same state.

The GENERAL SIX-PRINCIPLE BAPTISTS have four churches and nearly three hundred members in Rhode Island and Pennsylvania. The body was organized as early as 1653 at Providence, as a result of a controversy over the necessity of "laying on of hands." The practice is still observed, "not, however, as a mere form, but as a sign of the reception of the gifts of the Holy Ghost." [23] The six principles are repentance, faith, baptism, laying on of hands, resurrection of the dead, and eternal judgment.

The FREEWILL BAPTISTS (BULLOCKITES) have practically disappeared. In 1926 there were but two churches and thirty-six members, but those churches made no reports in the census of 1936. In 1835 John Buzzell, Charles Bean, and Jeremiah Bullock led a defection from the Free Baptists, which group had been organized in 1780 by Benjamin Randall. Later, Bullock again seceded and his followers formed a Freewill Baptist sect which was nicknamed "Bullockite."

Other Small Baptist Sects. Several Baptist sects observe Saturday as the

---

[23] *Census of Religious Bodies,* 1936 II, 157.

Christian Sabbath. All of these save one are of German lineage and are listed among the Dunkers.

The SEVENTH-DAY BAPTISTS are included in the regular Baptist category. These claim to trace their ancestry back to apostolic times and find among their forebears such sects as the Nazarenes, Cerinthians, Hypsistari, and certain groups of the Albigenses and Waldenses.[24] They first figure definitely in history, however, in England about the time of Cromwell. In 1664 a Seventh-Day Baptist, Stephen Mumford, came from London and settled near Newport, Rhode Island, where he united with the Newport church. As a result of his labors several converts were made in the congregation, and in 1671 a schism occurred which resulted in the establishment at Newport of the first Seventh-Day Baptist Church in America. The sect has been in existence since that period and today has over sixty congregations and seven thousand members in this country.

The Seventh-Day Baptists are in general agreement with Calvinistic Baptists save in their Sabbatarian views. In recent years they have departed from the practice of closed Communion and invite all Christians to their altars. They are among the few small sects which adopt a liberal and modern attitude toward religious education and are quite active in missionary and other forms of benevolent activity. Alfred University, at Alfred, New York, is under the control of the denomination, which also operates schools at Milton, Wisconsin, and Salem, West Virginia.

The SEPARATE BAPTISTS are found in Kentucky, Tennessee, Indiana, and Illinois, where are ninety churches with six thousand adherents. These emerged from the Great Awakening, which occurred under the preaching of Whitefield, the Tennants, and their fellow evangelists. Among the "New Lights" were numerous Baptists. These held to a milder form of Calvinism than was generally prevalent among the regular Baptists of the period, and looked with some favor upon infant baptism, and on these points they incurred the hostility of other groups. In 1754 the first Separate Baptist church was organized at Sandy Creek, North Carolina, by Shuball Stearns, who brought eight families from Boston. From this point evangelistic work was carried on and similar congregations were formed in various Southern states. In the course of time many of these merged with the regular Baptist associations, but the Separate sect has preserved its identity. The group still leans to the Arminian theory of the Atonement, is extremely conservative in its view of the Bible, and observes foot washing as an ordinance along with baptism by immersion and the Lord's Supper. It maintains Sunday schools, but has no foreign missions or educational institutions, though it does not oppose them.

[24] *Ibid.*, II, 159.

REGULAR BAPTISTS are found mainly in the Southern states. They claim to "represent the original English Baptists before the distinction between Calvinistic or Particular, and Arminian or General became prominent." [25] In general they occupy a middle position relative to the Atonement, though some of the churches in Tennessee, Virginia, and West Virginia lean toward the views of the Primitive Baptists. Relatively few Sunday schools are in operation, though as a group the sect does not oppose them. The Regular Baptists are conservative and literalistic in Scriptural interpretation, practice foot washing, and insist on closed Communion. They have 250 churches and 17,000 members, nearly all in rural territory, and are declining in numbers.

UNITED BAPTISTS are also found in the rural South, principally in Kentucky. They are almost exactly similar to Regular Baptists; they have no tenets or practices which distinguish them from the other mildly Calvinistic groups, and their churches not infrequently affiliate with the Southern and Northern Conventions. They owe their independent existence mainly to the isolation of the communities in which they are found. They are strict communionists and practice the rite of foot washing. There are about 275 United Baptist churches enrolling 25,000 members.

The DUCK RIVER AND KINDRED ASSOCIATIONS OF BAPTISTS, otherwise known as the Baptist Church of Christ, is a sect found in the hill country of Tennessee and Alabama. They represent a schism from the ultra-Calvinistic Elk River Baptist Association, which eventuated in 1825, on the universality of the Atonement. The Duck River Association resulted, the members of which occupy a middle position, believing in the "persevering of the saints," but tempering their Calvinism with the statement that "Christ tasted death for every man and made it possible for God to have mercy upon all who come to Him on Gospel terms." [26] A later division came about over the legitimacy of missionary operations. The Duck River Baptists have no missions, missionary societies or benevolent organizations, and very few Sunday schools, though they deny that they are to be classed among the antimission groups. They have no salaried ministers. Three ordinances are acknowledged as scriptural and perpetually obligatory—immersion, foot washing, and the Communion. The sect numbers ninety churches and eight thousand members.

The INDEPENDENT BAPTIST CHURCH OF AMERICA is a small body of Swedish Baptists in Minnesota and other states of the North. It was organized in 1893 as the Swedish Independent Baptist Church, later becoming the Scandinavian Independent Baptist Denomination of America. In 1912 there was a schism, one group being incorporated as the Scandinavian

[25] *Ibid.*, II, 194.
[26] *Ibid.*, II, 207.

Independent Baptist Denomination of the United States of America, and the other becoming the Scandinavian Free Baptist Society of the United States of America. In 1927 the two groups reunited under the present name. The sect is a typical Baptist group of the mildly Calvinistic or near-Arminian type. The members refuse to participate in war. There are about half a dozen churches and one hundred members in the body.

The AMERICAN BAPTIST ASSOCIATION was organized formally in 1924. It boldly claims that its associations "represent the direct continuance of the Baptist order from the time of Christ." [27] It refuses to affiliate with any other religious group and insists that all Baptists who "work through the conventions" have departed from the scriptural standard. It has missionary and Sunday-school "committees," however, but regards them "as the servants of the churches." In doctrine these Baptists are strict fundamentalists, denouncing "so-called modern science" and standing for the "infallible verbal inspiration of the whole Bible," including "the Genesis account of creation." They are found exclusively in Southern states, mainly in Texas, Arkansas, and Oklahoma, where they have nearly 1,500 churches and 118,000 members, mostly in the country areas.

The Dunkers. The Dunkers, of which there are five sects in the United States, are German Baptists who derived their religious principles from the German Pietists. Under the leadership of Philip Jacob Spener and August Herman Francke, founders of the famous Orphan School at Halle, this group cultivated personal religious life in protest against what they conceived to be defects in Reformation theology and practices. As a result of their study of the scriptures, Alexander Mack and seven others became convinced that the New Testament taught the doctrine of trine immersion for penitent believers only, whereupon one person selected by lot baptized Mack three times in the river Eder and Mack proceeded thus to baptize the others. This was in 1708. From this rite the name of Dunkers, Tunkers, Dunkards, or Taufers, from the German word "tunken," to dip, was derived.

The society thus organized was a strictly legalistic sect, seeking to reproduce in faithful detail the exact conditions pertaining in the primitive church. They waived apostolic succession, refused subscription to all written creeds, and sought to derive all their principles direct from the New Testament. Central in worship was the agape, or love feast; it was held in the evening, preceded by foot washing, and consisted of a full meal followed by wine and unleavened bread. In further conformity to the New Testament pattern the Dunkers greeted each other with a kiss, anointed their sick with oil, covered the heads of their women during services, wore

[27] *Ibid.*, II, 243.

the plainest clothing, refrained from all amusements, and refused to take oaths, bear arms, or engage in lawsuits. These are their fundamental principles to the present day, though certain groups have in some degree departed from the stricter practices, as will be noted. They are known among themselves as the Brethren.

The CHURCH OF THE BRETHREN (CONSERVATIVE DUNKERS) dates from 1723. As a result of persecution a company of the Brethren emigrated to America in 1719, under the leadership of Peter Becker, and settled at Germantown, Pennsylvania. In 1729 the remaining members, with Mack himself, came over. Their first church was organized in 1723 at Germantown, with Peter Becker as the minister. This was the Church of the Brethren, known now as Conservative Dunkers. As the movement grew, other congregations were formed in Pennsylvania and neighboring states and a flourishing denomination resulted. The Dunkers were thrifty, prosperous, and peaceable farmers, strict in adherence to their peculiar observances and manner of dress. To this day the conservatives among them have preserved their peculiarities. The Church of the Brethren (Conservative Dunkers) now has more than 1,100 churches with 180,000 members, well distributed throughout the country, but strongest in Pennsylvania, Indiana, Ohio, and Virginia. They are still largely a rural people.

The first defection from the main body of the German Brethren occurred in 1728, when Johann Conrad Beissel withdrew and founded the famous Ephrata monastic community. Beissel was a man of mystical temperament and became convinced that Saturday should be observed as the Christian Sabbath, that there should be community of goods, and that celibacy should be practiced. In the Ephrata settlement these principles were enforced. Men and women lived in separate houses and all property was held in common. At Ephrata various industries were developed, a school was established, one of the earliest in that section, and the printing press became famous. Late in the nineteenth century communism and celibacy were abandoned, but the strictly religious principles persisted in the community. The old cloister still stands, an object of great historical interest, occupied by a company of Dunkers known as SEVENTH-DAY BAPTISTS (German, 1728), not to be confused with another Seventh-Day Baptist Church. The sect today has only 4 churches and 140 adherents. In all doctrines and practices, save only the Sabbatarian principle, the little body is similar to all the other Dunker groups.

The CHURCH OF GOD (NEW DUNKERS) was founded in Indiana, in 1848, by George Patton and Peter Eyman. The name seems to be the only difference between this group and the main body of Dunkers. The malcontents claimed that "Bible things should be called by Bible names," and that the only name authorized by Scripture as properly applicable to a church is the Church of God, which designation was "foretold by prophecy as the new name." The common practices of trine forward immersion, foot washing, the holy kiss, and anointing of the sick are faithfully observed. The New Dunkers have eight congregations and five hundred members.

A great split among the Dunkers occurred in 1881 and 1882. Modern movements were influencing the people, particularly modifying the traditional plainness of dress. Two schools arose, one insisting that the Dunkers were departing from the ancient scriptural standards, the other insisting that still greater liberality should be allowed. Both parties split off and formed separate sects, but the largest group occupied a middle position and remained in the original Church of the Brethren (Conservative Dunkers).

The reactionary group organized as the OLD ORDER BAPTIST BRETHREN in 1881. They are the Dunker die-hards, and are ultraconservative in belief and practice. They dress after the old-time manner of extreme plainness, oppose missions, Sunday schools, and educational institutions, and have no salaried ministers. In adherence to the landmarks of trine forward immersion, anointing with oil, foot washing, refusal to take oaths or bear arms, and strict abstinence from intoxicants they are at one with all other conservative Dunkers. There are 65 Old Order churches with 3,500 members.

At the other extreme stands the BRETHREN CHURCH (PROGRESSIVE DUNKERS), organized in 1882, when Henry R. Holsinger of Berlin, Pennsylvania, was expelled from the church. He was a radical and objected to the authority of the annual meeting, advocated the autonomy of the local congregation, and insisted on such innovations as missions, an educated and salaried ministry, and modernity in the manner of dress. He was followed by a considerable number, and the Brethren Church occupies the liberal and progressive position on the points named. In doctrine and practice the sect is in general agreement with other Dunker bodies. The Brethren Church has 160 congregations and 17,000 members.

Polity is much the same in all the Dunker churches. It is congregational. Ministers are elected by the local body and bishops are similarly chosen from the ministry. Most of the preachers are not specially educated and are unsalaried, though among the more progressive churches, and especially in the Brethren Church, educated and full-time pastors are more and more employed. Among all the bodies the legalistic principle persists in the insistence on the peculiar form of baptism, foot washing, and anointing with oil after the primitive apostolic pattern.[28]

[28] See Kurtz, *Brethren's Encyclopedia*; Brumbaugh, *History of the German Baptist Brethren in Europe and America*; Falkenstein, *History of the German Baptist Brethren Church*; Holsinger, *History of the Tunkers and the Brethren Church*; Gillen, *The Dunkers*.

Other Brethren Sects. The RIVER BRETHREN date from a revival in 1770 among the Germans in Lancaster County, Pennsylvania— various groups more or less detached from the regular churches. Many of these believed in trine forward immersion and organized as "brother-hoods," while the others gradually drifted back to their former ecclesiastical affiliations. These brotherhoods were designated by the communities in which they were located. The principal group was in the southern part of the county, "down by the river," and baptized its converts in the river, hence the name of River Brethren. An organization was effected about 1820. In the course of time controversy over alleged departures from the original principles concerning nonconformity to the world in the matter of dress, nonresistance, and ceremonial detail arose and two schisms resulted.

Some of the points raised were trivial. In the matter of foot washing the "one mode" school believed that washing and drying should be performed by the same person, and the "two mode" adherents insisted that the two acts should be performed by different individuals. There was controversy as to whether the elements of bread and wine in the Sacrament should be placed on the table with the general supper or be brought forward after the supper had been eaten.

The OLD ORDER BRETHREN date from 1843, when a group in York County, called the "Yorkers" or "Yorker Brethren," withdrew and formed the sect known as the Old Order or Yorker Brethren.

The UNITED ZION'S CHILDREN date from 1852, when a second group seceded and formed, in 1855, the "Brinsers," after their leader Matthias Brinser, later becoming the United Zion's Children. The others remained in the original River Brethren organization.

The BRETHREN IN CHRIST arose during the Civil War, when there were difficulties over the doctrine of nonresistance, and to avoid military service a denomination was formed under the name of Brethren in Christ.

These three bodies are still in existence, confined mainly to Pennsylvania and Ohio, though having scattered congregations in other states. The approximate statistics are as follows:

Sect	Churches	Members
Brethren in Christ	100	5,500
Old Order Brethren	7	250
United Zion's Children	20	1,000

The Old Order or Yorker Brethren are the most conservative. They have no church edifices but hold their services in large barns.

In doctrine and polity the River Brethren are practically identical with the Dunkers. They practice trine forward immersion, anoint the sick with oil, observe the Communion meal with the Sacrament, dress in the plainest manner in opposition to all modern fashions, cover the heads of their women with a veil or light cloth, have few or no salaried ministers, are pacifist in their attitude to war, oppose secret societies and labor unions, generally refrain from participation in politics, and do not indulge in amusements, strong drink, tobacco, slang, or other "worldly" practices. Musical instruments are forbidden in churches, and photographs, fairs and exhibitions, life insurance, and lightning rods are also forbidden.

As examples of the legalism of these Brethren may be cited the matters of dress and head covering. While no regulation or uniform attire is prescribed, all clothing is of the plainest kind. The hair must not be "broidered" or plaited (I Tim. 2:9-10; I Pet. 3:3-5). Gold or pearls cannot be worn (I Tim. 2:9, 10). "Silks, laces, trimmings, and all goods of glistening, glaring, and loud colors" are likewise taboo.[29] The hair covering is derived from I Cor. 11:2-16. This is

not mere custom, or localism, but a doctrine, truth, principle. . . . Paul anchors his argument in creation . . . and would we dare ignore it, thus impeaching the inspired Word of God? It carries us far beyond custom or localism when the apostle nails it down in creation by his three indisputable reasons and treats it as a universal doctrine. . . . The man shall bare his head while the woman shall veil her head and thus recognize their relative positions as assigned by Jehovah. The Scripture does not state what shall be done with a man who violates this injunction; but as to the woman it says, if she be obstinate, and refuse to wear the veiling, "Let her be shorn." . . . The head veiling of holy women stands for sacred subjection to holy men as divinely decreed; and also for the authority to pray or prophesy in public as well as man. He who insults it, insults God, who is back of it. . . . The sacred writer associates much importance with this topic, an evidence of its magnitude in his mind. It is evident that if Christendom would adhere to all the underlying truths and principles of the head veiling that divorce, fornication, and adultery would be unknown in the professed Church of Christ.[30]

Churches of Christ. These were one of the results of the antimission movement in the early years of the nineteenth century and disrupted the Baptist churches. This propaganda had even more serious results in the ranks of the Disciples of Christ; for while in the case of the Baptists it separated from the main body a few backwoods sects, it carried away from the Disciples approximately one fourth of the entire body and left definite fissures in the main group remaining.

As previously mentioned, Alexander Campbell was a Baptist from 1813 to 1830, and during this period, and for a dozen years or more thereafter, he advocated antimission views. Though he later reversed himself, there was

[29] Revision of Article XXXI, Conference Minutes of 1929, program of the general conference of the Brethren in Christ Church, 1930.

[30] *The Scriptural Head Veiling* (leaflet) issued by the Brethren in Christ.

a strong reactionary party in the Disciples of Christ denomination which he formed. Controversy was intense from the birth of the body until the most vehement objectors to "innovations" made good their schism in the opening years of the twentieth century. The points in dispute were the matter of closed or open Communion, use of the title "reverend," the modern pastor or "one-man system," adoption or publication of what looked like a creed in Isaac Errett's "Synopsis" of the Disciples' position, installation of organs in the churches, and organization of missionary and other societies. It was on the last two points that disruption finally eventuated.

The missionary society question has already been discussed. In the early pioneer stage of existence no churches used musical instruments; poverty, if no other reason, prevented. As culture advanced and modern ideas exerted an influence, instruments came into use, and their appearance gave rise to controversy among all the sects. These quarrels were passing incidents and left no permanent divisions, however, save among the Baptists and Disciples. The organ was a serious matter with the latter. At one time there was controversy over the use of songbooks with printed notes, but nothing came of this.[31] Before 1860 organs were so rare that there was little occasion for agitation. In 1859 a melodeon was placed in a church at Midway, Kentucky, and controversy began in dead earnest. One Adam Hibler is alleged to have stolen "the instrument of Satan" in the dead of night, and with the help of a Negro servant, Reuben, carried it away in a sleigh. It has been recovered and is treasured as a historic relic in the Kentucky Female Orphan School at Midway.[32]

The attack on the organ was led by Elder Benjamin Franklin, J. W. McGarvey, W. K. Pendleton, editor of the *Millennial Harbinger*, and others. The arguments were mainly on scriptural grounds. "No element of public worship is legitimate which is not explicitly authorized in the New Testament. Instrumental music is not so authorized. Therefore it is not legitimate." [33] There were other objections also. The organ was not a help in worship but a hindrance; worshipers would neglect singing in admiration of the organist's skill. It was a separate and novel innovation. It was not to be classed with pulpits, pews, stoves, stained glass, printed Bibles, and hymnbooks, because the organ, unlike these, was an *element* of worship, and as such needed scriptural warrant.[34] *Lard's Quarterly* in 1864 declared:

Let every preacher resolve never to enter a meetinghouse of our brethren in which

[31] Garrison, *Religion Follows the Frontier*, p. 235.
[32] Louisville *Courier Journal*, August 23, 1931.
[33] Garrison, *op. cit.*, p. 235.
[34] *Ibid.*, p. 236.

an organ stands. Let no one who takes a letter from one church ever unite with another using an organ. *Rather let him live out of a church than go into such a den.* Let all who oppose the organ withdraw from the church if one is brought in.[35]

J. H. Garrison was refused support from the First Church in St. Louis for his paper the *Christian,* when he declared the publication would not represent the antiorgan party. At one time the St. Louis First Church had in its purchased building an organ which it refused to use while the Central Church in the same city, a pro-organ congregation, had no instrument. The conservatives contended that the pro-organ group should submit because, after all, the question could not be with the latter a matter of conscience but only of preference, to which it was replied that the liberal people had consciences of their own!

Gradually the pro-organ and antiorgan factions drifted into separate congregations, but both were Disciples. In the course of time, however, the antiorgan groups began calling themselves Churches of Christ. In 1906 the division was sufficiently marked for the census authorities to make a separate listing of the latter, and in the returns for 1926 the schism was complete. The Disciples of Christ now have eight thousand churches and nearly two million members. The Churches of Christ do not collect statistics, but the census (1936) reported 3,800 churches and over 300,000 members. About 85 per cent of the Churches of Christ are in the rural districts, and their stronghold is in the South, mainly in Texas, Tennessee, Arkansas, Oklahoma, Alabama, and Kentucky. It is the largest Protestant group showing pronounced sectarian characteristics, though loudest in protestation that it is not a sect or "denominational church" but the "true Church of Christ," conforming in every detail to the apostolic and scriptural pattern.

The Churches of Christ are fundamentalist. Their basic principle is that they "speak where the Scriptures speak and are silent where the Scriptures are silent," but like all such sects they decide for themselves, and against the consensus of Christian opinion, just what the Scriptures command and what they forbid. In typical fashion they select a few injunctions (but more silences) for observance and ignore all the others. They do not wash feet, heal the sick, anoint with oil, speak in unknown tongues, or cover the heads of their women; but they practice immersion, which at least is a doubtful injunction, observe the Communion each Sunday, which is also doubtful, and oppose the use of musical instruments and church societies and organizations of all kinds, which they base on the Bible's silence. The use of the radio, songbooks, stained-glass windows, and other concomitants

[35] *Ibid.,* p. 237.

of religious service, all unknown to the Scriptures, they justify as being not *elements* of worship but only aids to it.

In theology they occupy the common evangelical position. There is nothing distinctive about them save their "anti" attitude in the matter of organs and missionary societies, which, as has been seen, is not peculiar to this particular group. They carry on no organized home mission, social service, or other benevolent activity, though they are intensely evangelistic and some of their local congregations maintain social and benevolent institutions. They are not opposed to foreign missions and some of their ministers are working in foreign lands. Persons desiring to be foreign missionaries must find congregations to support them, after which they proceed very much as they please; if the congregational support fails they must return home and seek others to maintain them.

In polity they are the strictest of all congregationalists. Their ministers are unordained and are chosen by the local groups; the field is open to any individual who wants to preach. They have no conferences, presbyteries, synods, assemblies, or other ministerial or ecclesiastical bodies. This lack of organization is jealously guarded, even interchurch committees being unscriptural. There is no publishing house or editorial board; any person who cares to do so may start a paper and secure what patronage he can; commercial concerns may, and do, employ writers and publish Sunday school and other literature and sell it to all who will buy. Other bodies are referred to as "denominational churches." The Churches of Christ practice open Communion, but do not fraternize or affiliate with any interdenominational agency. They are zealous in debate; their periodicals teem with reports of public disputations with representatives of other sects. An examination of all the weekly issues of the *Gospel Advocate* for 1932 revealed that each paper, without an exception, contained several reports of converts won from the Baptists, Methodists, or Disciples.

The schism of the Churches of Christ was not the only disruption suffered by the Disciples of Christ as a result of controversies on the various points already mentioned. No other body has actually withdrawn from the main group, however. Not all objectors accepted the full program of the conservatives; some opposed the organ while favoring the missionary society and vice versa, others favored or opposed both but considered Sunday schools as unscriptural, and one party opposed the acceptance of alien immersion. The historian of the Disciples has found

at least six mutually hostile and exclusive groups: (1) the pro-music, pro-organized-missions group, known as the United Christian Missionary Society, with publishing headquarters at St. Louis; (2) the pro-music, anti-organized-missions group, with publishing headquarters at Cincinnati; (3) the anti-music, anti-organized-missions group, with rival publishing headquarters at Nashville, Louisville, Cincinnati, and elsewhere; (4) the anti-music, anti-organized-missions, anti-church-school group with publishing headquarters in Indianapolis; (5) the anti-music, anti-organized-missions, anti-alien-immersion group, with publishing headquarters at Austin, Texas; (6) the anti-music, anti-organized-missions, anti-Sunday-school group with publishing headquarters at Dallas, Texas.[36]

Christadelphians or Brethren of Christ. This sect has about 100 congregations and 2,500 members. It is an Adventist-Unitarian body which, strangely enough, branched off from the "reformation" movement led by Alexander Campbell, founder of the Disciples of Christ. It is one of those bodies which might be included under two or three of the categories in this book.

The moving spirit among the Christadelphians was an English physician Dr. John Thomas, who came to America in 1830. He was then only twenty-five years old. He identified himself with Campbell's movement, and as a result of his studies he became convinced that the Bible taught doctrines much different from those being preached in the "reformation." About the middle of the century he left Campbell's camp, was rebaptized, abandoned the practice of medicine, and gave himself to the promulgation of his belief in both America and Europe. On both continents he established little groups called *ecclesias*. In 1851 he founded at Richmond, Virginia, a periodical called the *Herald of the Kingdom and Age to Come,* which continued for several years. At the present time several papers are published by Christadelphians in this country, England, and Australia.

Christadelphians reject the trinitarian theology and hold that Christ was not "God the Son" but "Son of God"; he did not exist from eternity but was begotten in the Virgin Mary by the Holy Spirit emanating from God. They are likewise ardent millenarians. At the second coming of Christ the saints will be endowed with immortality and the wicked will be destroyed. Christ and his followers will occupy the land of Canaan and from Jerusalem will rule the world.

In polity the Christadelphians are congregationalists. Baptism is by immersion, and "alien immersion" is accepted if the subject believed in Christadelphian doctrine at the time of baptism. There are no clergymen in the accepted sense, but each church or *ecclesia* elects "serving brethren," who are divided into "managing brethren," "presiding brethren," and "lecturing brethren." No educational institutions or missionary enterprises are maintained. Closed Communion is practiced among the churches.

These people do not vote, hold office, or participate in war. They have

[36] Garrison, *op. cit.,* pp. 297, 298, quoting from an unpublished manuscript by C. C. Klingman.

been "called out of the world" and are not a part of nations or governments. "The saints of the Most High have no kingdom until the kingdom shall be given to them at the coming of Christ." [37]

[37] Thomas' works, wherein he sets forth details of Christadelphian doctrine and polity, are *Elpis Israel, Eureka, an Exposition of the Apocalypse, The Apostasy Unveiled, Catechesis, The Revealed Mystery.*

CHAPTER VIII

CHARACTERISTICS OF THE SMALL SECTS

AN ATTEMPT HAS BEEN MADE TO GROUP THE SMALL SECTS INTO PSYCHO-logical and theological categories according to their outstanding tenets, but much overlapping has been unavoidable. In the main features the sects are much alike. Most of them might be called pessimistic, since they believe in the more or less imminent end of the world order and set little or no store by social processes in the realization of their ends. Both the communistic and charismatic groups are essentially perfectionistic. Nearly all are legalistic in that they regard the Bible as an objective authority and insist upon ob-servances drawn therefrom. Some sects are so nearly identical that the impartial student is unable to discover any differences, and in the case of many the differences are trivial. This chapter will summarize the findings and point out some general characteristics of the small sects. In the nature of the case this will involve repetition of certain material already set forth in previous chapters.

Refuges of the Poor. Many of these small bodies are the refuges of the disinherited. The influence of economics in the rise of sects was discussed in the first chapter. It was pointed out that such groups are formed among the religiously neglected poor. As they develop into conventionalized de-nominations of the cultured and well-placed, those left behind in the eco-nomic struggle begin to feel themselves out of place, and these draw apart into congenial bands, obtaining satisfaction in the emotional freedom and naïve supernaturalism which the parent body has outgrown, and exalting into moral virtues the simple manners which their poverty makes necessary. Thus another sect is born, which usually begins in the next generation to repeat the process.

When labor struggles and the revolts of the poor have been tinged with religion, which was nearly always the case until recent times, millennial ideas have appeared, and, as has been seen, these notions are prominent in most of the small sects which follow the evangelical tradition. Premille-narianism is essentially a defense mechanism of the disinherited; despairing of obtaining substantial blessings through social processes, they turn on the world which has withheld its benefits and look to its destruction in a cosmic cataclysm which will exalt them and cast down the rich and powerful.

The earmarks of poverty are found in most of the small sects. The Church of the Nazarene frankly avows that its mission is to the poor. In the struggling days of American Methodism Bishop Asbury wrote in his *Journal,* "Religion is reviving here among the Africans. These are poor; these are the people we are more immediately called to preach to." Reference has been made to Wesley's dread of the prosperity accruing to his Methodists as a result of the very virtues he had taught them, his prediction that affluence would rob them of their religion and stop the revival, and his proposal that they give away the money they earned. His keen psychological insight and prophetic soul enabled him correctly to discern the course Methodism was destined to take.

It is a strange fact that these sects of the poor make little or no attempt to ameliorate the condition of their adherents. None have any program of social reform, except insistence on temperance and opposition to the liquor traffic. Not one takes an active hand in the labor struggle; most of them, indeed, look upon such matters as political questions to be wholly avoided. Some sects do not even allow their members to vote or hold public office. However they may work and practice thrift as individuals, as Christians they seem to have settled down into a state of resignation, and they expect God to reward them in the world during the millennium or in heaven after death.

One accordingly finds here a fervent supernaturalism and otherworldliness which has all but departed from the great denominations. This is most pronounced in the millennial hopes entertained. Even where these are not present, the members are consciously preparing for heaven. The listener nearly always hears this note in their preaching, but rarely from the pulpits of the great denominations.

This is especially pronounced in sectarian hymnology; the gospel hymns abound in references to heaven and the second coming of the Lord. These people who have sought the spiritual refuge of the small sects, like the frontier Christians in an earlier period, sing of the life beyond the grave because life here is hardly worth living. The hymnbooks of two or three generations ago were filled with "otherworldly" songs. Methodists and others sang "Beulah Land," "Gates Ajar," "Angel Band," "A Land That Is Fairer than Day," "Where Sickness and Death Never Come," "We Shall Meet on That Beautiful Shore," and other having similar sentiments. Such hymns have been progressively eliminated as life became more endurable and the prospects of golden streets and starry crowns less alluring than the creature comforts of a well-placed *bourgeoisie.* Streets of gold and chariots of fire cannot compete with concrete roads and modern automobiles, or mansions in the skies with steam heat and air conditioning! So our effete Christians sing for the Lord to "walk the city's streets again," but not to "bear me away on your snowy wings!" The larger denominations have shifted the emphasis to the mundane sphere and are intent on inculcating religion as a way of life which will result in human brotherhood and the correction of social ills; the sects continue to spurn this evil world and to regard the natural man as a vile worm of the dust, to be transformed and made ready for a world into which ills never come.

The Puritan Morality. The small sects usually stress the puritan type of personal behavior. It has been pointed out that their morality is in considerable degree a corollary of their economic state, arrived at by a process of elevating the manners they cannot well escape into moral virtues established by the will of God. Vices are the practices of the rich, the very practices they themselves or their children would be likely to follow if sufficiently affluent.

Over and over it has appeared that certain sects place under the ban all worldly amusements such as dancing, theater attendance, and the use of tobacco. Some Mennonites taboo such expensive luxuries as radios, telephones, top buggies, pictures, and rugs. Gold and costly raiment are prohibited by a large number of sects. Some regulate the very speech of their adherents and frown upon slang expressions. The Amish, to make certain that they will not fall into evil ways, denounce modern fashions, strictly prescribe the cut of coats and dresses, and even go to the length of banning buttons and suspenders, for no reason other than that their fathers in Germany used hooks and eyes and coats without lapels.

Austerity of life, humility, self-denial in things naturally desired, simplicity, abstinence and mortification of the flesh and worldly promptings are the moral fundamentals of the sects. The social effects of indulgence have little or nothing to do with this opposition. The Churches of Christ and others frankly base their objection to missionary societies on the fact that money is essential thereto, and their opposition to musical instruments is an echo from the period when organs could not be afforded by the poverty-stricken frontier churches.

Refuges of the Emotionally Starved. The small sects are the refuges of the emotionally starved. This also is in some degree a corollary of the economic status of the poor, since they cannot afford, or do not have access to, the recreations, associations, social functions, and cultural activities wherein the prosperous find outlets for their emotions. The emotional element has all but passed from the religion of the great churches, to their very great loss, and they have developed "worship programs" and "decision day services" and "religious emphasis weeks" in an endeavor to make up for the passing of great emotional experiences that plumbed the depths of men's souls, changed lives, emotionalized conviction and attitude, and left an irreducible appreciation of spiritual values. The naïve and simple people of the sects cling to the feeling element. They deliberately adopt devices to stir the emotions and attribute the results to the direct operation of the Holy Spirit.

Perfectionist sects believe that an emotional reaction constitutes proof that the soul has come into direct relationship with God, and this for them is the final authority. In some measure all Protestant groups make authority reside in personal experience, but the more sophisticated denominations encounter difficulty in defining just what religious experience actually is, and here lies the main difficulty with their theory. The sects are at no loss at this point; to them experience means feeling. Hence they covet "blessings," gifts, and outpourings of the Holy Spirit. These are arranged in an ascending series: first, conversion or forgiveness; then holiness or the "second blessing," which purges the nature of inbred sin; finally, in many cases, the gift of tongues or other ecstatic phenomena which correspond roughly to the mystical "spiritual marriage." It has been seen to what extremes the emotional element is carried by the Pentecostals and other sects of the charismatic order. In all this there is the fundamental assumption which lies at the heart of evangelical theology—that God may be directly apprehended and that he reveals himself to man through the feelings. The sects follow Wesley in the theory that "I know because I feel."

The sects preserve the revival technique, the most effective device ever developed for stimulating the emotions. They demand a regenerated church membership secured by insisting on conversion. Nearly all Protestants, in theory, expect conversion, but with the passing of the emotional element most of them are forced to give a very loose and indefinite meaning to the term. But the sects know exactly what it means: God enters the soul through an emotional upheaval which leaves a consciousness of sins forgiven and a great and joyous witness thereto. This whole field has in these modern days been left to the sects. It is small wonder that the emotionally starved flock to them.

The Craving for Objectivity. Many small sects reflect the craving for objectivity on the part of large numbers of people. Modern Protestant theologians who insist that final authority in religious matters resides in personal experience make the mistake of believing that experience is highly valued by all persons. Such is not the case. There are thousands who care little or nothing for personal experience, being temperamentally incapable of very deep feeling. What these most desire is *something that they can do,* an outward rite or observance that they can practice. Given this, the religious life becomes easy and certain.

This element is to a varying extent present in all religious groups; those that magnify experience, but think clearly, regard the observances merely as aid to worship, but the more ignorant are prone to accept them as possessing divine significance in themselves. Something very like idolatry frequently results, as in the case of Catholics who venerate images, pictures, and medals. Sometimes the craving for definiteness runs near to magic, as in transubstantiation, the transmission of grace through the repetition of a carefully prescribed formula or the touch of ordained fingers, and securing safety by the use of medals and insignia.

Most of the sects regard the Bible as a divinely inspired and infallible book, hence an objective authority. From its pages are drawn the things to be done. They "speak where the Scriptures speak and are silent where the Scriptures are silent." Baptism, foot washing, wearing of head coverings, and laying on of hands are among the commonest of the practices insisted upon. Sometimes the craving for objectivity takes a negative turn and worshipers are more intent on "being silent where the Scriptures are silent" than on "speaking where the Scriptures speak." This is most clearly seen among the Churches of Christ; their only distinctive tenets are the exclusion of organs and opposition to church organizations, authority for which they do not find in the Bible. They do not wash feet, wear veils, salute each other with a kiss, or lay on hands, though these are plainly written in the Book. Sometimes one encounters the utmost meticulousness and high evaluation of trivialities. Certain Brethren have split over such questions as whether baptism should be in running water or calm, forward or backward, with one plunge or three; whether the elements of the Communion should be on the table with the sacramental meal or on a side table; whether they should be prepared simultaneously with the meal or subsequently thereto; whether foot washing and drying should be performed by the same or different persons. The observances are not, it should be repeated, regarded as psychological aids to worship; God is interested in them and they possess moral significance in themselves.

Most interesting is the practice, already frequently pointed out, of selecting a few biblical injunctions or silences and ignoring others equally plain. Nobody follows the Book "from cover to cover," though many profess to do so. One group washes feet but pays no attention to Paul's advice about covering women's heads, while others observe the latter and ignore the former. The Bible is no more silent on melodeons and missionary societies than on pews, songbooks, and stained-glass windows in churches, or, for that matter, on churches themselves. Some persons are so psychologically constituted, or socially conditioned, that they must have an objective something to which they may cling, and they select one or two or three things and are satisfied.

Sectarian Conservatism. The small sects are nearly aways conservative. They insist on the commonplace and the ancient in theology, practice, and manner of life. Even the "Uncle Sam's religion" of the Liberal Church of America, which substitutes the constitution for the Bible, is a glorification of the Fourth of July type of patriotism. The sects seem to believe that all persons must think alike, and departures in minute details of doctrine are sufficient to cause lasting schisms. The conservatism which resists change of every sort is one of the clear marks of sectarianism.

Such sects hark back to the first century and believe it their duty to reproduce the primitive church. One that frankly avowed the purpose of perfecting an organization best suited to modern conditions would be an oddity. Such adaptations as are made are usually forced upon them over the protests of many of their adherents, or ensue so gradually that the changes are unnoticed. This attitude follows from belief in the Bible as infallible and inerrant and that the faith, including details of organization and administration, was "once for all delivered to the saints." Many carry their conservatism to matters of nomenclature, and insist that "Bible things must be called by Bible names." A large number trace their ancestry back to Christ and the apostles and regard themselves as the "true church." Sects of insignificant size and influence insist that all save themselves have departed from or corrupted Christianity, and declare their purpose of converting all Christendom to their way of thinking and incorporating all Christians in their own tiny body. Worship of the remote past, coupled with mistrust of modernity, is found in many sects.

A deep-seated suspicion of all others save themselves is a characteristic of many sects. Only a handful will enter upon any real program of co-operation with other bodies; even so great a group as the Southern Baptists refuses to affiliate with interdenominational co-operative movements. The Churches of Christ refer to others as "denominational churches" and to themselves as "the church," and they regard other flocks as a fair field for their evangelistic endeavors. Sometimes this antagonism to those who differ is carried to extremes of bitterness. The *Pentecostal Herald,* a holiness journal, published a boxed editorial on its front page headed, "Not This Man, but Fosdick." After reciting the story of the multitude clamoring for the release of the robber Barabbas and the crucifixion of Jesus, it was pointed out that the followers of the distinguished preacher, Harry Emerson Fosdick, were committing a similar sin.[1]

Very many small sects are inimical to modern scholarship, which they call "modernism." The most hated heresy is the hypothesis of organic evolution, which is considered as contradictory of the Genesis creation stories, and hence false and degrading to man. Scarcely less is their aversion to the

[1] January 25, 1933.

findings of geological science relative to the creation and age of the earth. Modern scholarship, subsumed under the term "higher criticism," is despised. Books and brochures flow from the presses, and colleges are founded in opposition to modern science, "falsely so-called." Yet the sects are usually loud in their protestations of fidelity to education—their statements always being followed by a significant "but."

Distinctive Principles Lost with Growth. The distinctive principles of the small sects are usually lost as the groups grow large. This has already been pointed out in connection with the rise of denomintions, which depart from their original principles as they wax strong and prosperous. Culture and prosperity are the main causes of such defections. Size also is a factor. As previously mentioned, the Church of the Nazarene illustrates this. It is still a sect of the poor and uncultured, but that it is already somewhat ashamed of its original position is shown in the elimination of the words "holiness" and "pentecostal" from the names of all its institutions of learning. Gaddis attributes the change in character to the growth of the body; its bishops and officials have developed power, machinery has been set up, the body has become interested in its statistics, and its democratic character and spontaneity are accordingly departing.[2]

Democracy and simplicity are essential to the naïve faith and worship of the small sects. In the case of Methodism, which has spawned so many sects, the protests were against its allegedly autocratic episcopacy quite as much as against its departure from original Wesleyan perfectionism. Several splits were occasioned by the former alone. Every group that has gone away has democratized its government. Now size is incompatible with thoroughgoing democracy and simplicity. Authority is a necessity in large bodies. Further, the class meeting and revival technique are hampered by the unwieldiness of size. The more numbers increase, the more certain are diverse elements to enter. More money is needed and emphasis is necessarily placed on collections, hence the prosperous exercise a large influence. So the well-known economic factor begins to operate and the sect is modified accordingly. It is vital to the distinctive principles of the sects that they remain small.

The Bizarre and Fantastic. Bizarre and fantastic notions, interpretations, and practices abound among the small sects; they offer a fertile field for what David Starr Jordan called "sciosophy" or "systematized ignorance." Multitudes are always ready to follow spectacular leaders like "King Benjamin" of the House of David and Father Divine of the Peace Mission. The former persuaded the gullible that he was the "seventh messenger," and firm in their belief that he was a sort of divinity, they followed him until

[2] Gaddis, *Christian Perfectionism in America,* manuscript in the library of the University of Chicago, pp. 507-8.

his sexual escapades became an open scandal and were suppressed by police interference. The members of the Church of God and Saints of Christ regard the Santa Fe cook, William S. Crowdy, as "a prophet sent from God" with the revelation that the American Negroes are in reality the Jews of the "lost tribes," and they are willing to turn over all their earthly possessions, including their labor, to his successor, their "Great Father Abraham."

The colored saints of the House of Prayer regard Bishop Grace in a similar light and have profound faith in his healing and saving power. In *Psalms of Grace,* published by the House of Prayer, appears this poetic effusion, one of many which express similar sentiments:

> Bishop Grace is a Holy Prophet,
>   An Angel and a Holy man;
> He has the key to the kingdom,
> It is always in his hand.
>
> Bishop Grace is Prophet Elijah;
>   He came to prepare the way of the Lord,
> And God gives him victory
>   Anywhere he chooses to trod.
>
> Bishop Grace is that Angel
>   That ascended from the East
> To seal the servants of God in their foreheads,
>   And prepare them for the heavenly Feast.
>
> Bishop Grace is the chief cornerstone,
>   The only Savior of the world;
> While he is with us we'd better obey;
>   The world will end when he is gone." [3]

Examples of strange interpretations of Scripture have appeared over and over again in the discussion of sectarian tenets. The "chiefess" of the Church of the Living God, Christian Workers for Fellowship, Mrs. Ethel L. Christian, proved from the Scripture that Jesus Christ was a Negro: He was the "son of David," and the 119th psalm, which she assumed was written by David, declares, "I am become like a bottle in the smoke." Several sects cover the heads of their women with "prayer veils" in obedience to Paul's dictum: "Every woman that prayeth or prophesieth with her head uncovered dishonoreth her head" (I Cor. 11:5). But the House of David makes this same Scripture teach that a *man's hair* should never be cut: *man is the head of woman,* and when a woman prays or prophesies her head, *the man,*

[3] *Psalms of Grace,* pp. 76-77.

must be covered with long hair! [4] This peculiar twisting of the text justifies the long tresses of the men, in spite of the plain statement in the same section, "Doth not even nature teach you that if a man have long hair, it is a shame unto him?"

Many sects, especially those with premillenarian leanings, delight in the search for hidden meanings in the Bible. Daniel and Revelation are the favorite hunting grounds. By deciphering the codes men have been fixing the exact or approximate date for the end of the world for many centuries, and the practice still goes on. The identity of the beast with the number 666 has always intrigued such persons and much exegetical ingenuity has been called forth. The preponderance of opinion since the Reformation favors the pope, but Napoleon, the Kaiser, and many other worthies have been put forward. A more recent interpreter identified Hitler with the beast, by the familiar device of adding the numerical value of the letters in his name, according to the Greek system; Hitler was to be in power three and a half years and the world order should have ended in 1936.[5]

The strange practices indulged in by many sects have already been mentioned. When the customary inhibitions have been broken down and rational control is lost under high emotional excitement, persons shout, laugh, dance, jerk, swoon, bark, and indulge in a variety of motor phenomena. The Pentecostal and several Negro sects specialize in such behavior. Talking in unknown tongues is one of the commonest practices. The murder of a woman in a cult sacrifice in Kentucky and the handling of poisonous snakes in worship are the most extreme.

In March, 1937, a Separate Baptist farmer named Jackson Whitlow, in Sequatchie County, Tennessee (near Chattanooga), was "called by the Lord" to "purify himself" for a great task by undergoing a fast. This he endured for nearly sixty days, spurning entreaties to take food as "tricks of the devil to outwit" him, until near the point of death. Then he announced that God had informed him the divine purpose was accomplished and the fast could be broken, whereupon he assumed the "burden" of preaching. A few years previously national attention was attracted to a "Godite" preacher named Teester at Sylva, North Carolina, who confounded scoffers by publicly allowing a rattlesnake to bite him. Teester recovered, claimed the promise of Mark 16:18 was thus vindicated, and he became a "seven days' wonder" as a revivalist. The Penitentes of New Mexico whip each other and cut crosses in their flesh with knives or sharp stones. Such exercises are not confined entirely to the small sects. Roman Catholic authorities have explained the multiplicity of fragments of "the true cross" by asserting that the wood of that instrument miraculously multiplied itself, and volumes

[4] *Shiloh's Messenger of Wisdom*, 27. No. 4, 8.
[5] Earl H. Pendell, in the *Christian Century*, June 7, 1933, p. 759.

could be written about the miracles performed by bones and other alleged relics of dead saints.

A backwoods preacher near Summerville, Georgia, was "led by the Lord" to serve a fatal "salvation cocktail" to one of his followers. He was acquitted of manslaughter by the courts, and among those who gathered to congratulate him was the mother of the victim.

Early in 1949 nation-wide publicity was given to Marjoe Gortner, a four-year-old preacher who performed a marriage ceremony at Long Beach, California. The child was an ordained minister of the Old Time Faith, Inc. This sect was formed by Mrs. Essie Binkley, so-called "angel of Skid Row," who conducts the Sunshine Mission in the slum area of Los Angeles. Mrs. Binkley ordained the child.

Unusual elements are prominent among certain cults and movements that should not be classed among the small sects being considered in this book because they are not Christian bodies and sometimes are only quasi-religious. Several of these cults flourish in California, but they are also found elsewhere. As extreme examples two will be cited here.

An interesting one is known as the Great I Am. It developed in Los Angeles under the leadership of G. W. Ballard. He claimed to be in touch with certain "ascended masters," chief of whom was St. Germain, and from these long-departed spirits he received the revelations which constituted the subject matter of his teachings. The revelations of St. Germain and Ballard's comments thereon were printed and circulated among the adherents of the cult. The climax of supernatural contacts was reached when both St. Germain and Jesus Christ personally appeared and allowed an artist to paint their portraits from life. Reproductions of these pictures were sold to the believers. The Ballards were convicted of using the mails to defraud, but the verdict was reversed by the Supreme Court.[6]

Another Los Angeles cult is known as the Temple of Yahweh, which was founded in 1946 by Joseph Jeffers, a former Baptist preacher. It teaches that there is unusual virtue in the "vibrations" involved in the use of the Hebrew name for God, Yahweh, and for the same reason Jesus is called Yahoshua. It denies the doctrine of the Virgin Birth, rejects baptism, does not observe Christmas or Easter, and accepts Friday as the original Sabbath day.

This group believes that the Anglo-Saxon-Celtic people are descendants of the "ten lost tribes" and are therefore the true Israelites. Ephraim is represented by the United States and Manasseh by Great Britain; a "remnant" from Ephraim, plus a few from other nations, will constitute the "little

---

[6] The California judge who passed sentence on and excoriated the Ballards was a Roman Catholic, and the *Converted Catholic Magazine* (March, 1947) pointed out that the Catholic Church regularly accepts money for influencing supernatural powers and securing the release of souls from purgatory.

flock" that will inherit the kingdom of Yahweh. The approaching "battle of Armageddon" will be an atomic war in which most of the people on earth will be destroyed, but Yahweh will preserve the "little flock" by hiding them in a safe place. Heaven, hell, and purgatory have no existence, but Yahweh is a real person who has his headquarters on the constellation Orion. Jeffers claims to receive messages from Yahweh and to transmit messages to him, as a result of which the cult leader is able to predict important events, interpret dreams, and heal the sick.

This cult has been involved in various scandals and many rumors have been circulated about the services at the temple. Jeffers claims that he has vast wealth stored on Orion. In 1945 the leader was sent to a federal penitentiary for stealing and transporting an automobile belonging to one of his former wives. He was paroled after serving eighteen months, but the parole was revoked and he was returned to prison for a similar offense shortly thereafter. His third wife carried on the work of preaching and publishing the sect's magazine Kingdom Voice during his absence.[7]

The archbishop of the Brotherhood of the White Temple at Denver claims that he is able to transport his spirit to Tibet for consultations with the lamas and mystics of that country. He has undertaken to build a shambulla ashrama in the "valley of survival" on a 1,600-acre mountain site. This is to be a stronghold for the protection of members of the sect during an atomic holocaust which is expected to occur shortly. Membership in the inner circle of the ashrama requires a contribution of five hundred dollars.

Religious Education and the Sects. No intensive study of religious education among the small American sects can be attempted here. The subject is of such importance for the evaluation of the place of such bodies in our contemporary religious life, however, that it should not be entirely neglected. A few outstanding facts revealed by the data in hand will therefore be mentioned:

1. Practically all the groups profess to believe in religious education and conduct Sunday schools. All that have sufficient strength maintain colleges or other institutions of learning. Only a handful, like the Primitive Baptists, Yorker Brethren, and two or three little Mennonite bodies, are in opposition to Sunday schools and even such stanch "antis" as the "hard-shell" Baptists are weakening at this point. The census statistics show that the sects have nearly as many Sunday schools as churches.

2. A study of the materials used in these Sunday schools yields a discouraging picture when tested by the standards prevalent in the great churches.

[7] See Kingdom Voice, August, September, October, 1947. The Los Angeles newspapers published accounts of Jeffers' troubles in the summer of 1947. I received the statement of doctrines direct from Mrs. Jeffers in January, 1948.

Relatively few sects have general boards or committees for the direction of their Sunday-school work, and in some cases the agency supposed to be in existence does little or nothing. The local congregations are left to shift for themselves in all things pertaining to their program of religious education.

Not many small sects produce their own literature and curriculum materials. A few produce one or two items, usually a "quarterly" or lesson discussions published in the official weekly paper. The others secure their materials from various denominational publishing houses or independent commerical concerns. Sometimes the literature thus secured bears the imprint of the sect but in no other regard is it distinctive. Two independent houses in New York supply the Plymouth Brethren and other fundamentalist bodies, and the Free Methodist literature is popular among the holiness groups. The Churches of Christ, which are energetic in Sunday-school work but antagonistic to any form of overhead organization, purchase materials from commercial printers, who employ preachers of the sect as editors. It is interesting to note that many of the "true church" sects, which stress most strongly their own peculiar tenets and regard all other bodies with great suspicion, nevertheless use the curriculum materials of the offending bodies in their Sunday schools.

These materials at their best are the old "uniform lessons" based on the International subjects; the same lesson is studied by every age group, the only difference being the manner of treatment. Investigation reveals that the variation between age groups is mainly a matter of simpler words, the approach and treatment being essentially the same. No sect uses graded literature; in one or two cases where grading was reported investigation showed that it meant only a simpler treatment of the International subjects. The whole curriculum is "material centered" and exclusively biblical in nature; in all the literature studied not one lesson was discovered of an "extra-biblical" character, as that term is understood by modern religious educators.

3. The small sects are confused as to the philosophy of religious education and have no very clear ideas as to its aims and purposes. Instruction in the Bible seems to be the main objective. Along with this is an indefinite notion that knowledge of Bible texts will carry over into character or prick the conscience and result in conviction and conversion. Investigation of the curriculum shows that the materials are not such as might be expected to bring about that consummation. Practically none of the groups believe that *religion can be taught*. Religion itself is conceived of in terms altogether mystical and supernatural; the Spirit of God must descend from an outside source into the human soul. Psychological processes such as conviction, repentance, and emotional reactions are indeed essential, but these are

regarded as being produced by God and are preparatory to conversion and regeneration, which, in the last analysis, are works wrought by God.

Conversion is assumed even when it has never occurred—at least when nothing has occurred which is covered by any reasonable or accepted definition of that experience. This is true not alone of the sects, however, but even more of the great denominations. Most of the latter also hold in theory to the necessity of conversion and insist theoretically on a converted membership; at least few would care to admit that they welcomed unconverted persons into the fold. But relatively few of their members, have ever experienced conversion in the New Testament sense or even in the plain English meaning of that term. A study of more than two thousand individuals, mostly young people, of the major Protestant groups has shown that above 66 per cent never underwent any kind of an experience which could be called conversion, but attained to such a degree of religious consciousness as they possessed by a process of gradual growth unmarked by recognizable emotional features; more than 27 per cent had no experience other than the slight emotional stimulus involved in joining the church or responding to a "decision day" appeal; and only 6.7 per cent remembered a definite crisis type of experience.[8] The same study showed that the percentage of those in the last group was much larger among persons above forty years of age, those taught the older and sterner "heaven and hell" theology, and those whose religious training had been inadequate. Thus the trend is definitely away from conversion experiences under the influence of a milder theology and modern religious culture. To preserve the theory of conversion it has been necessary to so define the term as to empty it of its former accepted meaning.

Growth of the Small Sects. Most of the small sects in America have had a long history; many of them have been here from the earliest colonial days. That they have maintained themselves seems proof that they have considerable survival value. They appeal to types of mind that could never be comfortable in the conventional folds of the great denominations.

Many of the small sects are declining; others are growing much more rapidly than the larger groups. When the percentage of growth of the small sects is compared with that of the great denominations for the past three census decades, it is found that the former expanded much more rapidly. Between 1906-16 the growth of all religious bodies was 18.9 per cent, while that of the small sects was 39.3 per cent; between 1916-26 the figure for the former was 17.6 per cent and for the latter 22.4 per cent; between 1926-36 only five large Protestant bodies registered as much as the norm of 17.6 per cent in growth, while 43 sects went beyond the norm, many of them far beyond it.

[8] Clark, *Psychology of Religious Awakening*, ch. ii.

It is of course true that the smallness of the sects makes a *percentage* growth easier, and that their *numerical* growth is insignificant in comparison with that of the great bodies. On the other hand the large denominations have the advantages of social prestige, less exacting conditions of membership, and the wealth and machinery necessary to promotion. All things considered, it is interesting and significant that the sects thrive so well in these modern days.

The great Protestant bodies commonly insist that a well-developed and scientifically based system of religious education is necessary to the life and growth of the church. It is almost their sole method of propaganda at the present time; it is commonly asserted that 90 or 95 per cent of all new members come through their Sunday schools, and the success of their programs of religious education is attributed largely to the fact that they have incorporated the findings of modern educational psychology. The leaders in this field are firm in the belief that without this sort of religious education the churches would decline and perhaps die. Yet the small sects ignore nearly all the principles of modern religious education, and not only survive but flourish and often outstrip denominations that employ them all. Nothing could be more repugnant to the modern educational theory than the suppression of the normal promptings of youth; yet some Mennonites insist that their boys and girls wear clothing that subjects them to ridicule, and deny them the pleasures of the radio. Total depravity is in conflict with the very fundamentals of modern educational theory, but it is the first principle of most of the sects. In curriculum building the sects defy everything that modern religious education teaches. Still the sects average well with their competitors in winning and holding the people. Such facts challenge the workers in the field of religious education to inquire whether, after all, the modern developments are really as efficient as they are claimed to be, and whether the sects do not possess elements of value which others have omitted and might well incorporate.

EGOCENTRIC OR "NEW THOUGHT" BODIES

EGOCENTRIC SECTS EMPHASIZE BODILY HEALTH AND HAPPINESS BY MEANS OF correct mental attitudes and are frequently referred to as healing or "psychology" cults. They sprang largely from the idealistic thinking of such persons as Emerson, Thoreau, Margaret Fuller, and R. W. Trine. They are numerous throughout the country and usually hold meetings in halls or hotels. In many points of theology they hold the general Protestant position. The following are a few typical groups:

AQUARIAN MINISTRY: This movement was started in 1918 by George and Louise Brownell and centers at Santa Barbara, California. Its purpose is to heal the sick and "show the value of right thinking and right living in building a grand and noble life-structure for one's self." The name is taken from Aquarius, the "sign of the Zodiac now influencing Mankind."

BIOSOPHICAL INSTITUTE: Founded in 1923 by Frederick Kettner, this body has its headquarters in a New York City hotel and claims three other branches.

BOSTON HOME OF TRUTH: This group was formed at Boston in 1891 by Annie Rix Militz.

CHAPEL OF TRUTH: Founded in 1923 by Mary L. Butterworth, it carries on a healing ministry. Its only group is in Philadelphia.

CHURCH OF CHRIST, SCIENTIST: The largest of all the healing groups, based on the teachings of Mary Baker Eddy. It denies the existence of sin and sickness, holding them to be "errors" of the mind. No statistics are given out, but in 1936 the census reported 2,113 churches and 268,915 members. Its healers or practitioners are found in all the larger cities.

CHURCH OF TRUTH: This body was founded in 1910 by Albert C. Grier at Spokane, Washington, where its headquarters are located. There are eight groups, most of them in the West.

DIVINE SCIENCE: This body was founded in 1898 by Nona L. Brooks, Aletha Brooks Small, and Fannie Brooks James. Its headquarters are at Denver, Colorado, and it has about two dozen churches or centers.

FELLOWSHIP OF DIVINE TRUTH: This sect declares that it was founded in 1934 by "Hilarion, the Master of Wisdom." Its headquarters are at Philadelphia and there is a branch at Elizabeth, New Jersey. Jeanette and Otis Swafford are its leaders.

MINISTRY OF THE HIGH WATCH: This was organized in 1924 to promulgate the "messages of the High Watch," based upon the teachings of Emma Curtis Hopkins. It is a mystical movement centering at Cornwall Bridge, Connecticut.

NEW HISTORICAL SOCIETY: This society, which seeks a universal government and religion, was founded in 1929 by Lewis Stuyvesant Chanler and Mirza Ahmad Sohrab. Its only chapter is in New York city. It is not a healing cult but seems to lean to the Bahai philosophy.

PSYCHIANA: This movement was started in 1928 at Moscow, Idaho, by Frank B. Robinson, who claimed that he had seen God and talked with him face to face.

SOCIETY OF LIFE: This group is a Christian Science offshoot and originally called itself the Christian Science Parent Church.

UNITY SCHOOL OF CHRISTIANITY: This movement was founded in 1889 by Myrtle and Charles Fillmore and has headquarters at Kansas City, Missouri. It does not regard itself as a church, but it is prolific in the circulation of literature and its groups meet in halls in many American cities.

UNIVERSAL PEACE INSTITUTE: This group was founded in 1934 by Lillian K. Daniel. It has a center or retreat near Mount Rose, Pennsylvania. There are no branches.

APPENDIX B

ESOTERIC OR MYSTICAL BODIES

ESOTERIC SECTS ARE THE MYSTICAL GROUPS THAT CLAIM TO BE IN POSSESSION
of, or to have access to, truth that is unknown to ordinary mortals but which can
be revealed by various processes. Some of them operate very much like correspondence schools, while others have leaders who conduct seances and receive and transmit messages from spiritual sources.[1] The following bodies are representative of
the class:

BROTHERHOOD OF THE WHITE TEMPLE: The leader of this group is Maurice Doreal of
Denver, Colorado, who is styled "archbishop." He claims to be able to transport his
spirit to Tibet for consultations with the mystics there. Under the title of Shambulla
Ashrama, Inc., the group attempted "to build a sanctuary called the Valley of Survival," which would protect the cultists against an impending holocaust.

GREAT I AM: (See p. 227.)

INSTITUTE OF MENTALPHYSICS: The leader of this movement is Edwin J. Dingle of
Los Angeles, California, who claims that he received healing and a mass of mystic
knowledge from the lamas of Tibet, who regarded him as one of themselves in reincarnation. The leader imparts this wisdom to students by mail.

MAYAN TEMPLE: Under the leadership of "Pontiff" Harold Davis Emerson, in New
York city, this group seeks a restoration of the faith of the ancient Mayans or pre-
historic people of South America. It is claimed the Indians were the original created
race, since the Hebrew word from Adam should be translated "red earth." The leader
says he is a descendant of the last high priest of the Mayans.

ROSICRUCIANS: The Ancient Mystical Order Rosea Crucis or the Rosicrucian Order has
headquarters at San Jose, California. It is not a religious society or a church. It claims
to be a very ancient body which has possession of truths which were known to the
great minds of the past but which became lost in the course of the centuries. The
mission of the order is to reveal those truths to its students or members. It is a
secret brotherhood which sells its lessons and operates like a correspondence school.

ROYAL FRATERNITY OF MASTER METAPHYSICIANS: This is a metaphysical study group
founded by James Bernard Shafer in New York city. There are no branches but

[1] A letter from Helen Templeman of Los Angeles says she is the earthly contact for Washington,
Lincoln, Shakespeare, Franklin, Roosevelt, Lord Northcliffe, Plato, Aristotle, Plutarch, Darwin,
Dante, Hypatia, King Thotma, Wesley, Spurgeon, Emerson, Lord Cameron, Beethoven, Lord
Falconer, Woodrow Wilson, Coolidge, Edison, Burbank, Luther, Napoleon, John the Baptist, and
others. She allegedly receives messages from them which she publishes.

the group operates a retreat on Long Island known as "Peace Haven, the House of the New Commandment."

SPIRITUALISTS: Spiritualism took form in the United States in 1848, when certain phenomena, especially rappings and knockings, were observed at Rochester, New York, and other places, and which were attributed to the spirits of the dead. Spiritualists have many theological tenets, most of which correspond more or less closely to those of the Protestant churches, but their distinguishing mark is the belief in the possibility of communication with the spirit world through sensitive persons who are called "mediums." These hold "seances" at which the spirits are contacted and messages received, usually by raps upon a table. Deception has often been charged against mediums and many "exposures" have been published. There are four Spiritualist bodies in the United States: National Spiritualist Association, Progressive Spiritual Church, National Spiritual Alliance, and General Assembly of Spiritualists. These have over four hundred churches or local groups and nearly thirty thousand members.

SWEDENBORGIANS: The Church of the New Jerusalem or the New Church, which exists in two branches, teaches the philosophy of the Swedish theologian Emanuel Swedenborg (1688-1772). He experienced an illumination and received revelations direct from God, and his theology is based on hidden spiritual meanings in certain books of the Bible. The two New Church sects in the United States have around one hundred churches and six thousand members.

TEMPLE OF YAHWEH: (See p. 227.)

THEOSOPHISTS: Theosophy is an occult movement based on the revelations of the Russian prophetess Madam H. P. Blavatsky, who came to America and founded the first Theosophical Society at New York in 1875. She claimed to be in touch with certain mahatmas or lamas of Tibet who transmitted their messages to the world through her. She was investigated by the Society of Physical Research and denounced as fraudulent and there were certain scandals in her career. The movement has split into several branches: Theosophical Society in America (Wheaton, Illinois), Theosophical Society (Covina, California), United Lodge of Theosophists (Los Angeles).

VEDANTA SOCIETY: This society inculcates the Vedanta philosophy of Hinduism. It grew out of lectures delivered by Swami Vivekananda at the World Parliament of Religions at the Chicago World's Fair in 1893. It has about a dozen small groups in this country.

YOGODA SAT-SANGA: This group, otherwise called the "Self-Realization Fellowship," instills the Hindu practice of yoga or the withdrawal of senses from the external world and concentration of thought within. Lectures by Hindu yogis are delivered in halls and hotel parlors in many cities.

AHMADIYYA MOVEMENT: This is a movement or sect of Islam or Mohammedanism which was founded by Hayrat Ahmad, who is recognized as the "Promised Messiah and Mahdi and the expected Messenger of all nations." He died in 1908. The present head of the movement is Hazrat Mirza Bashirud-Din Mahmud Ahmad. The movement regards itself as the "true and real Islam" and has missions in many countries. It has headquarters at Chicago and Pittsburgh and publishes a quarterly periodical called *The Moslem Sunrise.*

BIBLIOGRAPHY

Angus, S.: *The Religious Quests of the Graeco-Roman World*, New York, 1929. *The Mystery Religions and Christianity*, New York, 1928.

Asbury, Francis: *Journal of Rev. Francis Asbury*, New York, 1821.

Atkins, Gaius Glenn: *Religion in Our Times*, New York, 1932. *Modern Religious Cults and Movements*, New York, 1923. *Procession of the Gods*, New York, 1930.

Anderson, Paul B.: *People, Church and State in Modern Russia*. New York, 1944.

Augur, Helen: *An American Jezebel: The Life of Anne Hutchinson*, New York, 1930.

Bach, Marcus: *They Have Found a Faith*, New York, 1946.

The Bahai Centenary, 1844-1944, Wilmette, Ill., 1944.

Bahai Procedure, Wilmette, Ill., 1942.

Bahai, The Coming World Religion, Wilmette, Ill., 1946.

Baird, Robert: *Religion in America*, New York, 1866.

Baker, Alonzo L.: *Belief and Work of Seventh-Day Adventists*, Mt. View, Calif., 1938.

Bass, Archer B.: *Protestantism in the United States*, New York, 1929.

Beet, Joseph Agar: *The Last Things*, London, 1905.

Betts, George Herbert: *The Beliefs of 700 Ministers*, New York, 1929.

Bicknell, E. J.: *The Christian Idea of Sin and Original Sin in the Light of Modern Knowledge*, London, 1923.

Binder, Louis Richard: *Modern Religious Cults and Society*, Boston, 1933.

Blackstone, William E.: *Jesus Is Coming*, Chicago, 1908.

Boas, Ralph and Louise: *Cotton Mather, Keeper of the Puritan Conscience*, New York, 1928.

Boehm, Henry: *Reminiscences, Historical and Biographical, of Sixty-Four Years in the Ministry*, New York, 1865.

Bolshakoff, Ser...
the Soviet...

Braden, Charles...
Religion,...
lieve, New...

A Brief Accoun...
Friends, Ph...

Brown, W. S.:...
gow, Ky., 1...

Buber, Martin,...

Campbell, James...
Christ, New...

Carpenter, Ellswo...
Very Soon),...

Carroll, Charles:...
Image of Go...

Cartwright, Peter:...
wright, New...
a Presiding El...

Case, Shirley Jack...
Chicago, 1918 —

Caylor, E. H.: The...
Spirit Medium,...

Chamberlain, W....
New York, 19...

Chapman, J. B.: A...
Nazarene, Kans...

Christ Coming in H...
Refuted, New Y...

Clark, Elmer T.: T...
Awakening, New...

Cohon, Samuel S.: W...
cinnati, 1931.

Coke, Thomas, Journa...

Cole, Stewart G.: H...
New York, 1931.

A Collection of Psalm...
Worship, Boston,...

Corwin, Charles E.: A...
Church in Ameri...

Curnock, Nehemiah...
Wesley, 8 vols., L...

* This has been restricted to books which are more or less accessible, altho...
a relatively small part of the materials used, as the references in the footnotes
pages of primary sources are listed in the first edition of this work.

the group operates a retreat on Long Island known as "Peace Haven, the House of the New Commandment."

SPIRITUALISTS: Spiritualism took form in the United States in 1848, when certain phenomena, especially rappings and knockings, were observed at Rochester, New York, and other places, and which were attributed to the spirits of the dead. Spiritualists have many theological tenets, most of which correspond more or less closely to those of the Protestant churches, but their distinguishing mark is the belief in the possibility of communication with the spirit world through sensitive persons who are called "mediums." These hold "seances" at which the spirits are contacted and messages received, usually by raps upon a table. Deception has often been charged against mediums and many "exposures" have been published. There are four Spiritualist bodies in the United States: National Spiritualist Association, Progressive Spiritual Church, National Spiritual Alliance, and General Assembly of Spiritualists. These have over four hundred churches or local groups and nearly thirty thousand members.

SWEDENBORGIANS: The Church of the New Jerusalem or the New Church, which exists in two branches, teaches the philosophy of the Swedish theologian Emanuel Swedenborg (1688-1772). He experienced an illumination and received revelations direct from God, and his theology is based on hidden spiritual meanings in certain books of the Bible. The two New Church sects in the United States have around one hundred churches and six thousand members.

TEMPLE OF YAHWEH: (See p. 227.)

THEOSOPHISTS: Theosophy is an occult movement based on the revelations of the Russian prophetess Madam H. P. Blavatsky, who came to America and founded the first Theosophical Society at New York in 1875. She claimed to be in touch with certain mahatmas or lamas of Tibet who transmitted their messages to the world through her. She was investigated by the Society of Physical Research and denounced as fraudulent and there were certain scandals in her career. The movement has split into several branches: Theosophical Society in America (Wheaton, Illinois), Theosophical Society (Covina, California), United Lodge of Theosophists (Los Angeles).

VEDANTA SOCIETY: This society inculcates the Vedanta philosophy of Hinduism. It grew out of lectures delivered by Swami Vivekananda at the World Parliament of Religions at the Chicago World's Fair in 1893. It has about a dozen small groups in this country.

YOGODA SAT-SANGA: This group, otherwise called the "Self-Realization Fellowship," instills the Hindu practice of yoga or the withdrawal of senses from the external world and concentration of thought within. Lectures by Hindu yogis are delivered in halls and hotel parlors in many cities.

AHMADIYYA MOVEMENT: This is a movement or sect of Islam or Mohammedanism which was founded by Hayrat Ahmad, who is recognized as the "Promised Messiah and Mahdi and the expected Messenger of all nations." He died in 1908. The present head of the movement is Hazrat Mirza Bashirud-Din Mahmud Ahmad. The movement regards itself as the "true and real Islam" and has missions in many countries. It has headquarters at Chicago and Pittsburgh and publishes a quarterly periodical called *The Moslem Sunrise*.

BIBLIOGRAPHY *

Angus, S.: *The Religious Quests of the Graeco-Roman World*, New York, 1929. *The Mystery Religions and Christianity*, New York, 1928.

Asbury, Francis: *Journal of Rev. Francis Asbury*, New York, 1821.

Atkins, Gaius Glenn: *Religion in Our Times*, New York, 1932. *Modern Religious Cults and Movements*, New York, 1923. *Procession of the Gods*, New York, 1930.

Anderson, Paul B.: *People, Church and State in Modern Russia*. New York, 1944.

Augur, Helen: *An American Jezebel: The Life of Anne Hutchinson*, New York, 1930.

Bach, Marcus: *They Have Found a Faith*, New York, 1946.

The Bahai Centenary, 1844-1944, Wilmette, Ill., 1944.

Bahai Procedure, Wilmette, Ill., 1942.

Bahai, The Coming World Religion, Wilmette, Ill., 1946.

Baird, Robert: *Religion in America*, New York, 1866.

Baker, Alonzo L.: *Belief and Work of Seventh-Day Adventists*, Mt. View, Calif., 1938.

Bass, Archer B.: *Protestantism in the United States*, New York, 1929.

Beet, Joseph Agar: *The Last Things*, London, 1905.

Betts, George Herbert: *The Beliefs of 700 Ministers*, New York, 1929.

Bicknell, E. J.: *The Christian Idea of Sin and Original Sin in the Light of Modern Knowledge*, London, 1923.

Binder, Louis Richard: *Modern Religious Cults and Society*, Boston, 1933.

Blackstone, William E.: *Jesus Is Coming*, Chicago, 1908.

Boas, Ralph and Louise: *Cotton Mather, Keeper of the Puritan Conscience*, New York, 1928.

Boehm, Henry: *Reminiscences, Historical and Biographical, of Sixty-Four Years in the Ministry*, New York, 1865.

Bolshakoff, Serge: *The Christian Church and the Soviet State*. London, 1942.

Braden, Charles S. (ed.): *Varieties of American Religion*, Chicago, 1936. *These Also Believe*, New York, 1949.

A Brief Account of the Rise of the Society of Friends, Philadelphia, 1889.

Brown, W. S.: *Bible Defence of Slavery*, Glasgow, Ky., 1853.

Buber, Martin, *Hasidism*, New York, 1948.

Campbell, James M.: *The Second Coming of Christ*, New York, 1919.

Carpenter, Ellsworth: *Coming to Earth! (Very, Very Soon)*, New York, 1940.

Carroll, Charles: *The Negro a Beast; or, In the Image of God*, St. Louis, 1900.

Cartwright, Peter: *Autobiography of Peter Cartwright*, New York [1856]. *Fifty Years as a Presiding Elder*, New York, 1871.

Case, Shirley Jackson: *The Millennial Hope*, Chicago, 1918.

Caylor, E. H.: *The Late Dr. Sedgwick and the Spirit Medium*, Dayton, Ohio, 1900.

Chamberlain, W. H.: *The Russian Enigma*, New York, 1943.

Chapman, J. B.: *A History of the Church of the Nazarene*, Kansas City, 1926.

Christ Coming in His Kingdom, Millenarianism Refuted, New York, Chicago, Boston, n. d.

Clark, Elmer T.: *The Psychology of Religious Awakening*, New York, 1929.

Cohon, Samuel S.: *What We Jews Believe*, Cincinnati, 1931.

Coke, Thomas, *Journal*, Dublin, 1916.

Cole, Stewart G.: *History of Fundamentalism*, New York, 1931.

A Collection of Psalms and Hymns for Publick Worship, Boston, 1799.

Corwin, Charles E.: *A Manual of the Reformed Church in America*, New York, 1922.

Curnock, Nehemiah (ed.): *Journal of John Wesley*, 8 vols., London, 1909.

* This has been restricted to books which are more or less accessible, although these constitute only a relatively small part of the materials used, as the references in the footnotes show. More than twelve pages of primary sources are listed in the first edition of this work.

Cutten, George Barton: *The Psychological Phenomena of Christianity*, New York, 1908.

Dakin, Edwin Franden: *Mrs. Eddy: The Biography of a Virginal Mind*, New York, 1930.

Davenport, Frederick Morgan: *Primitive Traits in Religious Revivals*, New York, 1905.

Dimond, Sydney G.: *Psychology of the Methodist Revival*, London, 1926.

Dorchester, Daniel: *Christianity in the United States*, New York, 1888.

Dow, Lorenzo: *Perambulations of Cosmopolite; or, Travels and Labors of Lorenzo Dow in Europe and America*, New York, 1855.

Dow, Peggy: *Vicissitude; or, The Journey of Life*, Rochester, 1842.

Dresser, Horatio W.: *A History of the New Thought Movement*, New York, 1919.

Dugger, A. N., and Dodd, C. O.: *A History of the True Church*, Salem, W. Va., 1936.

Duren, William Larkin: *The Top Sergeant of the Pioneers*, Atlanta, 1930.

Eaton, E. L.: *The Millennial Dawn Heresy*, New York, 1911.

Edwards, Jonathan: *A Narrative of Many Surprising Conversions in Northampton and Vicinity; Together with Some Thoughts on the Revival in New England*, Worcester, 1832.

Elliott, Charles: *History of the Great Secession from the Methodist Episcopal Church in the Year 1845, Eventuating in the Organization of the New Church Entitled the "Methodist Episcopal Church, South,"* Cincinnati, 1855.

Farrar, Frederick W.: *History of Free Thought*, New York, 1888.

Fee, William I.: *Bringing in the Sheaves; Gleanings from Harvest Fields in Ohio, Kentucky, and West Virginia*, New York, 1896.

Ferguson, Charles W.: *The Confusion of Tongues, a Review of Modern Isms*, New York, 1929.

Ferm, Vergilius (ed.): *Religion in the Twentieth Century*, New York, 1948.

Finley, J. B.: *Autobiography of Rev. James B. Finley*, New York, n. d. (1853). *Sketches of Western Methodism; Biographical, Historical, and Miscellaneous, Illustrative of Pioneer Life*, Cincinnati, 1854.

Finney, Thomas M.: *The Life and Labor of Enoch Mather Marvin*, St. Louis, 1881.

Flack, J. V. B.: *Life History of J. V. B. Flack, D.D.*, Excelsior Springs, Mo., 1912.

Flew, R. Newton: *The Idea of Profection*, London, 1934.

Fowler, W. Warde: *The Religious Experience of the Roman People*, London, 1922.

Frodsham, S. H.: *With Signs Following, the Story of the Latter-Day Pentecostal Revival*, Springfield, Mo., n. d.

Fry, C. Luther: *The U. S. Looks at Its Churches*, New York, 1930.

Funk, John F.: *The Mennonite Church and Her Accusers*, Elkhart, Ind., 1878.

Gaddis, M. E.: *Christian Perfectionism in America*, MS Dissertation, University of Chicago.

Gaddis, M. P.: *Footprints of an Itinerant*, New York, 1873.

Garber, Paul Neff: *That Fighting Spirit of Methodism*, Greensboro, N. C., 1928.

Garrison, Winfred Ernest: *The March of Faith*, New York, 1933. *Religion Follows the Frontier, a History of the Disciples of Christ*, New York, 1931.

Grant, Helen: *Peter Cartwright, Pioneer*, New York, 1931.

Greenstone, Julius H.: *The Jewish Religion*, Philadelphia, 1929.

Hall, Thomas Cuming: *The Religious Background of American Culture*, Boston, 1930.

Hare, Edward: *A Refutation of the Charges Against the Methodists, Advanced by the Rev. Doctor Magee*, London, 1810.

Hastings, James (ed.): *Encyclopedia of Religion and Ethics*, New York, 1910-1927.

Haygood, A. G.: *Our Brother in Black, His Freedom and His Future*, Nashville, 1881.

Haynes, Carlyle B.: *Seventh-Day Adventists, Their Work and Teachings*, Washington, D. C., 1940.

Horton, Walter Marshall: *A Psychological Approach to Theology*, New York, 1931.

Hoshor, John: *God in a Rolls Royce: The Rise of Father Divine, Madman, Menace or Messiah?* New York, 1936.

Howell, Emma E.: *The Great Advent Movement*, Washington, D. C., 1935.

Idelsohn, Abraham: *The Ceremonies of Judaism*, Cincinnati, 1930.

Irvine, W. C.: *Heresies Exposed*, New York, 1937.

James, William: *The Varieties of Religious Experience*, New York, 1908.

Jenkins, James: *Experience, Labours and Sufferings of Rev. James Jenkins*, 1842.

Jennings, Walter Wilson: *Origin and Early History of the Disciples of Christ*, Cincinnati, 1919.

Jennings, Samuel: *An Exposition of the Late Controversy in the Methodist Episcopal Church; of the True Objects of the Parties Concerned Therein, and of the Proceedings by Which the Reformers Were Expelled*, Baltimore, 1831.

The Jewish People, Past and Present, Vols. I-II, New York, 1948.

Johnson, H.: *Soviet Russia Since the War*, New York, 1947.

Judd, Charles Hubbard: *The Psychology of Social Institutions*, New York, 1926.

Kauffman, Daniel: *The Mennonite Church and Current Issues*, Scottdale, Pa., 1924.

Koerber, Fred: *Bible Prophecy of Today's Events*, Hickory, N. C., 1942.

Kraft, Celia, and Preece, Harold: *Dew and Jordan*, New York, 1946.

Kuhn, Alvin Boyd: *Theosophy*, New York, 1930.

Lamont, Corliss: *Humanism as a Philosophy*, New York, 1949.

Landham, Isaac: *The Universal Jewish Encyclopedia*, Vols. I-X, New York, 1939.

Langhan, John: *The Era of Frauds in the Methodist Book Concern in New York*, Baltimore, 1896.

Lauterbach, R. E.: *These Are the Russians*, New York, 1945.

Lee, Jesse: *A Short History of the Methodists in the United States of America*, Baltimore, 1810.

Lee, Umphrey: *The Historical Background of Early Methodist Enthusiasm*, New York, 1931. *John Wesley and Modern Religion*, Nashville, 1936.

Leftwich, W. M.: *Martyrdom in Missouri, A History of Religious Proscription, the Seizure of Churches and the Persecution of Ministers of the Gospel, in the State of Missouri, During the Late Civil War, and Under the "Test Oath" of the New Constitution*, St. Louis, 1870.

Long, Lindley G.: *A Layman's Look at Prophecy*, Louisville, 1948.

Loud, Grover C.: *Evangelized America*, New York, 1928.

Loughborough, J. N.: *The Great Second Advent Movement, Its Rise and Progress*, Washington, 1909.

Mains, George Preston: *Premillennialism*, New York, 1920.

Mathews, John: *Peeps into Life* (no place or date).

Maude, Aylmer: *A Peculiar People, The Doukhobors*, New York, 1904.

Maury, Reuben: *The Wars of the Godly, the Story of the Religious Conflict in America*, New York, 1928.

Maxon, Charles Hartshorn: *The Great Awakening in the Middle Colonies*, Chicago, 1920.

McCaine, Alexander: *The History and Mystery of Methodist Episcopacy, or a Glance at "The Institutions of the Church, as We Recieved Them from Our Fathers,"* Baltimore, 1827.

McComas, Henry C.: *The Psychology of Religious Sects*, New York, 1912.

McCown, Chester Carlton: *The Promise of His Coming*, New York, 1921.

McDaniel, S. C.: *The Origin and Early History of the Congregational Methodist Church*. (No place or date.)

McElreath, Walter: *Methodist Union in the Courts*, New York, 1946.

MacFarland, C. S., and Bell, Herman F., eds.: *Religion Through the Ages*, New York, 1948.

McFerrin, J. B., et al.: *History of the Organization of the Methodist Episcopal Church, South, Comprehending All the Official Proceedings of the General Conference; The Southern Annual Conferences, and the General Convention; With Such Other Matters as Are Necessary to a Right Understanding of the Case*, Nashville, 1845.

McKenzie, John G.: *Psychology, Psychotherapy and Evangelism*, New York, 1940.

Miliukov, Paul: *Outlines of Russian Culture* (Part I, "Religion and the Church"), Philadelphia, 1942.

Mode, Peter G.: *The Frontier Spirit in American Christianity*, New York, 1923.

Moore, S. W.: *Our Church in Sandburg*, Nashville, 1874.

Musser, Daniel: *The Reformed Mennonite Church, Its Rise and Progress, with Its Principles and Doctrines*, Lancaster, Pa., 1878.

Myles, William: *A Chronological History of the People Called Methodists of the Connexion of the Late Rev. John Wesley*, London, 1803.

Nagler, A. W.: *Pietism and Methodism*, Nashville, 1918.

Neal, Julia: *By Their Fruits, the Story of Shakerism in South Union, Kentucky*, Chapel Hill, 1947.

Neely, Thomas B.: *American Methodism, Its Divisions and Unification*, New York, 1915.

BIBLIOGRAPHY

Neve, J. L.: *Churches and Sects of Christendom,* Burlington, Iowa, 1940.

Newman, Albert Henry: *A History of the Baptist Churches in the United States,* New York, 1915.

Nichol, Francis D.: *The Midnight Cry,* Washington, D. C., 1944.

Niebuhr, H. Richard: *The Social Sources of Denominationalism,* New York, 1929.

Norwood, J. N.: *The Schism in the Methodist Episcopal Church, 1844; A Study of Slavery and Ecclesiastical Politics,* Alfred, N. Y., 1923.

Noyes, George Wallingford: *Religious Experience of John Humphrey Noyes, Founder of the Oneida Community,* New York, 1923.

O'Donnell, Elliott: *Strange Cults and Secret Societies of Modern London,* New York, 1936.

Olsen, M. Ellsworth: *A History of the Origin and Progress of Seventh-Day Adventists,* Washington, 1926.

Pardington, G. P.: *Twenty-Five Wonderful Years, a Popular Sketch of the Christian and Missionary Alliance,* New York, 1914.

Parker, Robert Allerton: *The Incredible Messiah, the Deification of Father Divine,* Boston, 1937.

Penny, Norman (ed.): *The Journal of George Fox,* New York, 1924.

Phelan, M.: *The New Handbook of All Denominations,* Nashville, 1930.

Phillips, C. H.: *History of the Colored Methodist Episcopal Church in America,* Jackson, Tenn., 1925.

Platner, John Winthrop, and others: *The Religious History of New England,* Cambridge, 1917.

Plyler, A. W.: *The Iron Duke of the Methodist Itinerancy,* Nashville, 1925.

Pratt, James Bissett: *The Religious Consciousness,* New York, 1920.

Preece, Harold, and Kraft, Celia: *Dew on Jordan,* New York, 1946.

Reformation Principles Exhibited by the Reformed Presbyterian Church, in the United States of America, New York, 1892.

Richardson, Simon Peter: *The Lights and Shadows of Itinerant Life: An Autobiography of Rev. Simon Peter Richardson,* Nashville, 1901.

Rivers, R. H.: *Life of Bishop Paine,* Nashville, 1884.

Roberts, B. H.: *The "Falling Away," or the World's Loss of Christian Religion and Church,* Salt Lake City, 1931.

Sangster, W. E.: *The Path to Perfection,* New York, 1943.

Saunders, Charles F.: *The Taproot of Religion and Its Fruitage,* New York, 1931.

Schaff, Philip: *Creeds of Christendom,* 3 vols., New York, 1919.

Schaff-Herzog: *Encyclopedia of Religious Knowledge,* 12 vols., New York, 1909.

Schou, H. I.: *Religion and Morbid Mental States,* New York, 1928.

Sheldon, Henry C.: *Studies in Recent Adventism,* New York, 1915. *Christian Science So-Called,* New York, 1913.

Shogi, Effendi: *God Passes By* (Bahai), Wilmette, Ill., 1944.

Shook, Charles A.: *The True Origin of the Book of Mormon,* Cincinnati, 1914. *The True Origin of Mormon Polygamy,* Cincinnati, 1914.

Silver, Jesse Forest: *The Lord's Return,* New York, 1914.

Simpson, Matthew: *Cyclopedia of Methodism,* Philadelphia, 1881.

Skinner, Otis A.: *The Theory of William Miller Concerning the End of the World in 1843 Utterly Exploded,* Boston, 1840.

Smith, C. Henry: *The Mennonites,* Berne, Ind., 1920.

Smith, George G.: *The Life and Letters of James Osgood Andrew,* Nashville, 1882.

Smith, Joseph Fielding: *The Way to Perfection,* Salt Lake City, 1931.

Spalding, Arthur: *Pioneer Stories of the Second Advent Message,* Nashville, 1942.

Spicer, Wm. A.: *Pioneer Days of the Advent Movement,* Washington, D. C., 1941.

Stiles, Henry Reed: *Bundling, Its Origin, Progress, and Decline in America* (reprinted privately, N. J.), 1871.

Stratton, George Malcolm: *Social Psychology of International Conduct,* New York, 1929.

Stroup, Herbert H.: *The Jehovah's Witnesses,* New York, 1945.

Stuber, Sidney I.; *How We Got Our Denominations,* New York, 1948.

Swedenborg, Emmanuel (translated by John Faulkner Potts): *The Doctrine of the New Jerusalem Concerning the Lord,* New York, 1929.

Sweet, William Warren: *Circuit-Rider Days in Indiana,* Indianapolis, 1916. *The Methodist Episcopal Church and the Civil War,* Cincinnati, n. d. (1912). *The Rise of Methodism in the West,* New York, 1920. *Men of Zeal, the Romance of American Methodist*

Beginnings, New York, 1933. *Religion on the American Frontier, The Baptists,* New York, 1931. *The American Churches,* New York, 1948.

Swift, Arthur L., Jr. (ed.): *Religion Today,* New York, 1933.

Swihart, Altman K.: *Since Mrs. Eddy,* New York, 1931.

Tawney, R. H.: *Religion and the Rise of Capitalism,* London, 1928.

Taylor, E. R.: *Methodism and Politics, 1791-1851,* Cambridge, 1935.

Telford, John (ed.): *Letters of John Wesley,* 8 vols., London, 1931.

Tennant, F. R.: *The Origin of Sin,* Cambridge, 1908.

Theodosia, or the Heroine of the Faith, or Ten Days' Travel in Search of the Church, Nashville, 1857.

Thomas, Daniel Lindsey and Lucy B.: *Kentucky Superstitions,* Princeton, N. J., 1921.

Thomas, Wendell: *Hinduism Invades America,* New York, 1930.

Tillett, Wilbur F.: *A Statement of the Faith of World-Wide Methodism,* Nashville, 1906.

Tomlinson, Homer A., ed.,: *Diary of A. J. Tomlinson,* New York, 1949.

Tucker, R. L.: *The Separation of the Methodists from the Church of England,* New York, 1918.

United States Census of Religious Bodies, 2 vols., Washington, 1926, 1936.

Van Baalen, J. K.: *The Chaos of Cults,* 6th ed., Grand Rapids, 1947.

Warfield, Benjamin Breckinridge: *Studies in Perfectionism,* 2 vols., New York, 1931.

Warner, W. J.: *The Wesleyan Movement in the Industrial Revolution,* London, 1930.

Waterman, Philip F.: *The Story of Superstition,* New York, 1929.

Weaver, William B.: *History of the Central Conference Mennonite Church,* Danvers, Ill., 1926.

Weber, Herman C. (ed.): *Yearbook of American Churches,* New York, 1936.

Weber, Julius A.: *Religion and Philosophies in the U. S. A.,* Los Angeles, 1931.

Webster, Hutton: *Primitive Secret Societies,* New York, 1908.

Wenger, John C.: *Glimpses of Mennonite History and Doctrine,* Scottsdale, Pa., 1947.

Wheeler, Ruth: *His Messenger,* Washington, 1939.

White, Alma: *The Ku-Klux Klan in Prophecy,* Zarephath, N. J., 1925. *Klansmen: Guardians of Liberty,* Zarephath, N. J., 1926. *The Truth in Satire Concerning Infallible Popes,* Zarephath, N. J., 1929. *Heroes of the Fiery Cross,* Zarephath, N. J., 1929. *Looking Back from Beulah,* Zarephath, N. J., 1929.

Wightman, William: *Life of William Capers, Including an Autobiography,* Nashville, 1859.

Wilbur, Earl M.: *A History of Unitarianism,* Cambridge, 1946.

Wiley, Austin: *The History of the Antislavery Cause in State and Nation,* Portland, Me., 1886.

Williams, Michael: *The Shadow of the Pope,* New York, 1932.

Williams, Norman Powell: *The Ideas of the Fall and of Original Sin,* London, 1927.

Willoughby, Harold R.: *Pagan Regeneration, a Study of Mystery Initiations in the Graeco-Roman World,* Chicago, 1929.

Wilson, Samuel Graham: *Bahaism and Its Claims,* New York, 1915.

Wood, Clement: *The Woman Who Was Pope,* New York, 1931.

Worcester, William L.: *The Language of Parable, a Key to the Bible,* New York, n. d. (Swedenborgian).

Wright, R. R. (ed.): *Encyclopedia of African Methodism.* Philadelpha, 1916.

Yahn, S. G.: *History of the Churches of God of North America,* Harrisburg, Pa., 1926.

Zerfoss, S. G.: *The Ephrata Cloister,* Little, Pa., 1921.

INDEX OF RELIGIOUS BODIES IN THE UNITED STATES

THIS LIST OF RELIGIOUS BODIES, WHILE NOT ENTIRELY COMPLETE, IS THE MOST extensive list that has ever been published. A great many more groups are included than are treated in the text. The names of those discussed are followed by page references. Some of the groups, such as the Rosicrucians, are only quasi-religious; others, such as Buchmanism and Youth for Christ, are religious movements and not organized bodies; many others are independent local groups rather than denominations in the accepted sense. Little information is available about some of them.

Church of the Living God, The Pillar and Ground of Truth, 120
Churches of the New Jerusalem (Swedenborgian):
General Convention of the New Jerusalem in the U.S.A.
General Church of the New Jerusalem
Cicero Bible Church (Cicero, Illinois)
Commandment Keepers or Black Jews, 163-64
Community of True Inspiration. See Amana Society
Congregational Christian Churches
Congregational Church of God
Congregational Holiness Church, 108
Cooneyites or Go-Preachers, 184
Cosmic Science Church, Inc.
Cosmopolitan Church of Liberality
Covenant Keepers

Disciples of Christ, 19, 61, 155, 200, 212-16
Divine Art of Swing Studio
Divine Science, 12, 24, 232
Divine Science College and Church
Divine Truth, 12
Dukhobors, Canadian. See under Mennonite Churches
Dunkers. See Brethren, German Baptists

Eastern Orthodox Churches, 14, 164-65
Albanian Orthodox Church, 165
American Holy Orthodox Catholic Apostolic Eastern Church, 165
Apostolic Episcopal Church, 165
Bulgarian Orthodox Church, 165
Greek Orthodox Church (Hellenic), 165
Holy Orthodox Church in America (Eastern Catholic and Apostolic), 165
Romanian Orthodox Church, 165
Russian Orthodox Church, 164-65
Serbian Orthodox Church, 165
Syrian Antiochan Orthodox Church, 165
Ukranian Orthodox Church in America, 165
Episcopal Church, 14, 21, 157. See also American Episcopal, Protestant Episcopal, Reformed Episcopal
Erieside Church
Evangelical and Reformed Church
Evangelical Congregational Church, 70
Evangelical–United Brethren Church. See under United Brethren Churches

Faith Tabernacle (California)
Father Divine's Peace Mission, 124-27, 224
Fellowship of Divine Truth, 232
Fellowship of the Reformation
Fire-Baptized Holiness Church, 107, 110-11
First Born
First Church for Spiritual Healing
Fellowship of Encircling Good
Fort Wayne Gospel Temple, 47
Forward Movement Bible School and Headquarters, 104

Free Christian Zion Church of Christ, 14, 119-20
Free Church of God in Christ, 119
Free Pentecost Church
French Evangelical Church (Huguenots)
Friends (Quakers), 14, 20, 32, 54, 186
Ohio Yearly Meeting of the Friends Church
Oregon Yearly Meeting of the Friends Church
Primitive Friends, 72
Religious Society of Friends (Central Yearly Meeting)
Religious Society of Friends (Conservative), 72
Religious Society of Friends (General Conference), 71-72
Religious Society of Friends (Kansas Yearly Meeting)
Religious Society of Friends (Philadelphia and Vicinity)
Full Gospel Church
Full Salvation Union

Garr Auditorium (Charlotte, N.C.), 104
Good Hope Mission
Good Tidings Tabernacle (New York, N.Y.)
Go-Preachers. See Cooneyites
Gospel Mission to the Jews (New York, N. Y.)
Gospel Speaking Association (Elder Michaux)
Grace Full Gospel Assembly
Great I Am, 12, 227

Hebrews, 27. See also Jewish Congregations
Hephzibah Faith Missionary Association, 78
Hindu Society (Ramikrisna-Vivekanauda Centers)
Holiness Church, 44, 100, 114-15
Holiness Church of God, Inc.
Home of Truth (Boston), 232
House of David, 23, 135, 153-54, 224-25
House of God, Holy Church of the Living God, The Pillar and Ground of the Truth, House of Prayer for All People, 129
House of Israel, 164
House of Prayer (Bishop Grace), 15, 119, 122-24, 129, 225
House of the Prince of Peace
House of the Lord, 129-30
Huguenots. See French Evangelical Church
Humanist Society (American Humanist Association)
Hutterian Brethren. See Mennonite

Independent Fundamental Churches of America
Institute of Mentalphysics, 234
Institute of Religious Science and Philosophy
International Chain-Ring-Key
International Church of the Foursquare Gospel, 115-16
International Council of Christian Assemblies
International Sufi Movement
Irvingites. See Catholic Apostolic Church
Israel Gospel Church, 109

GENERAL INDEX

For references to the individual sects, see Index of Religious Bodies in the United States (pp. 241-46).